FROM SECULARISM TO JIHAD

FROM SECULARISM TO JIHAD

Sayyid Qutb and the
Foundations of Radical
Islamism

Adnan A. Musallam

PRAEGER

Westport, Connecticut
London

Library of Congress Cataloging-in-Publication Data

Musallam, Adnan.
    From secularism to Jihad : Sayyid Qutb and the foundations of
radical Islamism / Adnan A. Musallam.
        p. cm.
    Includes bibliographical references and index.
    ISBN 0–275–98591–1 (alk. paper)
    1. Quòtb, Sayyid, 1903–1966. 2. Islamic fundamentalism—Egypt. 3.
Scholars, Muslim—Egypt—Biography. I. Title.
BP80.Q86M85   2005
320.5'57'092—dc22   2005018672

British Library Cataloguing in Publication Data is available.

Library of Congress Catalog Card Number: 2005018672
ISBN: 0–275–98591–1

First published in 2005

Praeger Publishers, 88 Post Road West, Westport, CT 06881
An imprint of Greenwood Publishing Group, Inc.
www.praeger.com

Printed in the United States of America

The paper used in this book complies with the
Permanent Paper Standard issued by the National
Information Standards Organization (Z39.48-1984).

10 9 8 7 6 5 4 3 2 1

Contents

Preface

> Religious violence preceded Sayyid Qutb. It would have continued its existence even if Sayyid Qutb had not been born. . . . It would have looked for another thinker, another justification and another interpreter on whom it is based. . . . The ultimate injustice is to leave out all the thinking of Sayyid Qutb and to take from it only what he said—in a time of adversity. *('Adel Hammuda, Sayyid Qutb from the Village to the Gallows, 1996)*

> There is nothing more clear and more audacious in excommunicating the nation than the texts of Sayid Qutb. It is useless to quote his previous writings which were written prior to his *Milestones on the Road*, because the possibilities of defending him dwindle. *('Abd al-Ghani 'Imad, The Hakimiyyah of God and the Authority of the Jurisprudent, 1997)*

From Secularism to Jihad: Sayyid Qutb and the Foundations of Radical Islamism is a historical reading and inquiry into the life and thought of Sayyid Qutb (1900–1966). This book describes Qutb's transformation from a secular literary figure, a man of letters in the 1930s and 1940s, to an independent Islamist in the late 1940s and early 1950s. The content of this book focuses on Qutb's emergence as a radical Islamist in the prisons of the late president Gamal 'Abd al-Nasser of Egypt, 1954–1964; his rearrest, trial and execution in 1965–1966; his posthumous fame, 1966–present; and the impact of his controversial thought on current Islamic resurgence and global jihadists.

Islam is an Arabic word which means complete submission and obedience to Allah (God). More than a billion persons, or a fifth of humankind, are Muslims who follow the Islamic religion. Islamism, on the other hand, is a political ideology which insists that Islam is a way of life encompassing the religious, political, economic, social, and all other spheres of life. Islamism advocates a society based on strict Shari'ah (Islamic law) to replace the un-Islamic secular-oriented governments and societies prevalent in both the Arab and other Muslim countries throughout the world.

The existence of totalitarian and corrupt regimes in the twentieth century led to the rise of socialist ideas as viable alternatives. With the collapse of the Soviet Union and the end of cold war, however, leftist ideologies lost influence. Islamism in the Arab world gained momentum with the defeat of Egypt and the Nasser regime in the 1967 war, the repeated humiliations of Arabs at the hands of Israel, and the victory of the Khomeini revolution in Iran in 1979. More radical and revolutionary Islamism emerged in Egypt with the assassination of President Anwar el-Sadat in 1981, while global revolutionary Islamism appeared in the aftermath of the Soviet Union's invasion of Afghanistan in 1979. Thousands of young Arab and Muslim volunteers from Saudi Arabia, Egypt, Algeria, Yemen, Sudan, and other Muslim countries joined this global holy war against the Soviets. Sayyid Qutb became an ideologue whose writings are a manifesto for these revolutionary Islamists.[1]

Sayyid Qutb of Egypt was a poet, educator, journalist, critic, controversial Islamic ideologue, and radical Islamist. Together with many members of the Muslim Brothers, Qutb was imprisoned between 1954 and 1964. He was arrested again in 1965 and was accused of heading a secret apparatus that conspired to topple the regime of the late President 'Abd al-Nasser of Egypt.

Qutb is famous for his revolutionary zeal. He promoted what he considered the inevitable establishment of "the Islamic society" instead of "al-Jahili society" that prevailed in the Muslim world including Egypt. By "al-Jahili society," Qutb meant the contemporary features of the pre-Islamic pagan Arab society in which God's law on earth (al-Hakimiyyah) is violated by human beings' deification of their fellow humans and their aggression against each other. Western civilization is no longer valid for leading humanity because it is morally bankrupt. Islam alone has values that can liberate the oppressed man from the servitude of their fellow human beings. It is inevitable to resurrect the Islamic nation and to establish the Islamic society through "jihad" (exertion of one's power so as to spread the belief in Allah through the tongue, heart, hand, or sword) led by an Islamic vanguard whose banner, creed, and method are the belief that is based on "There is no god but Allah." Qutb provides guidance for this belief in his work *Ma'alim fi al-tariq* (Milestones on the Road).[2]

The revolutionary thought propounded in Qutb's *Milestones on the Road* was used as evidence by the office of the attorney general of the Egyptian State Security during an investigation of Qutb and during his trial in 1965 and 1966. It was one of the important factors that sent Sayyid Qutb to the gallows in August 1966. The execution of Qutb added a new martyr to the contemporary Islamic movement. Truly, the writings of Sayyid Qutb have become a basic part of the Islamic revival in the last forty years, a revival that derives much of its strength, among other things, from the utter failure of the Arab regimes to build viable societies, and from the repeated humiliation of the Arabs in their confrontation with Israel.

Despite the fact that *Milestones on the Road* made its appearance in 1964, some concepts posited in this book such as "al-Hakimiyyah" (God's rule on earth), "al-Jahiliyyah" (ignorance of the Divine Guidance), "al-Tali'ah" (vanguard) and "al-'Uzlah al-shu'uriyyah" (separation or isolation from others through feelings) still arouse much controversy in Arab and Islamic circles.[3]

Qutb's execution and thus his inability to clarify his controversial terms, led to radical interpretation of his writings and eventually to the emergence of excommunicating jihadist Islamists in Egypt and the Muslim world who were influenced by his thought.

NATURE OF THE RESEARCH

This research offers a historical study of the ideas that reflect the Egyptian social, economic, and political conditions. This book preserves the chronological sequence of events in its presentation of Qutb's intellectual career. Transformations in Qutb's life and thought are given chronologically in order to keep track of his development from a literary critic to an Islamic propagator. In order to show the extent of transformations in Qutb's view of life, I attempted in this research to compare Qutb's philosophy and thought in the 1930s and 1940s with that of the 1950s and 1960s.

The analysis presented in this study describes and interprets Qutb's published books and articles dealing with politics, literature, religion, and society. This study also includes attention to unpublished materials and the available biographies and studies of Qutb as well as valuable material that one finds on Sayyid Qutb when researching web sites.

This book posits a crucial question about the transformation Qutb experienced in the 1940s: What were the factors that led Qutb to change his outlook on life from a secular man of letters to an Islamic propagator?

Many answers were given for this question. For example, a study about Sayyid Qutb attributes the basis of Qutb's commitment to an Islamic ideology to one of the lectures of Hassan al-Banna, the founder and leader of the Society of Muslim Brothers in Egypt, and to its supposed magical effects on him.[4] Such an interpretation, however, should not be taken seriously, because it lacks documentation and evidence. This answer and similar superficial answers do not take into consideration multiple forces, such as his upbringing, his religious education, his personal background, and the state of Egyptian life and society in the first half of the twentieth century that formed Qutb's personality and his view of life.

In order to understand the changes that occurred in Qutb's view of life, it is necessary to trace the different stages of his life within the framework of the intellectual, political, religious, and social environment prevailing between 1919 and 1966. The first chapter of this study thus explains the intellectual and political transformations in Egypt between 1919 and 1952. In subsequent chapters, this study recounts Qutb's childhood and his emergence as a poet and a critic (1906–1938), his emergence as a student of the Qur'an (1939–1947), his alienation (1939–1947), his emergence as an independent Islamic ideologue (1947–1948), his experiences in and impressions of America (1948–1950) and the aftermath of his return (1950–1952), his radicalization (1952–1964), his arrest, trial, execution and martyrdom, and his posthumous fame and impact (1965–present).

PROBLEMS IN RESEARCHING QUTB'S LIFE AND THOUGHT

The road taken by a researcher in Qutb's controversial life and works is extremely difficult. One of the difficulties is the fact that many works that have been produced on Qutb are characterized by excessive lack of objectivity and by excessive bias. There are some writings that portray Qutb as a saint and others that portray him as a devil. For example, *The Crimes of the Muslim Brothers Gang* (Cairo: 1965) was written by supporters of the regime of the late President 'Abd al-Nasser in order to demonize the Muslim Brothers and to portray them and Sayyid Qutb as evil forces conspiring against the Islamic religion. There are also many articles that attacked Sayyid Qutb and his book *Milestones on the Road*, such as the supplement of the Cairene magazine *Rose El-Yousuf* (September 12, 1965), the article of Nash'at al-Taghlibi, "Milestones on the Road: The Constitution of the Brethren," in the Egyptian *Armed Forces Magazine* (October 1965) and Sharif Yunis, "Sayyid Qutb: Milestones on the Road of Killing," *al-Qahira* (Cairo), November 1994.

In addition, the biographies of Sayyid Qutb are replete with misinformation and mistakes. For example, a booklet written in English by the Pakistani writer S. Badrul Hassan entitled *Sayed Qutb Shaheed* (Karachi: 1980) recounts the following wrong information: "He was appointed a professor in this college because of his intelligence which God endowed him with. For some time he demonstrated his abilities at Cairo University." As we shall see in Qutb's biography, he did not work at Cairo University after his college graduation. Rather, he was appointed a teacher of Arabic language and literature in elementary government schools until he was transferred in the late 1930s to technical posts in the Ministry of Education in Cairo.

Further problems are seen by Islamist researcher Salah 'Abd al-Fattah al-Khalidi, who studied different aspects of the life and thought of Sayyid Qutb. He wrote the following:

> I would like . . . to point out a mistake committed by Islamists as they look at Sayyid Qutb and admire his Islamic thought. They were interested in knowing his life and his thought after he had joined the Muslim Brothers movement, but they were not interested in him before this stage. By so doing, they overlooked important aspects of his life and thought. They left out forty-five years from his life which were replete with events and developments. . . . They admired Sayyid Qutb when he was at the pinnacle of Islamic thought. It pleased them to look at him with admiration and dazzlement in his sublime position. . . . However, they were neither inter-

ested to know the road—and it was full of extreme
hardships—nor to understand the suffering of Sayyid as
he stepped in this road.[5]

As for the opponents of Sayyid Qutb, they did much to destroy
his literary and intellectual heritage. According to the researcher
'Abd al-Baqi Muhammad Hussayn:

> There was a time when the writings of Sayyid Qutb in-
> cluding his poetry were burned in the libraries and pub-
> lishing houses. Owning any of his writings was
> considered a crime. Furthermore, mere mentioning of
> the name of Sayyid Qutb, reference to his writing or
> using them in a research or a scientific study was con-
> sidered a punishable felony. Research necessity obliged
> a researcher to deal with a portion of his heritage or to
> benefit from it, but without declaring Qutb's name. In
> addition, some authors who reprinted their writings
> after the (1965) ordeal, omitted what they had written
> about Qutb in the first editions that were published be-
> fore his ordeal.[6]

In view of the difficulties one encounters in researching Sayyid
Qutb, I attempted in the context of this research to aim at objectivity and to avoid the partisanship which characterizes biased writings.

Thus, a major goal of this study is to help Arab, Muslim, and
Western readers gain a better understanding of the rise of one of the
most controversial Arab and Muslim thinkers in the past forty years.
If I ultimately succeed in presenting a comprehensive and human picture that is to a large extent objective and devoid of partisanship, I
will have achieved the desired goal.

Acknowledgments

I would like to thank the members of the editorial board of the refereed and scholarly journals *The Muslim World*/Hartford Seminary, the *Journal of Islamic Studies*/Oxford, and the *Journal of South Asian and Middle Eastern Studies*/Villanova University who published my articles on Sayyid Qutb which are documented in this research. I value the efforts of Professor Trevor LeGassick of the University of Michigan, Ann Arbor, Michigan, who read the manuscript and who provided me with many critical comments. My heartfelt thanks to Mr. John Eilts, the Middle East librarian at Stanford University, Stanford, California, and to Dr. Dave Weaver, Professor of Journalism at Indiana University, Bloomington, Indiana, for their advice, support, and deep friendship.

My deep appreciation goes to Stephen Magro, formerly of Praeger/Greenwood Publishing Group, who supervised the birth of this research project on Sayyid Qutb, and to Dr. Heather Staines and her assistants at Greenwood, and to Deborah Masi of Westchester Book Services, whose dedication and meticulous editorial work have made the realization of the project possible.

Many thanks to Mrs. Samia Srour of Bethlehem University for her excellent secretarial work and to Dr. Hanna Tushyeh and Mr. Sami Kirreh, my colleagues at Bethlehem University, who read the manuscript.

Last but not least, I express my deep appreciation to my wife, Salwa, and daughters, Anissa, Hiyam, Gena, Ameera, and Jessica, whose patience and support encouraged me to realize this work on Sayyid Qutb.

CHAPTER 1

INTELLECTUAL, POLITICAL, AND SOCIOECONOMIC TRANSFORMATIONS IN EGYPT, 1919–1952

INTRODUCTION

The period from 1919 to 1952 is the formative stage of Sayyid Qutb's life and thought and the time when he emerged as an independent Islamic ideologue. It is a period of transition from tradition to modernity. It is a colorful period full of vitality and contradictions. It is also the formative stage for contemporary thought, literature, theater, and cinema, among other things, in modern Egypt. The Westernization process which had begun early in the nineteenth century was by now fully evident in all aspects of life in Egypt. A secular educational structure dominated the nation, widening the gulf between those with secular and those with religious education.

The liberal nationalist forces that drew much of their inspiration from the Western world appeared to have gained the upper hand in the aftermath of the 1919–1922 revolt and the introduction of the constitutional parliamentary system of government in Egypt in 1923. The liberal nationalists in Egypt managed to leave their mark on the intellectual life of the country in the 1920s and to open the doors for the emulation and mimicry of Western civilization. However, the more the Westernizers proceeded and gained momentum, the more violent was the reaction of the religiously oriented Egyptians, and the more polarized that country became.

By the mid-1930s, a widespread reaction against rampant Westernization, Western suppression of the nationalist movements in the Arab East and Arab West, and the failure of the liberal nationalist establishment to achieve the independence of the Nile Valley and to solve society's pressing problems was taking place, even among the liberal literati. World War II and its adverse effects on the political, social and economic life of the Egyptians further alienated the onetime adherents of the liberal nationalist ideal and discredited the liberal nationalist politicians. Following the war, the country slipped into a period of increasing violence and the breakdown of law and order.

Thus, in the seven-year period preceding the July 1952 military revolt, the country was dominated by a sense of anger, grief, and despair at the established political institutions, which was only exacerbated by the Egyptian defeat in the 1948 Palestine War. As a result, many Egyptians defected to the camps of the two viable alternative groups who were prepared to challenge the existing order, namely, the Marxists and the Muslim Brothers.

Within this context, the transformations in Sayyid Qutb's life and thought will be examined in this book.

WORLD WAR I AND ITS IMPACT ON THE NATIONALIST MOVEMENT

With the outbreak of World War I in 1914, a formal British protectorate was declared and martial law was imposed which, inter alia, gave sweeping powers to the British high commissioner, including the dismissal of the pro-Ottoman Khedive 'Abbas Hilmi. British wartime measures, especially those carried out in the wake of the Palestine campaign in 1917 and 1918, led to ever-increasing demands for labor, food, and animals. The burden of these demands naturally fell on the shoulders of the peasants. Urgent demands for new recruits and volunteers to man the Labor Corps (Fayaliq al-'Amal) and the Camel Transport Corps led indirectly to the restoration of forced labor in the provinces, which was carried out by the local Egyptian government. These wartime measures caused much resentment against the British and caused the rise of pan-Islamic and pro-Ottoman sentiments in the country. Likewise, the war years caused many liberal nationalists, including some with records of pro-British leanings such as Saʿd Zaghlul, to become embittered nationalists by 1918. The transformation of Zaghlul's opinions of Britain paralleled those of most Egyptians. At the beginning Zaghlul advocated moderation and patience. He believed that cooperation with the British would bring its rewards after the war. British heavy-handedness during the war, however, united the country in a demand for early independence.[1]

THE LEADERSHIP OF THE 1919–1922 REVOLT

By 1918, a strong nationalist movement was in the making, spearheaded by Saʿd Zaghlul and colleagues from the defunct legislative assembly who were associated with the prewar liberal nationalists and the secular disciples of Muhammad ʿAbduh, such as Qasim Amin and Ahmad Lutfi al-Sayyid.

It is beyond the scope of this study to give a detailed account of the 1919–1922 popular revolt in Egypt. It suffices to mention that Saʿd Zaghlul and the Egyptian delegation al-Wafd al-Misri, or Wafd Party, which came into existence on November 13, 1918, became the unchallenged leaders and representatives of all Egypt, Muslims and Christians alike. In their demand for the liberation of Egypt and the Nile Valley from the British, Zaghlul and the Wafd Party were able to unite "the unlimited poverty of some and the insultingly bloated fortunes of others, the demand for change and the demand for conservatism, reaction and movement."[2] From this pluralistic background, which was full of contradictions, the Wafd Party and its leadership emerged to dominate the Egyptian political scene for the next thirty years. The contradictions, however, planted the seeds of disintegration within the party and explained the recurring splits among rank-and-file members throughout its history.

The leadership of the 1919–1922 revolution was dominated from its inception by secularists whose records in the pre-1919 period indicated that they were under "the spell of European thought and who were willing to adopt not only European ideas, but the very institutions that grew in Europe."[3] This was not, however, indicative of any grassroots support for the secular ideals of the Wafd. The life of the Egyptian masses continued to be shaped by Islam, its unitary worldview and its social and ethical principles. As Nadav Safran points out, "A relatively small class of Western educated and Western-oriented liberal nationalists had managed to ride to a decisive political victory on the wave of two elemental and hitherto inchoate forces that moved the large masses of the people: hatred of a religiously alien power born of a Muslim view of the world, and excessive economic suffering."[4]

It can be said further that the failure of Muslim reformists and other Islamic groups to become the rallying point for the Egyptian masses in the 1919–1922 revolution clearly indicates the absence of a viable alternative Islamic movement and program at that time. As Hisham Sharabi points out, "By 1914 Islamic revivalism had run its course; nationalism and its demands, not the problems of Islamic reform, had become the central social force in both Egypt and the Fertile Crescent."[5] Thus, the secularists and the masses shared a common nationalist vision: the liberation of the motherland from alien rule. This further explains why the secular leadership managed to ride to a decisive political victory in the 1919–1922 revolution.

SECULARISM ON THE OFFENSIVE: REVOLT AGAINST TRADITION

The assumption of power by the liberal nationalists was enhanced by Britain's unilateral declaration of Egypt's semi-independence in 1922, followed by the promulgation of a parliamentary constitutional monarchy in 1923 and the holding of general elections in 1924. If the triumph of the secular leadership of the nationalist movement did not necessarily imply the triumph of the secular nationalist ideology among the masses, it did at least, according to Safran, mean "the coming to power of a group of people who were motivated by that ideology and who could therefore use the important instruments of the state, such as legislation, public education, and other means, to foster its promotion and general acceptance by the public."[6]

The predominance of liberal nationalists in centers of power in Egypt during this period partially explains why secular forces appeared on the offensive in the 1920s, challenging the traditional Islamic ethos and causing much public uproar and panic among Muslim conservatives and Muslim reformists alike. Thus, in the aftermath of Mustafa Kamal Ataturk's abolition of the Ottoman caliphate in 1924, the question was raised as to whether the position of caliph was indeed necessary in Islam, and if so, who would succeed the Ottoman Sultan Muhammad VI. King Fuad of Egypt, through discreet efforts, was one of the claimants aspiring for the title.

In 1925, in the midst of this controversy, the jurist 'Ali 'Abd al-

Raziq, a disciple of Muhammad 'Abduh, published his controversial work *al-Islam wa-usul al-hukm* (Islam and the Principles of Government).[7] 'Abd al-Raziq argued both that the caliphate had had a disastrous effect on the progress of the Muslims and that it was unnecessary on the grounds that, while the Qur'an and the Sunnah had imposed moral precepts binding on the individual conscience, they were not concerned with the problems of political power. 'Abd al-Raziq's conclusion was that religion and politics should be separate. 'Abd al-Raziq's work raised much controversy and, as a result of the opposition of the royal court and various Islamic groups, he was dismissed from his position of judge in the religious courts.[8]

An even more provocative work than that of 'Abd al-Raziq appeared in 1926, entitled *Fi al-shi'r al-jahili* (On Pre-Islamic Poetry), later reissued in 1927 as *Fi al-adab al-jahili* (On Pre-Islamic Literature), by Taha Hussayn, a former student of al-Azhar and Muhammad 'Abduh. Using the principles of Cartesian logic, the author cast doubt on both pre-Islamic poetry and the Qur'anic stories of Abraham and Ismail, and in the process created a public uproar. Had it not been for the intervention of the constitutionalist liberal prime minister 'Abd al-Khaliq Tharwat, Hussayn probably would have lost his teaching post at the Egyptian University.[9]

One can observe in the literature of the period strong signs of a general rebellion against traditional methods. A prime example is the emergence of the modernist Diwan school of poetry, which was spearheaded by 'Abbas Mahmud al-'Aqqad, 'Abd al-Rahman Shukri, and 'Abd al-Qadir al-Mazini. The Diwan school directed bitter criticism at the neoclassical principles of such well-established literary figures of the time as Ahmad Shawqi, Hafiz Ibrahim, and Mustafa Sadiq al-Rafi'i. Salma Khadra Jayyusi points out that "the neo-classical school had been conforming to a concept of poetry which, left unopposed, would have entrenched itself so strongly that to arrive at modernity would have become an extremely arduous task. Backed by Shawqi's talent, it had acquired a great hold on the minds of the Arabs."[10]

According to R. C. Ostle, *al-Diwan: Kitab fi al-naqd wa-al-adab* (The Diwan: A Book on Criticism and Literature, Cairo, 1921) of al-'Aqqad and al-Mazini should be viewed in the same category as the controversial works of Taha Hussayn and 'Ali 'Abd al-Raziq, in that they all reflect the cultural and political crisis of the period. On the nature of the Diwan group's poetry and its relation to the time, Ostle points out that "it is hardly surprising that poetry should have been showing more subjective, egocentric tendencies throughout a period when the writings and activities of figures such as the feminist Qasim Amin and the political theorist Lutfi al-Sayyid were concerned basically with the significance of the individual in social and political terms." He adds that popular leaders such as Mustafa Kamil and Sa'd Zaghlul "gave broad sections of the Egyptian population the conviction that they too as individuals had a part to play in the struggles and the destiny of the newly emerging nation state."[11]

In addition to the literati, other secularists began to quicken the pace of attack on traditional Islam and its teachings. There was, for example, more discussion of Darwinian and social evolutionary theories, which had been put forward earlier by Shibli Shumayyil, Salama Musa, Ismail Mazhar, Hussayn Fawzi, and others. They had, in fact, carried on an extensive criticism of religious thought and had "declared Islamic civilization and culture as dead and useless and advocated the adoption of Western civilization and culture without reservation as the only way for the advancement of their country." These nonliterati intellectuals brushed aside Islamic reform and dubbed the famous nineteenth-century Islamic reformer Jamal al-Din al-Afghani (1838–1897) an "ignorant reactionary." Only "evolution, science and a positivist philosophy constituted the formula which they advocated for the advancement of Egypt."[12]

Traditional society came under attack in other fields as well. Since Qasim Amin publicized the case for women's emancipation, there had been repeated attempts to elevate the cause of female liberation to the national level, chief among them attempts by Malak Hifni Nasif in her *al-Nisa'iyyat* (Women's Affair, c. 1910), 'Abd al-Hamid Hamdi in the weekly journal *al-Sufur* (Unveiling, c. 1919), and Huda Sha'rawi and the Feminist Union in Egypt (founded in 1923). The feminist cause was further enhanced by legislative acts from 1923 to 1931 that challenged the traditional Islamic conception of marriage. The erosion of traditional values was further advanced by a reassertion of Pharaonism, that is, renewed interest in the ancient history and civilization of Egypt, which was given impetus by the discovery of the tomb of Tutenkhamon in 1922 and which assumed an important place in the writings of prominent secular Egyptian literati such as Muhammad Hussayn Haykal and Tawfiq al-Hakim in the 1920s. This current was an integral part of the liberal constitutional experiment which "undermined Islam not only as a basis of community and a source of legislation but also as a determinant of national feeling and identity."[13]

Taha Hussayn once again published a highly controversial work in 1938, *Mustaqbal al-Thaqafah fi Misr* (The Future of Culture in Egypt), in which he attacked traditional institutions and ethos and called for the elimination of the Arabic language college at al-Azhar and a greater role for the government in supervising Arabic language instructions at al-Azhar. Failure to do so, according to Hussayn, would undermine the natural unity of mentality among the educated and would instill in the children reactionary principles that would conflict with the secular education they were pursuing. Likewise, Hussayn asserted that Egypt and Europe have shared a common intellectual heritage since the time of the Pharaohs, and he claimed that Egypt is a Western, not an Eastern, nation.[14]

RESURGENCE OF ISLAMIC SENTIMENTS

Already in 1927 there was evidence of a renewal of Islamic sentiments resulting from the reaction of a number of Muslims who, according to J. Heyworth-Dunne, "were sad to see their heritage disappear, to be substituted by the Western system." This renewal took the form of active Islamic associations such as Jam'iyyat al-Shubban al-Muslimin (The Young Men's Muslim Association). This society was founded in November 1927 by prominent Muslims with the express purpose, inter alia, of opposing irreligion and libertinism, reviving the glory of Islam by restoring its religious law and its supremacy, spreading the knowledge best suited to the modern way of life, and making use of the best of Eastern and Western cultures while rejecting what was bad in them.[15]

A year later, in 1928–1929, Jam'iyyat al-Ikhwan al-Muslimin (the Society of Muslim Brothers), which was destined to play a significant role in Egyptian political and religious life in the 1940s and early 1950s, was founded by Hassan al-Banna (1906–1949).[16]

EASTERNISM

The resurgence of Islamic sentiments in the late 1920s, when examined within the larger intellectual trends of the period, can be seen as an integral part of a more active and general concern to return to the cultural roots of Egyptian society and to reject the blind mimicry of Western civilization. A case in point is the development of the in-

tellectual current of al-Sharqiyyah (Easternism), or al-Rabitah al-
Sharqiyah (the Eastern League) in the 1920s and the 1930s and the
growing distinction in the writings of many intellectuals in Egypt and
the Arab East between the "spiritual" East and the "materialistic"
West, the "oppressed" East and the "imperial" West. Such intellectuals included Ahmad Amin, Tawfiq al-Hakim, 'Abd al-Wahhab 'Azzam,
Muhammad Hussayn Haykal, Mikha'il Nu'aymah, and Fahmi al-
Mudarris (from Iraq), who attacked blind imitation of the West and
called for the rejuvenation of Eastern cultural roots. According to
Ibrahim Iskandar Ibrahim, the attempt to revive and glorify the East
appeared at a time when Egyptians were searching for cultural identity
as well as political independence. Eager to assert themselves, these intellectuals tended to stress the alleged spirituality of the East and Eastern civilization and to emphasize the materialistic character of Western
civilization.[17]

'Abd al-'Azim Ramadan points out that the current of Easternism
was a transition between the prewar current of pan-Islamism and
the later notion of pan-Arabism which developed in the late 1930s
and 1940s. This transitional stage occurred at a time when Egyptians were going through a period of ambivalence, searching for their
roots, and gradually rediscovering their Arabic Islamic heritage.[18]

INTEREST IN ISLAMIC SUBJECTS

Further evidence of the search for cultural heritage in the 1930s
was the renewed interest of liberal literati such as Taha Hussayn,
Ahmad Amin, 'Abbas Mahmud al-'Aqqad, Muhammad Hussayn
Haykal, and Tawfiq al-Hakim in Islamic subjects.[19]

Safran categorizes this period as the "reactionary phase" of Egypt's
intellectual development in the liberal nationalist era, 1919–1952. In
this phase, "the writers had surrendered their previous guide and
bearing—rationalism and a Western cultural orientation—without
being able to produce viable Muslim inspired alternatives."[20]

Charles D. Smith disagrees with Safran's thesis and asserts that
"the shift of intellectuals, and particularly Taha Hussayn and Hussayn Haykal, was a device designed to placate the religious and political opposition of the time and that, rather than seeking
Muslim-inspired alternatives, the intellectuals were trying to achieve
their previous goals by different means because of the resurgence of
Islamic sentiment which had occurred."[21]

Safran's controversial categorization of intellectual development into a "progressive phase" and a "reactionary phase" is an oversimplification of the complexities involved in the development of intellectuals in a transitional society and reflects the author's own distinctively Western value judgments. Charles D. Smith's thesis, on the other hand, is relevant in the case of Taha Hussayn. Hussayn published his Islamic work in 1933 and followed it in 1938 with his controversial work *The Future of Culture in Egypt*, in which he advocated Egypt's close affinity with European culture. Smith's thesis, however, fails to take into consideration the fact that intellectuals, as integral members of Egypt's transitional society, were genuinely reflecting society's quest for cultural roots and heritage.

Ibrahim explains the interest in Islamics in a more convincing manner. In his view, the intellectuals, especially the literati (Udaba'), never possessed a vigorous rationalist spirit which they later abandoned, as Safran suggests. "It is misleading to conceive them as systematic thinkers, who began as 'progressive' rationalists, glorifying reason, and ended as 'reactionary', attacking reason and advocating the superiority of passion." Ibrahim points out that these literati were masters of the traditional culture, that they were deeply influenced by their Islamic upbringing and by their profound knowledge of Arabic and its classical literature. In Ibrahim's view, "the impact of traditional life on the minds of this generation was so deep that it could occupy a large space in their autobiographies." Thus, the literati represented the "transitional" society that was in the process of formation. The literati grew up in a traditional society and attained adulthood "when the beliefs, culture and outlook of that society were disintegrating and finally came to experience life in another social structure which was obscure and to some extent confused." As a result, the literati were the product of two worlds which eventually merged to form a single unstable world. Hence, "their double weltanschauung."[22]

These literati, according to Ibrahim, were "enlightened" Muslims who, unlike such secularists as Salama Musa, Isma'il Mazhar, and Hussayn Fawzi, tried to renew, not refute, the traditional culture. They had much to admire in Western civilization, but were reluctant to accept it fully. Instead, they sought to reconcile the "technique" of the West with the "spirituality" of the East. Once this was achieved, a new Eastern civilization would emerge. The literati, therefore, were "neither totally emancipated from the hold of the old traditional culture, nor enthusiastic Westernizers. They were the connective link between tradition and modernity." Furthermore, in their writings the literati attempted to bridge the gap between East and West and to steer a middle course in a society which had been polarized, since Muhammad 'Abduh's death, into two camps: Westernizers, on the one hand, and Muslim reformers and conservatives on the other.[23]

FAILURE OF THE POLITICAL SYSTEM

The resurgence of Islamic and anti-Western sentiments in public life in the late 1920s and 1930s, as well as the emergence of mass movements in the 1930s, including the Society of Muslim Brothers, Young Egypt Party and Communist Party which functioned outside the political system can be attributed, inter alia, to the bankruptcy of the Egyptian liberal nationalist regime. A closer examination of the parliamentary monarchial regime of 1923 to 1952 attests to an undistinguished record of failure in the monarchial regime's efforts both to realize the ideals of the 1919–1922 uprising (the total liberation of the Nile Valley from British tutelage) and to solve the pressing problems of the nation.

Thus, whenever there was a free election under the provisions of the 1923 constitution, the Wafdists, who represented the nationalist forces under the leadership of Sa'd Zaghlul, and after 1927 under Mustafa Nahas, would inevitably come to power. King Fuad, and after 1936 his son King Faruq, both firmly believed that benevolent despotism, not liberalism, was best suited to Egypt, and therefore determined to govern as they pleased and sought to remove the Wafd, dissolving parliament and modifying or suspending the 1923 constitution. With the help of a coalition of anti-Wafdist forces which included the king's henchmen of Ittihadists (Union Party) and Sha'bists (People's Party), as well as other parties which were formed by successive splits from the Wafd, such as the Constitutional Liberals, the Sa'dists, and the Wafdist Bloc, the king was able to prevent the Wafd from enjoying the fruits of its constitutional victories. The Wafd mobilized mass support and organized mobs in the cities and towns to demonstrate against those who were usurping constitutional powers. The Wafd Party would remain in opposition until a quarrel between the king and the Constitutional Liberals or the Sa'dists (for example, in 1925 and 1949) or a change in Britain's policies toward internal politics brought about its return to power (as had happened in 1930, 1936 and 1942).[24]

Failure of the political system can also be attributed to British interference in the internal affairs of Egypt. Britain and its high commissioner (who often had the last word in Egyptian internal policy) manipulated the struggle between the king and the Wafd and opposition in the nationalist movement to Britain's strategic interests. The exploitation of Egypt's domestic front by the British can be seen clearly in the recall of the Wafd to power in 1936 and 1942; each time the Wafd's recall to power had disastrous effects on the Wafd's grip on the nationalist forces. The signing of the 1936 Anglo-Egyptian treaty, which provided for mutual defense and the continued presence of British forces in the Suez Canal area, was seen by many of the Wafd Party rank and file as a betrayal of the nationalist cause. They also saw it as a negation of the Wafd's role as the leader of the movement for complete independence, a role it had held from 1919 to 1935. According to P. J. Vatikiotis, students, professionals, and intellectuals left the Wafd, and many of them joined other mass movements including the Muslim Brothers and Young Egypt organizations.[25] Thus, it appeared that by the late 1930s and 1940s both internal and external factors were causing liberal nationalist ideology to lose ground. Internally, the liberal nationalist regime's failure to build viable democratic institutions for achieving complete independence from Britain in accordance with the ideals of the 1919–1922 revolution and its failure to solve the nation's ills discredited it.

Externally, the successful challenge put to Western democracies by Fascism and Marxism in the aftermath of the great depression of the late 1920s and the 1930s left a deep impression on Egyptians, further lowering the credibility of the liberal nationalist experiment. The liberal nationalist regime and institution at home were discredited moreover by Egyptians' increasing awareness that their fellow Arabs and Muslims were suffering at the hands of Western democracies such as Britain and France. As a result of the rapid growth of the Arabic press and the advent of Arab broadcasting, Egyptians became increasingly aware of the French suppression of the nationalist movements in the Levant and North Africa in the 1920s, 1930s, and 1940s, as well as of British sponsorship of the Jewish National Home in Palestine and their suppression of the Palestinian Arab nationalist movement. Awareness of these circumstances caused Egyptian nationalists to redirect their efforts. Instead of aiming to create an "Egypt for the Egyptians" modeled after Western democracies, Egyptian nationalists turned more and more to a vision of Arab and Muslim solidarity under Egypt's leadership.[26]

THE IMPACT OF WORLD WAR II ON EGYPTIAN SOCIETY, 1945–1952

The rapid growth of industry and Allied workshops and services in Egypt during World War II (1939–1945) created a great movement of people from the rural areas to the major urban centers, especially Cairo. Between 1939 and 1947 alone, Cairo's population increased more than 60 percent over the previous decade, while the population of Egypt as a whole for the same period increased 20 percent. According to Daniel Lerner, "the ancient metropolis has not the social capacity to absorb them as participants, and these urbanized nomads increase the nation's explosive rather than productive potential."[27] Furthermore, the years during and following World War II saw additional strain on the social and political spheres and continued erosion of popular support for the liberal nationalist regime. Charles Issawi points out that "the gap between rich and poor, already great, was further enlarged; the unskilled rural and urban laborer suffered severe privations; and the salaried middle and lower middle classes, whose money incomes rose very little, were relentlessly pressed down."[28]

When the Anglo-American Middle East Supply Center made Egypt the central focus of the Allied war effort during the war years in the Middle East and North Africa, relations between Egyptians and the occupying forces deteriorated. Peter Mansfield points out the following:

For the average British soldier, a typical Egyptian was a Cairo prostitute or a Port Said pimp selling Spanish fly and tickets to a blue film. After a few beers he would be ready to belch out the British army version of the Egyptian national anthem:

King Farouk, King Farouk
Hang your buttocks on a hook
Or
Queen Farida
Queen Farida of all the wogs

Mansfield points out that "most Egyptians knew enough English to understand and if they did not the sentiment was clear."[29]

This development should be seen in light of the ravaging impact of World War II upon Egyptian society. Safran writes that "the mass of well-paid, easy-spending, pleasure-seeking soldiers, themselves torn from their social roots and controls, spread a mood of eat and drink for tomorrow we die, . . . [which] was extremely provoking to Egyptians."[30]

The ethos of World War II is highly visible in the writings of Egyptian novelist Naguib Mahfouz (1911–), who won the Nobel Prize in literature in 1988. Mahfouz's 1947 novel *Zuqaq al-Midaqq* (Midaq Alley)[31] was received with much acclaim for its realistic portrayal of the impact of the war on the inhabitants of a blind alley in the Hussayni quarter of old Cairo, near al-Azhar. The residents of the Zuqaq are civilians, and the war invades their lives in the form of rising prices, well-paid jobs at Allied bases in Cairo and at the Suez Canal, and drastic changes in their personal lives.

Through the central characters of the novel—Hamidah, the restless beautiful maiden of the alley who is willing, at any cost, to leave the alley and its wretched conditions; Kirsha, the homosexual owner of the alley's coffeehouse; Zita, the kingmaker of beggars; Doctor Bushi, the self-appointed dentist and a partner of Zita; and Sayyid Radwan al-Hussayni, the dignified and philanthropic mystic who is loved by all—the reader gains an understanding of how the presence of large numbers of Allied forces in Egypt, and the social and economic ills that the war caused, affected Egyptians on a personal level as individuals and afflicted Egyptian urban society as a whole.

For example, Hamidah, the principal figure in the novel, represents the restless Egyptian youth who were overanxious to seek a more exciting life and better job opportunities in the Allied camps. Hamidah is lured by money and fine clothes, which she always desired, and by a pimp, Faraj Ibrahim, who trains her to cater to the pleasures of Allied soldiers. When her fiancé, 'Abbas al-Hulw, the barber of the alley who gave up his profession for a more lucrative job in a British army camp, discovers her entertaining a group of drunken British soldiers, he attacks her, only to be beaten to death by the soldiers.

Commenting on Mahfouz's *Zuqaq al-Midaqq*, Hamdi Sakkut writes: "The world of the Zuqaq exists as a criticism of the real world. . . . One admires Mahfouz for having the courage and humanity to describe in such detail a man like Zita, while most other people either try to pretend that such sordidness and filth do not exist, or else deny that this is a proper subject for a work of art."[32]

Another World War II development that had a far-reaching impact on Egyptian political developments in the postwar period was British imposition of a Wafdist cabinet on the king and the country.

The return of the Wafd to power on February 4, 1942, with the aid of Sir Miles Lampson, British high commissioner since 1933, and General R.C.W.H. Stone, commander of British troops and armor in Egypt, caused great anger and frustration among Egyptians. The incident caused a great rift between the humiliated king and the Wafd, as well as dismay among many of the Wafd's followers and young army officers. The late President Nasser, then a young army officer, writes in his *Falsafat al-Thawrah* (Philosophy of the Revolution, Cairo; Dar al-Ma'aref, 15) about the long-lasting impact of the events of February 1942 on young army officers, who deeply felt humiliated by the British action and as a result became determined to sacrifice themselves to restore the nation's dignity.

Mansfield points out that the February 1942 incident was a "seminal event in the history of modern Egypt. Its immediate effect was to upset the twenty-year-old triangular balance of forces in Egyptian political life. Ultimately it destroyed the monarchy, the Wafd, and in helping to provoke the 1952 revolution, the British position in Egypt."[33]

SOCIOECONOMIC AND POLITICAL TRANSFORMATIONS, 1945–1952

After the war ended, Egypt slipped into a period of increasing violence, chaos, and breakdown in law and order, which ended only with the overthrow of the monarchy and liberal nationalist regime by the Free Officers in July 1952. Following Egyptian and Arab defeat in the Palestine War, 1948–1949, a clandestine committee of Free Officers led by Lieut. Col. Gamal 'Abd al-Nasser was organized in 1949. The growing Egyptian middle class in 1945–1952 resented the concentration of power in the hands of the king and a few large landowners who dominated Egyptian life. These landowners, "representing less than one half of one percent (some 12,000) of the proprietors, owned 37 percent of the arable land, more than two million acres. They led the country's principal political parties, controlled parliament, determined what legislation would be enacted, and decided upon the government's domestic and foreign policy. Nearly all leading politicians were among the 0.4 percent of the population who owned more than 50 acres."

On the other hand, the majority of Egypt's population, the peasants, were poverty stricken and were infected with many diseases, such as liver fluke and bilharzia, which were associated with the misuse of the Nile water for drinking and washing, and the lack of sanitation and hygiene. Poverty was further exacerbated by overpopulation and the lack of enough agricultural land to accommodate the entire population. Eighty percent of Egypt's population lived in these rural areas. The landowners lived in large cities and had little empathy with the peasants and the poor and needy in the rural areas.[34]

In the industrial sector, "sharp fluctuations in production and a drive to intensify mechanization in the textile industry resulted in recurrent unemployment . . . (and) the cost of living index soared from 100 in 1939 to 331 in 1952, and real wages did not keep pace." These circumstances led to the radicalization of the working class.[35]

Breakdown of law and order between 1945 and 1952 can be seen in the epidemic eruption of waves of strikes among industrial workers and public employees, including the police force. Many of the strikers and demonstrators were violently suppressed. These strikes were accompanied by other violent outbreaks of discontent such as peasant collective actions against landlords between 1944 and 1952, the most notable of which was the uprising against the feudal estates of the Badrawi-'Ashur family at Buhut in June 1951.[36]

Frequent assassinations and attempted assassinations of public figures took place during this violent period. Those who were assassinated included Prime Minister Ahmad Mahir (1945), the Wafdist Anglophile Amin 'Uthman (1946), the secretary of the Cairo Court of Appeals (1948), the chief of Cairo's police force Salim Zaki (1948), Prime Minister Nuqrashi (1948), and the Supreme Guide of the Muslim Brothers, Hassan al-Banna (1949). Unsuccessful attempts were made to assassinate Wafdist leader Mustafa Nahas (1946 and 1948) and Prime Minister Ibrahim 'Abd al-Hadi (1949). Violent acts were also committed against public places, as can be exemplified in the bombing of Metro Cinema in May 1947, Cairo's Jewish quarter in 1948, and large department stores in Cairo in the summer of 1948.[37]

Under these wartime and postwar conditions, two alternative groups appeared on the Egyptian scene who were prepared to challenge the existing order. These two alternative groups were the leftist groups and the Islamic alternative led by the Society of Muslim Brothers. The leftist groups had gained much confidence by the defeat of fascism in Europe following two decades of agonizing struggle to formulate viable Marxist alternatives to the liberal nationalist regime. The Islamic alternative led by the Society of Muslim Brothers rose to prominence with years of discipline and experience behind it.

The Leftist Groups

The 1940s saw the proliferation of radical student and workers' committees and clubs in Egypt, which gave the nationalist movement a new direction. In 1945 these groups set up national committees of students and workers who challenged the regime by their continuous agitation. In addition, there was a proliferation of leftist political and cultural organs, including the Institute for Scientific Research and the Committee for the Propagation of Modern Culture, as well as the journals *al-Fajr al-Jadid* (The New Dawn), *al-Tali'ah* (The Vanguard) and *al-Jamahir* (The Masses) between 1945 and 1948. At the same time the National Popular University was created to train working-class leaders. During its six months of existence, the university offered evening classes in political economy, history, philosophy, literature, and international affairs, among other subjects.[38]

Vatikiotis points out that these Marxist groups combined a program of national liberation (i.e., the evacuation of British forces from Egypt) with the "liberation of the exploited masses from a capitalist minority . . . and played a major role in labor strikes and student demonstrations which followed from February 1946 until 1952." He adds that these groups influenced the "tactics and programs" of other well-established groups, which in turn adopted more radical reforms into their own political program. For example, the left wing of the Wafd took up "the cause of the urban proletariat" and attacked the "capitalists" and the state of the national economy in order to make the Wafd's program more appealing to the masses. The monthly review *al-Ba'th*, founded by the Wafdist man of letters Muhammad Mandur in 1944, became a platform for intellectuals who advocated a close link between the educated and the rural and urban working classes. In 1945 these intellectuals called for the limitation of land ownership and demanded the intervention of the state in bringing about radical economic and social change.[39]

The feminist movement expanded as well in this period, which was a time when a growing number of women were entering institutes of higher learning. Cairo University graduate and feminist Inji Aflatun founded the League of University and Institutes Women with other feminists in 1945. The League of University and Institutes Women represented a "Marxist-progressive-nationalist-feminist" current in the late 1940s and 1950s. In February 1951, Duriyya

Shafiq, a French-educated feminist activist, led "a sit-in at the parliament to demand the right for women to vote."[40]

In 1945, the Wafdists, the nationalist and communist intellectuals, and the trade unions formed a common front, the National Committee of Workers and Students, in order to demand the total British evacuation of Egypt, the internationalization of Egyptian demands and liberation from economic subjection. The National Committee's influence, according to Anouar Abdel-Malek, extended to universities, secondary and technical schools, the intelligentsia, the professions and the trade unions. The National Committee spearheaded mass action in the form of local committees, demonstrations, strikes, and armed struggles against the British.[41]

The Muslim Brothers

The inability of earlier Muslim reformers, such as Muhammad 'Abduh and Muhammad Rashid Rida, to translate their Islamic ideology into religious mass movements was overcome by their disciple Hassan al-Banna (1906–1949), who created a viable Islamic movement in the 1930s and 1940s.[42] This movement became known as the Society of Muslim Brothers. The Muslim Brothers had a unique opportunity to benefit from the failure of the Wafd in successive governments to solve the massive problems of society. The bulk of the Muslim Brothers' supporters and propagandists had come from the Wafd Party, which had already been losing members for several years. Heyworth-Dunne points out that "the greatest secession took place after the Wafd was dismissed in October 1944, when Makram Ebeid published his *Black Book* in 1945 on the misdeeds of the Wafd while in power, thus giving Hassan al-Banna all the materials he needed to attack the Wafd and to undermine its position."[43]

In addition to their call for a *Shari'ah*-based Muslim society to replace Western-inspired regimes, the Muslim Brothers' program for the rebirth of Egypt called for such economic reforms as the abolition of usury in all its forms, the nationalization of natural resources, the nationalization of financial institutions such as the Misr Bank, the industrialization of the whole nation, the reform of the tax system, the redistribution of land, the protection of farm renters from landowners, the introduction of labor reform measures in the agricultural and industrial sectors, and the institution of Zakat-based social security.[44]

Likewise, the Society of Muslim Brothers embarked upon a series of industrial and commercial enterprises to demonstrate the feasibility of an Islamic alternative to the Western-inspired economic system. The society's labor union activities, were intensive, and they were met with much success among transport, textile, utilities, and refinery workers. However, the withdrawal of the unions dominated by the society from the National Committee of Workers and Students, according to Richard P. Mitchell, "brought upon the Society the wrath of all 'progressive forces' in the leftist alliance, and signaled the renewal of internecine struggle between the leftist groups and the Muslim Brothers for the leadership of the masses."[45]

According to Vatikiotis, the Muslim Brothers were more successful than the leftists in winning a great number of followers from the masses. The leftists' leadership and spokesmen came from Westernized sectors of society, and their proposals for reform and change were based on foreign ideology.[46] The Muslim Brothers, on the other hand, had infiltrated the armed forces beginning in the 1940s, and some members of the clandestine Free Officers movement, such as Anwar el-Sadat and Gamal 'Abd al-Nasser who would lead the successful July 1952 coup, were in touch with the organization through military officers with Muslim Brothers' affiliation such as 'Abd al-Muni'im 'Abd al-Ra'uf and Mahmud Labib.[47]

INTELLECTUAL CURRENTS, 1945–1952

The decade preceding the military revolt in July 1952 was dominated by a sense of anger, grief and despair at the established sociopolitical and economic political institutions and their inability to solve the country's pressing problems. This is evident in the intellectual production of the period, which focused on social protest and demanded the total reform of Egyptian society.

Taha Hussayn

Between 1945 and 1950, Taha Hussayn, departing from his earlier controversial cultural works, published several works that criticized the established order and focused on social injustice, political corruption, and resistance to oppression and exploitation. These works included *Mir'at al-damir al-hadith* (The Mirror of Modern Conscience, 1949); *al-Mu'adhdhabun fi al-ard* (The Tormented on Earth, 1949), which was banned in Egypt; and *Jannat al-hayawan*

(Animal Paradise, 1950). Pierre Cachia points out that Hussayn's "fretting over the stationary conditions of the masses is genuine, and there are signs of a swing to the left and an unprecedented concern with moral issues, as though his earlier faith in the inevitable success of simple but fundamental formula—liberty, parliamentary democracy, natural evolution—had ended in disillusionment."[48]

Among the outstanding works of this genre is Taha Hussayn's work *al-Mu'adhdhabun fi al-'ard* (The Tormented on Earth), which was written in the last years of the monarchy. Hussayn explains why this book was confiscated. He points out that "the government's aim was to increase the prosperity of the affluent and to intensify the destitution of the sufferers, and the wretched." When he decided to write a book that would address the problem to enlighten Egyptians with the reality of their affairs, the book was confiscated.[49]

Hussayn dedicated the book "to those burning with their yearning for justice and those rendered sleepless by their fear of injustice. To those who have what they do not spend and those who do not have anything to spend." Taha Hussayn describes the way of life of the wretched and the poor as follows:

> His eye was capable of coveting objects of the farthest reaches of sight, yet his hand has no reach at all. He would see delicacies at arm's length, and his heart would long for them and the hearts of his sons and daughters would hug for them. Yet, when he attempted to grasp them, his hands would refuse to stretch out as though paralyzed, or as though bound to his body by the heaviest of chains.
>
> Wretchedness would only accompany this majority along with its friends: hunger, nakedness, sickness, humiliation, degradation, toil that consumes and is never exhausted, and anxiety that intensifies and never relents. The people felt the greatest hatred for these companions and were most weary of them. But they found no means of ridding themselves of such burdensome fellows, unless justice should come and drop a veil between them. But justice was excessively tardy in coming, as though walking in chains.[50]

Khalid Muhammad Khalid

Likewise, modernist religious Muslims attempted to reformulate Islam in a way that would make it more responsive to the requirements. A controversial work of the period that challenged the established religious institutions was Shaykh Khalid Muhammad Khalid's *Min huna nabda'* (From Here We Begin, 1950). The controversy surrounding his book was similar to the reaction that was provoked in 1925 by the publication of 'Ali 'Abd al-Raziq's work *al-Islam wa-usul al-hukm* (Islam and the Principles of Government). In his bitter attack against the status quo, the 30-year-old graduate of Egypt's leading religious school, al-Azhar, called for the purging of "priest-craft" (Kahanah) from Islam and charged that official faith often conspires with wealth against justice and mercy. He went on to insist on the indispensability of secular national government and of socialism for reconstructing a healthy and prosperous society. He also advocated the further emancipation and education of women. Khalid accused traditional religious institutions of being priestcraft (Kahanah) that totally contradicts the true spirit of religion (ad-Din). True religion interacts fully with the needs of the people, serves to guide and help them as they face new challenges and pressing needs and blesses them as they constantly attempt to leap forward to new horizons.[51]

Khalid further accused the priestcraft of being a religion of reactionaries who support the interests of the powerful and the rich and in the process justify poverty. He cites an example from his days as a student at al-Azhar where a leading figure of this priestcraft declared on the pages of a daily newspaper that al-Azhar should not mix the acquisition of knowledge with worldly things even though this same leading figure possessed many of these worldly things.[52]

Furthermore, Khaled accused the political establishment of subsidizing feudal lords, and in the process he quotes Ihsan 'Abd al-Quddus (Rose al-Yusuf, issue no. 1035), who put forth the following:

> Taking a look at the national Egyptian budget is enough to incite a person to become a communist or at least to become convinced that communism is right and that those who are rebelling against class divisions in Egypt are not mere hatemongers. . . . [The] government budget shows that taxes imposed on agricultural land owners are 4,700,000 Egyptian pounds whereas [the] budget allocation for irrigation systems for the same agricultural lands totals 6,200,000 Egyptian pounds. That is the state subsidizes landowners the like of Badrawi Ashur and Abbud Pasha with a total of 1,500,000 Egyptian pounds generated from taxes imposed on ordinary people . . . from cigarettes, textiles, foodstuff and basic necessities of life.[53]

Immediately, the book was censored by the Azhar religious circles, and the public prosecutor ordered a stop to the release and distribution of the book. The Cairo Court of First Instance finally ordered the release of the book on the grounds that the charges leveled against the author, which included the charges that he assaulted Islam, that he called for changes in the basic laws of society by force and terror and that he incited the public against capitalists, have no bases.[54]

The Arab Idea

Egyptian affinity and empathy with the Arab idea and Arab causes at this stage were growing. The Palestine problem, 1936–1939; Egyptian involvement in Arab affairs in the same period; the emergence of pan-Arab activities such as the Society for Arab Unity, organized by Muhammad Ali 'Alluba in 1942; the Union of Arabism, established by students at Cairo University; activities of prominent pan-Arabs such as 'Abd al-Rahman 'Azzam and Ahmad Hassan al-Zayyat; the formation of the Arab League in 1945; and the Palestine War in 1948–1949 were all important contributing factors. In addition, Egypt's central role in Arab publishing and mass media, including radio, music, and cinema, increased Egyptians' interest in Arab affairs and eventually led to the emergence of the Arab component of Egyptian collective cultural identity. This cultural identity would become more prominent during the administration of President Nasser in the 1950s and the 1960s.[55]

THE END OF THE LIBERAL NATIONALIST REGIME, 1948–1952

The Defeat of the Arabs in Palestine

Within this context of wartime and postwar social, economic, and political crises, the disintegration and collapse of the liberal nationalist order became evident. The period 1945–1952 saw the culmination of the liberal nationalist era in the breakdown of law and order, the rise of radical Islamic and leftist groups determined to challenge the status quo, and the emergence of radical ideas encompassing a whole spectrum of thought. Egyptian and Arab performance in the Palestine War in 1948–1949 led to further hopelessness and anger. The decision of the Egyptian government to intervene in May 1948 gave it "some short-term relief from the ceaseless round of strikes and riots, and for a time a rigid censorship was able to conceal the disastrous course of the war."[56] The utter defeat of the Arab forces in Palestine could not be hidden for very long, however. There were also scandals over inferior army equipment, and "king and governments were blamed for treacherously letting down the army in which there developed an intense feeling of shame. . . . And the ground was immensely fertile for the growth of a resistance movement."[57]

The Failures of the Wafd and the Breakdown of Law and Order, 1950–1952

The return of the Wafdists to power in 1950–1952, through free general elections, retarded this process but was unable to reverse it. Despite their introduction of reforms such as free secondary and technical education, the distribution of land to landless peasants and aid to the working classes such as compensation for sick leave and cost of living allowances that were geared to alleviate socioeconomic problems, Egypt's problems were simply too overwhelming by this time for these limited solutions to have any far-reaching effect. For example, the results of the educational reforms were for practical purposes disastrous. Vatikiotis points out that "the original objective of making elementary education universal in the country to eradicate illiteracy suffered. Secondary schools in particular manifested the drawbacks of a centralized uniform syllabus and examinations . . . an over emphasis on language and theoretical subjects; overcrowding because of poor and limited physical facilities; a shortage of qualified teachers; and consequent low standards of teaching."[58]

Furthermore, the Wafd Party was fatally polarized. The struggle between the right wing, which was dominated by large landowners such as Fu'ad Siraj al-Din, the head of the party's apparatus, and the Marxist-oriented left wing, which offered radical solutions in concert with other leftist groups in Egypt and which controlled the party press, prevented the party from sponsoring any revolutionary measures to combat the nation's ills. The Wafdist government's indecisiveness was apparent in the Anglo-Egyptian confrontation of 1951–1952. The failure of Anglo-Egyptian negotiations and the resulting Wafdist government's unilateral abrogation of the 1936 treaty and the 1899 Sudan Condominium Agreement in October 1951 provided the party with an excellent opportunity to restore its credibility and to reassert its leadership of the masses. Instead of capitalizing on this very popular move, however, by forging a unified Egyptian response against the British military presence in Egypt, the Wafdist government hesitated. Meanwhile, ad hoc Egyptian guerrilla bands consisting of large numbers of Muslim Brothers as well as students, workers, intellectuals, army officers and noncommissioned officers took matters into their own hands and carried out guerrilla operations against British troops in the Suez Canal. By late January 1952, it appeared that British forces had decided to take the offensive and were moving military forces toward Cairo. Opposition to the Wafdist government's unwillingness to commit regular armed units against the British or to take up the coordination and training of irregular forces became evident with more frequent demonstrations and strikes against both the government and the king.[59]

The killing of fifty Egyptian policemen and gendarmes by the British in Isma'iliyah on January 25, 1952, aroused the anger and frustration of the Egyptian people. The following day, mobs in Cairo went on a rampage and began burning the center of the city. Their targets were cinemas, hotels, sporting clubs, restaurants, and other establishments. The mobs prevented fire brigades from fighting the fires. Finally, the army was called in to quell the rioting. According to Mitchell, "the fire lumped together, in one massive rejection, the British, the West, the foreigner, the wealthy, and the ruler-king and pasha alike."[60]

The burning of Cairo demonstrated the weakness of the Wafd in the face of turmoil. The king, who had nothing but contempt for the Wafd, lost no time in dismissing the Wafdist cabinet on January 27, 1952. A six-month period elapsed between the burning of Cairo and the dismissal of the Wafdist government and the Free Officers' revolt of July 1952. During this time, four different interim governments were formed amid a general collapse of the institutions of the monarchial regime, including the police and security forces that had served as the mainstay of its rule. Meantime, the rift between the army and the king over the king's effort to reassert his authority over the military, by trying to force the unpopular general Hussayn Sirri 'Amir on the leadership of the Officers' Club and to place his brother-in-law, Colonel Ismail Shirin, over the Ministry of War and the Navy, grew worse.[61]

Emergence of the Free Officers

During this period, the army was the only institution in Egypt that had emerged intact from the chaos of the Palestine War and the burning of Cairo, and it was the only force left that had the power to restore law and order and govern with credibility if given the opportunity. In the meantime, the position of the Muslim Brothers continued to improve in the months preceding the July revolution. Their relations with the successive governments were excellent, and they emerged from the January–July chaos as the strongest noninstitutional group in the country, especially since the largest political group, the Wafd Party, was discredited and had lost much of its mass appeal. The Muslim Brothers had infiltrated the armed forces so that many in the rank and file and some members of the clandestine Free Officers movement including Nasser himself were at some time either members of or in close association with the society. The Free Officers needed the full support and cooperation of the society to execute their revolution.[62]

On the morning of July 23, 1952, the Free Officers movement, in the making since the early 1940s and given much impetus by Egyptian defeat in the 1948 Palestine War, seized the opportunity presented by the deteriorating state of the country to overthrow the monarchy and the liberal nationalist regime. Selma Botman describes the Free Officers as follows:

> The Free Officers, who actually carried the day, were not the military, not the army as such, but a political movement within the military in which all the opposition trends were represented—communists, Muslims Brothers and Wafdists. The genius of Gamal Abdul Nasser was that he was able to gather around himself a group of officers who agreed on a limited number of principles for the reshaping of Egypt. Through this representative military opposition, Nasser ultimately took control of the country. Nasser required all those who worked with him to discipline their relations with their own political organizations and avoid security leakages. He did not ask his collaborators to give up their ideology, only to veil organizational ties behind allegiance to the Free Officers' group.[63]

Seventy years earlier, in 1882, the British had occupied Egypt in order to reestablish the authority of the Khedival system that was threatened by the nationalist forces led by Ahmad 'Urabi. In 1952, however, the British military forces in Egypt did not attempt to interfere on behalf of the ousted liberal nationalist regime or to alter the course of events. According to Vatikiotis, "the moment they (the Egyptian government) severed their special relationship with Britain (abrogated the 1936 treaty)—which had also served as a prop for their rule—they had sealed their own fate in the country. It is unlikely they had expected an army coup; it is even highly probable that this eventuality hardly crossed their minds. Perhaps after the fiasco in Palestine it should have."[64]

CHAPTER 2

Qutb's Childhood and the Emergence of a Poet and a Critic, 1906–1938

I am like a navigator whose ship went astray and he is afraid of a fearful and desolate shore. What will be born on the day you are born, O! my morrow? *(Sayyid Qutb the Poet, 1934)*

Religion. . . . Religion. . . . This is the cry of the feeble and the weak who seeks protection in it whenever the current takes him away. . . . Say it one hundred times, for thank God, we are not ones who are terrified by such empty cries . . . and we studied religion more than you and we understand it more than you. *(Sayyid Qutb the Literary Critic, 1938)*

QUTB'S CHILDHOOD IN MUSHA, EGYPT, 1906–1921

Child from the Village

An account of Sayyid Qutb's childhood has been largely preserved in his autobiographical literary work *Tifl min al-qaryah* (Child from the Village), which was first published in Cairo in 1946 when Qutb was becoming firmly established as a literary critic in Cairo's leading literary reviews, especially *al-Risalah*.[1]

Egyptian society in the 1920s and 1930s had been going through a great cultural upheaval as a result of a clash between traditional and modern values, in which traditional values were being eroded but not replaced. In the meantime, imitation of the West was widespread and reaction against such mimicry was developing. Qutb's outlook on life at this formative stage of his own life reflects the transitional nature of the society to which he belonged.

In Qutb's autobiography, one can observe the conflicting forces of tradition and modernity that were working to shape his personality and worldview. One can see, for example, the shift away from traditional education to secular training, that is, from the kuttab (Qur'anic school) to the madrasah (modern elementary school). In the process one also sees the schism which was developing in the educational system and the gulf between those in Egyptian society who had received religious education as opposed to secular education. The hostility between Qutb and the kuttab children was just one example of the rift that was growing between tradition and modernity, between the tradition-bound students and sheikhs of the kuttab on the one hand, and urban-bound effendi class, the transitionals who were represented by the teachers and students of the 'madrasah,' on the other.

But one is also struck by the deep impact of traditional life on the mind and worldview of Sayyid Qutb, the adib (litterateur), by the large space he devotes in his autobiography to popular religious practices, to his Islamic upbringing, and the customs and manners of villagers. Similarly, one observes that Qutb at a very early age had mastered important aspects of traditional Egyptian Muslim culture, such as the memorization of the Qur'an and a thorough knowledge of the Arabic language, which paved the way for his membership in the ranks of the udaba' (literati) in the 1920s, 1930s and 1940s.

When Qutb moved to Cairo permanently in his teens (ca. 1921), he came to experience life in a different social structure, one which was modern, urban, and afflicted with cultural and other problems. As a result of this changing environment and his uprootedness at an early age, Qutb was the product of two worlds, traditional and modern, which eventually merged into one unstable world with two conflicting worldviews (double weltanschauung).[2]

The trauma produced by this uprootedness is reflected in Qutb's later writings. Following the death of his mother in 1940, Qutb describes himself, his brother, and his sisters as strangers who resemble branches whose roots have withered from estrangement from their native soil.[3] Ibrahim describes the Qutbs' feeling of uprooted-ness as a "nostalgic feeling toward the past, symbolized in the coun-tryside, the seat of purity, and in hatred of Cairo, the symbol of corrupted morality. Cairo for them is the new society, the new home which could never become theirs."[4]

Fashioned after Taha Hussayn's *al-Ayyam* (The Stream of Days),[5] one of Qutb's favorite prose works, *Tifl min al-qaryah*, is an account of rural life in upper Egypt in the early decades of the twentieth cen-tury. In addition to scattered details relating to the life of Sayyid Qutb and his family, one finds a wealth of information on various aspects of village life such as popular religious practices and super-stition, systems of education, agricultural life, public health and hy-giene, status of women, and political life. In dedicating his book to Taha Hussayn, his superior in the Ministry of Education from 1942 to 1944,[6] Qutb writes:

> To the author of *al-Ayyam*. . . . Some of the days which the child spent in the village resembled yours; however, most of them were different. The extent of these differences was that between one generation and another, one village and another, one life and an-other, one nature and another, one trend and another. But they were, after all, days from *al-Ayyam*.[7]

To elucidate the various forces that were shaping Qutb's person-ality and world outlook in his childhood, closer examination of the legacy of his parents, his educational training, association with the underprivileged, and the impact of folk religion and superstition are presented here.

THE LEGACY OF SAYYID QUTB'S PARENTS

Sayyid Qutb Ibrahim Hussayn Shadhili was born in 1906 in the Egyptian village of Musha, also known officially as "Balad al-Shaykh 'Abd al-Fattah" in reference to its native Muslim saint or holy man,[8] in the Asyut District (Markaz Asyut), 235 miles by rail south of Cairo. The chief city of this 'Markaz,' Asyut city, is the largest set-tlement of Upper Egypt and, like Musha, it is located on the west bank of the Nile between Cairo and Aswan.[9]

Qutb Ibrahim, Sayyid Qutb's father, was a prominent farmer in Musha whose ancestry, according to Sayyid Qutb, could be traced to his sixth great-grandfather, an Indian Muslim named 'Ubayd Allah.[10] Qutb Ibrahim's fortunes in the village dwindled gradually, however, and he was eventually forced to sell some precious parcels of land to pay back some debts that had accumulated due to the family's wealthy style of living. Sayyid Qutb became aware of his father's financial dilemma at the age of ten when his weeping mother, Fatimah, confronted him with this bitter reality and impressed upon him his future role in restoring his family's prestige and fortunes in the village.[11]

Qutb Ibrahim was an active member of the local branch of the Nationalist Party (al-Hizb al-Watani) and subscribed regularly to the party's organ *al-Liwa'*. During World War I, Qutb Ibrahim's home became a meeting place for party members.[12] The father left a deep impression on his son. In dedicating his book *Mashahid al-qiyamah fi al-Qur'an* (Scenes of Resurrection in the Qur'an) to the soul of his father, Sayyid Qutb writes:

> When I was a young child you imprinted on my senses the fear of the Day of Judgment. You never scolded me or restrained me, but your daily life was an example of a man who was always aware of the Day of Accounting. . . . The image of you reciting the *Fatihah* (The opening Chapter or Surah of the Qur'an) every evening following supper, and the dedication of the prayer to the souls of your fathers in their final abode, are vividly imprinted in my imagination.[13]

Sayyid Qutb's mother, Fatimah, came from a prominent family in the village whose fortunes, like those of the Qutb family, were declining gradually.[14] There is no doubt that she was, until her death in October 1940, a major force in her children's lives. This is clearly apparent in *al-Atyaf al-Arba'ah* (The Four Phantoms), an anthology dedicated to her memory by her children Hamidah, Aminah, Muhammad, and Sayyid Qutb, which appeared in 1945.[15]

Fatimah's influence on her son Sayyid was immense. She instilled in him a sense of mission in life in the face of her husband's deteriorating financial situation. As a first step in that direction, she wanted her son to obtain the best education possible in the village and then to go to Cairo to live with her brother Ahmad Hussayn 'Uthman, a graduate of al-Azhar, who was a teacher and a journalist, in order to continue his education.[16] Fatimah was deeply religious and wished all her children to learn the Qur'an. In dedicating his book *al-Taswir al-fanni fi al-Qur'an* (Artistic Portrayal in the Qur'an) to the memory of his mother, Sayyid Qutb writes:

> When you sent me to the primary school in the village your greatest wish was that Allah might open my heart to memorize the Qur'an and that He might provide me with a melodious voice so that I could chant it for you. . . . I have memorized the Qur'an and fulfilled a part of your wish.[17]

Sayyid Qutb's Educational Training

Sayyid Qutb's education began at the age of six (ca. 1912) when, after prolonged hesitation and considerable debate in the family, he was sent to a modern primary school, or 'madrasah,' in the village instead of the traditional 'kuttab.' Qutb grew fond and proud of his 'madrasah' and its teachers and developed a great contempt for the 'kuttab' and its students and sheikhs.[18] However, as a result of false rumors spread by the 'kuttab' teachers and others that the government intended to eliminate Qur'anic education from its modern elementary schools, Sayyid and some other village children were forced to attend the much-hated "dirty kuttab" for a brief period. But soon Sayyid was back at his "beloved madrasah" and, with fellow students in the modern school, they were organized into a Qur'anic memorization team to prove, through school contests with 'kuttab' students, that children of the 'madrasah' could be as good as, if not better, than 'kuttab' children in Qur'anic memorization. The frequent success of the 'madrasah' children in these contests gave Sayyid Qutb an overwhelming feeling of victory.[19] Later, when asked about his greatest wish in life, Qutb would answer that he would like to return to being a student at the "holy madrasah" to defend it against the 'kuttab' and the children of the 'kuttab.'[20]

By the end of his fourth year in the 'madrasah' (ca. 1916), Sayyid Qutb had memorized the Qur'an completely.[21] Although this did not give him deep insight into the meaning and significance of the Book, it did leave long-lasting impressions on his imagination in the form of strong and beautiful imagery and personal associations evoked by certain verses. The beauty and simplicity of the "Qur'an of childhood" was, according to Qutb, complicated by the Qur'anic commentaries that he later read and studied as an adult in Cairo in the 1920s and 1930s. In the late 1930s, however, Qutb returned to his "Qur'an of childhood" and became a student of its artistic imagery.[22]

Sayyid Qutb's career at the 'madrasah' was highly distinguished. In addition to being the pride of the school in its successful Qur'anic memorization program, Qutb excelled in his classes, especially Arabic, so that by the age of ten he was already reading his father's newspaper to the visitors who used to come to his house to hear the latest news.[23] His deeply felt mission in life of restoring the Qutb family's fortune seemed to have quickened his entry into the adult world. Soon he began to imitate the men of the village, attending their prayers at the mosque and staying out until late in the evening.[24]

Sayyid Qutb's intellectual growth was accelerated by his deep interest in reading and collecting books. He soon became famous for his collection of twenty-five books and was an excellent customer of "Uncle Salih" ('Amm Salih), the book peddler, who visited the village three or four days a year. Two books in his library, *Kitab Abi Ma'shar al-Falaki* on astrology and *Kitab Shamhurash* on folk rituals and magic, helped to spread the child's fame in the village. As a result, special requests for fortune telling from young and old alike began to pour in, which Sayyid sought to meet with the aid of these two books.[25]

Sayyid also became interested in more serious works that reflected the nationalistic mood of Egypt toward the end of World War I. For example, his schoolteacher lent him a nationalistic diwan (anthology of verse) by the political prisoner Thabit al-Jurjani and another nationalist historical work by Muhammad al-Khudari. Sayyid patiently copied out the verses of the diwan as well as the introduction of al-Khudari's work.[26] Thus, through the influence of his home, which was a meeting place of the local branch of the Nationalist Party, and the influence of his teachers, together with the prevailing nationalist mood sweeping the country, Qutb became aware of politics. When the revolution broke out in 1919 under the leadership of Sa'ed Zaghlul, thirteen-year-old Sayyid Qutb was already making speeches and composing nationalistic verse, which he recited at mosques and at public gatherings.[27]

Sayyid Qutb's Empathy with the Underprivileged

At home and in school, Sayyid Qutb was, by his own admission, pampered.[28] He was the only boy in the family in the early years of his childhood and thus received all the attention and love of his parents. In addition, he was surrounded at home by many poor villagers who served the Qutb Ibrahim family in return for clothing, fuel, and food.[29] At school he wore the best clothes, and he was not allowed to roam the streets after school for fear of dirtying his clothes and being influenced by the manners and foul language of the village children.[30] He was treated royally by his teachers because of his father's hospitality to them and because of Sayyid's generosity in supplying the school with sugar and tea. Sayyid and the other children of prominent and wealthy families in Musha received an education more akin to private tutoring.[31]

This privileged upbringing, however, did not prevent Sayyid Qutb from feeling compassion toward the underprivileged. His favorite childhood friend Jum'ah, for example, belonged to a less privileged section of the community.[32] Young Qutb also showed compassion in his treatment of transient workers from the Qana and Aswan areas who worked annually on his father's land. Sayyid helped them by reading and writing letters for them and by assisting them in sending money orders to their families. In return, Qutb learned many things from the laborers' way of life. He learned that they earned little money, that meat was a rare item to be eaten only on Id al Adha (Feast of the Sacrifice), that butter was an unknown item in their world, that wheat was unavailable, and that sugar was an item that only the rich possessed.[33]

The memory of these and other childhood experiences with the underprivileged were to haunt Sayyid Qutb later in life and make him feel that he was an exploiter of these workers and the millions like them who "planted the Nile valley with gold" in return for starvation. According to Qutb, if there had been a just law in the valley, it would have taken him to prison instead of the many people whom the existing laws considered thieves and criminals. Such was the feeling that overwhelmed Sayyid Qutb every time he sat down to eat or tried to enjoy life.[34]

Folk Religion and Superstition in the Village

Qutb was also deeply influenced in his childhood by the traditional folk religion and superstition which were deeply rooted in the culture of his village. In smooth-flowing prose which is simple, picturesque, and often humorous, which is typical of Qutb's style in *Tifl min al-qaryah,* Sayyid Qutb vividly describes the superstition surrounding Muslim holy men (awliya') and evil spirits ('afarit).[35]

For example, according to Qutb's account of folk religion in the village, insanity was the essential attribute of a holy man (wali), a person thus afflicted being regarded as a favorite of God. Qutb writes also of the procedure by which people were chosen to be holy men and the extent to which these insane (majadhib) awliya' were venerated as healers:

> He was a child under six years of age when people began whispering in the village about "the head sheikh." He heard them saying: He took a purgative and that it was hard on him. "The purgative?" He knows it well. He still remembers that one day he was afflicted with fever. So they forced him to drink that bitter liquid having the abhorrent taste and smell, with all means of enticement and threatening. Then came what is inevitable! But this man "the head sheikh" why does the purgative make him look like a terrified tramp who is out of his wits, gazing absent-mindedly and weird. What sort of purgative is this one which has such effects on people? The man was tearing up his clothes. He then wallowed in the mud or poured down soil on his head and his naked body until his skin was clothed with soil and mud in a robe other than the torn discarded robe! He used to go out in the alleys of the village shouting in a resounding and terrifying voice: *Allah! Allah! Allah*! Or he used to swell his chest with air and he jumped and sank with his stature as he cried out in a piercing voice: *Hayy! (Alive!) Hayy! Hayy!*[36]

He recalls, too, in great detail the village superstition concerning evil spirits ('afarit). The premature deaths of Qutb's childhood companion Jum'ah and Qutb's baby brother were attributed to these spirits. Despite the efforts of an enlightened teacher in the 'madrasah' who tried repeatedly to dispel such superstition by taking his students on night-time field trips to the alleged locations of the 'afarit to prove their nonexistence, and although Qutb tried very hard not to accept superstition himself, he admits that the world of spirits continued to be an integral part of his imagination even as an adult.[37] This could very well explain the predominance of the world of spirits as a theme in his mystical-oriented poetry in the 1930s.

Two years after the outbreak of the 1919 Egyptian revolt, Sayyid Qutb left his village for his uncle's house in Cairo to continue his education in accordance with his mother's wishes.[38] Sayyid's departure was surrounded by an air of importance that gave the impression that the boy was, in the words of an Egyptian proverb, "on his way to conquer Acre" (ka'innahu dhahib li-fathi 'Akka).[39] Perhaps his mission to restore his family's wealth and prestige in Musha appeared one step closer to realization.

THE EMERGENCE OF A POET

Early Years in Cairo and the Influence of al-'Aqqad

When Sayyid Qutb left his village around 1921, he was a highly literate and politically conscientious young man with a mission in life that had been engraved in his consciousness since he was ten. Qutb lived in the Cairo suburb of Zaytun with his maternal uncle Ahmad Hussayn 'Uthman for four years. He enrolled in a preliminary teachers' training school (equivalent to an intermediate school) known as Madrasat al-Mu'allimin al-Awwaliyah, and after graduating in 1928 he attended Dar al-'Ulum's preparatory high school, known as Tajhiziyat Dar al-'Ulum. A year later, in 1929, he began his college career, which lasted until 1933.[40]

During those early years in Cairo, Qutb maintained his excellence in Arabic language and literature and began to compose poetry and write essays that appeared in Cairo's publications, such as *al-Hayat al-Jadidah* (The New Life) and *al-Balagh* (Proclamation), which began to appear in the early 1920s. On January 16, 1925, at the age of nineteen, Sayyid Qutb published in the *al-Balagh* daily his earliest poem, in which he attacked British policies and defended Egypt's leader Sa'd Zaghlul.[41] At the same time, Qutb became closely associated with and influenced by the modernist and outspoken Wafdist journalist and leader of the new school of modern poetry, the Diwan school, 'Abbas Mahmud al-'Aqqad.

Qutb's first contacts with al-'Aqqad took place while Qutb was living with his uncle, who was a friend of al-'Aqqad and an active member of the Wafd Party. On many occasions, Qutb accompanied his uncle on his visits to al-'Aqqad's house, where the young man was highly impressed by the personality and thought of al-'Aqqad and, as a result, became an enthusiastic reader of books that he borrowed from al-'Aqqad's large personal library. Through the influence of his uncle and al-'Aqqad, Qutb became an active member of the Wafd and began to contribute poetry and essays to the party's newspaper, *al-Balagh*.[42] In addition, Qutb became an outspoken supporter of the new school of poetry in its rebellion against the well-established neoclassical school. Al-'Aqqad's influence on Qutb at this formative stage was considerable. According to Qutb, al-'Aqqad helped him to focus on the thought rather than the utterance (al-'in-ayah bi-al-fikr akthar min al-lafz) and steered him away from imitating the conservative prose styles of Mustafa Lutfi al-Manfaluti (1876–1924) and Mustafa Sadiq al-Rafi'i (1880–1937).[43]

Throughout his secular career, Qutb tried to emulate al-'Aqqad and to live up to his uncompromising standards in politics and literature. In order to grasp al-'Aqqad, Qutb recounted, he had to go beyond the literary culture of Arabic into the study of all materials, poetry, novels, and plays, translated from Western literature. He had to study modern psychology, including the theory of the unconscious (al-'Aql al-batini), psychoanalysis and behavioral psychology, biology, Darwinism, chemistry, Einstein and the theory of relativity, the structure of the universe, the analysis of atom and its relation to radiation, as well as modern scientific and philosophical theories in various fields of knowledge. When reading *al-Muqtataf* (Selection, Cairo), for example, Qutb recalled that he read first psychological, biological, and scientific subjects such as the smashing of the atom (tahtim al-dharrah) before he turned to literary subjects.[44]

From 1929 to 1933, Qutb attended Dar al-'Ulum in Cairo, where he was active in student, academic, and literary affairs. He was, for example, a leader in the formation of a student organization whose major goal was the strengthening of relations between Egyptian and "Eastern" students.[45] In addition, he was active in the promotion of changes and improvements in the educational curricula. This included the introduction of English language instruction and artistic criticism, the expansion of Arab language and religious studies and Hebrew education in a proposed preparatory year at the college.[46] In literature, Qutb distinguished himself as an outspoken partisan of the new school of poetry, especially the views advanced by al-'Aqqad, leader of the Diwan group, whose writings and theories appear to have been greatly influenced by English writers such as Hazlitt, Coleridge, Macaulay, Mill, and Darwin.[47]

Poetry of the Heart

The cornerstone of the view of al-'Aqqad's Diwan school was that poetry is subjective, a reflection of the heart and an interpreter of the soul, not merely an outer description of things. Poetry, therefore, is the result of natural and spontaneous talent and is a sincere expression of the poet's self. To the partisans of the new school, the deeply entrenched neoclassical poetry and its protagonists Ahmad Shawqi (1869–1932) and Hafiz Ibrahim (1871–1932) showed none of these characteristics. Salma Khadra Jayyusi points out that "the neo-classical school had been conforming a concept of poetry which, left unopposed, would have entrenched itself so strongly that to arrive at modernity would have become an extremely arduous task. Backed by Shawqi's talent, it had acquired a great hold on the minds of the Arabs."[48]

Sayyid Qutb's first major work on poetry and criticism appeared in 1932, while Qutb was still a student at Dar al-'Ulum. It clearly reflects a sensitive young mind which was greatly influenced by the Diwan group's subjective poetry of the heart. In his later writings, Sayyid Qutb would refer to this poetry as the poetry of psychological states (shi'r al-halat al-nafsiyyah).[49]

Qutb's work entitled *Muhimmat al-sha'ir fi al-hayah wa shi'r al-jil al-hadir* (The Mission of the Poet in Life and the Poetry of the Present Generation),[50] based on a public lecture delivered at the auditorium of Dar al-'Ulum in 1932, expounds the author's views on modern poetry as illustrated by the poetry of the younger generation of poets. In it, Qutb, like his mentor al-'Aqqad, attacks the poetry of the neoclassical school, especially that of Ahmad Shawqi.[51]

A Poet in Search of Eternity and the Highest Ideal

According to Qutb, poetry is one of the fine arts which serves as an intermediary between what is and what ought to be, and which draws us closer to the "highest ideal" (al-mathal al-a'la). Poetry addresses one's inner self, describing the sensitive feelings in a mysterious way, allowing one's feelings to be liberated and one's imagination to wander freely and without limit throughout the spacious world of the spirit.[52]

The poet, according to Qutb, is one who has a deep feeling for life and has been molded by life to serve as the intermediary between it and people. To fulfill his mission, the poet has to have a more precise (adaqq) and deeper (a'maq) feeling for life than that shared by the masses, but one which does not disrupt his links with them. He should express his feelings as he himself sees them, not as others see them. Furthermore, he should have a philosophy of his own which is derived from his personal feelings and in light of which he can explain life.[53]

Clearly, Qutb's elitist concept of the poet is a romantic image of a man of sensibilities whose superiority of imagination sets him on a higher level than others without disrupting his links with them. Armed with these and other concepts, Qutb composed poetry which was true to the spirit of the Diwan school and the poetry of the heart and soul he preached and which was a true mirror of his psychological state. The poems he published in the 1920s and early 1930s in many Cairene publications, including al-*Balagh*, al-*Muqtataf*, al-*Risalah*, *Sahifat Dar al-'Ulum*, al-*Wadi*, *Kawkab al-Sharq* and *Apollo*, were collected in his only published anthology, al-*Shati' al-Majhul* (The Unknown Shore), which appeared in January 1935.[54]

In these poems, one can discern a restless, troubled, often pessimistic man whose rebellious soul searches for the answers to human existence, ponders the meaning of death and ultimately escapes beyond the physical world into the mysterious world of spirits to attain the eternal happiness and existence for which he longs and which he cannot find in this troubled finite world. Qutb also composed love poetry which is characterized by an excessive idealization of the beloved. Even here, however, he rarely ventures outside the inner world of his subjective and spiritual experiences.[55]

Qutb's restlessness can be seen in his quest for the meaning of life and human existence and in his morbid fascination with death. He made frequent visits to the Valley of the Dead (Wadi al-Mawta) near Cairo at sunset or before sunrise. These visits culminated in the writing of his poem "al-Sirr aw al-sha'ir fi Wadi al-Mawta" (The Secret or the Poet in the Valley of the Dead). In this poem, Qutb writes as a troubled poet who continuously searches for the secret of life, but to no avail. He therefore attempts to question the dead who, having left the world's deceptions and vanities behind, will perhaps be able to provide the answer he seeks. But the dead do not know the answer and are ruffled by the poet's intrusion. Now realizing the futility of his queries, the poet concludes by wishing that death would come to him rapidly and thus alleviate his suffering.[56]

In his poem "al-Ghad al-majhul" (The Unknown Morrow), Qutb's disorientation is likewise made apparent in his fear of what might lie in store for him in the morrow. He describes himself as a sailor whose ship has been lost and who is afraid of the barren and forbidding shore that lies ahead. He is afraid that the love he now experiences will no longer be available, that the flowers whose scent now surrounds him will wither and that darkness will engulf him in loneliness.[57]

Examples of this romantic sadness are numerous in his 1935 collection of poetry. His love poetry, however, is quite different in spirit. Here one sees another Qutb, one who shows a great lust for life. "Al-Hayah al-ghaliyah" (Precious Life), "Da'i al-hayah" (Caller of Life), "hubb al-shakur" (Love of the Thankful), "al-Mu'jizah aw al-sahm al-akhir" (The Miracle or the Last Arrow) and other love poems reveal an invigorated and optimistic Qutb who often contrasts his troubled past with his newly discovered happiness.[58] This happiness does not endure, however, and he soon returns to his disorientation. Finally, Qutb escapes from the miserable finite existence of this world into "al-Shati' al-majhul" (Unknown Shore), the world of spirits, the eternal life after death for which he longs, where one cannot perceive the milestones of time and existence and where the soul is set free to roam the eternal world to discover new worlds and wonders.[59]

His collection of poems also included a sarcastic criticism of the socio-economic situation in Egypt. In a stanza in one of his poems, he writes:[60]

> O, you who are tender with animals
> Do not forget people who might groan and are hurt
> Dogs in Egypt might receive care
> While its people are deprived and shattered
> If there is some dignity in Egypt
> It will get angry and blood will boil on its side.

The writings of Sayyid Qutb will focus later on the topic of social justice, as seen in the 1940s and the early 1950s in his works *A Child from a Village*, *The New Thought* magazine, *Social Justice in Islam*, and *The Battle of Islam and Capitalism*.

REASONS FOR QUTB'S UNHAPPINESS

Why was Sayyid Qutb so restless and unhappy at this formative stage in his life? Qutb answers this question himself, at least partially, in his first work *Muhimmat al-sha'ir fi al-hayah*, where he rebuts those who accused the young poets of the new school of poetry of self-centeredness and excessive pessimism. He stresses that this pessimism and restlessness are a true reflection of Egyptian society of this period:

Look around you. Do you not see the confrontation between the rising generation and the circumstances surrounding them? Do you not hear the cries echoing with pain and protest from every side? Why can't poetry be the same when it is the most precise expression of the buried feelings? Why should poets sing hymns of happiness and exuberance? Have we won a military battle against the armies of the enemies? Have we attained our usurped independence? Everything in the country deserves complaint. Therefore, our young poets who are complaining and in pain are sincere in their feelings. They will leave behind them for future generations a clear picture of this confusing period.[61]

Commenting on the period of the early 1930s, Badawi writes that the political situation had deteriorated following the advent of the repressive regime of Prime Minister Isma'il Sidqi "with the result that young intellectuals were driven to escape from social and political reality into a solipsistic inner world of private sorrows and vague longings, and into excessive preoccupation with depopulated nature."[62]

Another clue to Sayyid Qutb's state of mind at this formative stage is, by his own admission, his great anxiety over the tremendous influence which 'Abbas Mahmud al-'Aqqad's overpowering personality was having on him. Qutb greatly feared that his imitation of his mentor could lead to the disappearance of his personality into that of al-'Aqqad (al-fana' fi shakhsiyat al-'Aqqad),[63] and Qutb attempted to overcome this dilemma by following an independent path in his composition of prose and poetry. As Qutb points out, al-'Aqqad was firmly convinced that reason and intellect alone guide people's actions. By contrast, Qutb was becoming increasingly interested in spiritual themes and was finally compelled to dissociate himself completely from al-'Aqqad in the 1940s.[64]

As the material situation of the family in Musha began to deteriorate, the task for which Qutb came to Cairo was transformed to merely saving the family from loss instead of retrieving the family's wealth and restoring its glory. The circumstances of his life in Cairo were difficult compared to the quiet and happy life of childhood he lived in his village of Musha with his father and mother. All the elements of easy life were available for Qutb in Musha. In Cairo, however, he aimed to realize his many dreams, including rescuing the standing of his family in the village and obtaining the proficiency certificate from the Primary Teachers' School. Obtaining a job in teaching was extremely difficult for him. When he found a job, it quickly became evident that the income did not suit the requirements of his life. Moreover, the great expectations that had accompanied the revolution of 1919 were soon transformed into violent conflicts and harsh conspiracies in Cairo in which all values and ethics were lacking and nothing remained except the feeling of loss, frustration and disappointment.[65] Sayyid Qutb expressed his wrath and rebellion against this life in his poems, as we see in the following verses written as early as 1929:[66]

Is this a life or is it hell fire
With its agitated fire ablaze?
No, there is a painful grief in my soul
From my life which is more than what is in death;
To whom shall I complain if I wish to complain
And to whom can I clarify my feeling?
Where is the one who can see what I see
in my feeling, except my soul and my conscience?
Get lost O! my life;
I hated poetry in a filthy atmosphere,
Get lost and be fraught with curses,
Get away from a wrathful, gloomy and bored person.

The death of his father during his final year at Dar al-'Ulum in Cairo (ca. 1933) and the family problems that developed as a result affected Qutb's psychological condition. The heavy burden of responsibility for the welfare and education of his brother and two sisters fell upon his shoulders when his family left Musha permanently to live with Sayyid in Cairo's southern suburb, Hulwan. Precisely what effects these developments had on Qutb are not specified in his writings. On his thirtieth birthday, however, he laments the days of his youth, which had been spent like the days of an old man, wasted without a joyous celebration of life:[67]

To the thirty we ride swiftly
O! nights;
Life's essence has elapsed from my age
So I do grieve for a dear thing,
The period of youth has gone as it came,
The period of wishes and imagination
It got lost in distress and disturbance
And it passed without celebration
So hurry up O! nights.

Following the publication of his *diwan* in January 1935, Qutb's career as a poet continued, and a second *diwan, Asda' al-zaman* (Echoes of Time), was planned for publication in December 1937. This did not materialize;[68] however, in analyzing the poems that appeared between 1935 and 1937, one finds the same subjective tone that characterized Qutb's 1935 collection: restlessness, unhappiness, quest for the eternal, idealization of the beloved and so on. In addition, one detects a preoccupation with morality and ethics which will become paramount in Qutb's thought in the 1940s, 1950s and 1960s. In "al-Khati'ah" (The Sin), for example, sin is portrayed as a snake that thrives on moral darkness and on the animalistic instincts of man. Only a conscience that is good and alive can abort sin's mission.[69] On the other extreme, one can also detect in this collection Qutb's concern with beauty. This can be seen, for instance, in his poem " 'ibadah jadidah?!" (A New Deification), where he presents a view, a spiritualization of beauty (jamal), which totally contradicts his religious stand in the late 1940s, 1950s and 1960s. Through beauty he sees the divinity which inspires worship; for him, therefore, beauty is a manifestation of the divinity and, as such, it is a legitimate object of worship.[70]

In "Filastin al-damiyah" (Bloody Palestine), the poet calls on the Palestinian Arabs during the Palestine Arab revolt (1936–1939) to continue on the path of bloody struggle as the only way to achieve independence. He attacks the savagery of the West for spilling the blood of the East, and assures Palestinians that Egyptians, both old and young, wholeheartedly support them and attach great importance to their struggle.[71]

Salah 'Abd al-Fattah al-Khalidi says that the poet Sayyid Qutb is rightly considered al-Sha'ir al-musawwir (the portraying poet) in the modern age as Ibn Al-Roumi was "the portraying poet" in the Abassid age.[72] As we shall see shortly, the precursor of Qutb's early artistic studies of the Qur'an will revolve around artistic portrayal in the Qur'an. In his seminal work *The Mission of the Poet in Life and the Poetry of the Present Generation*, which he wrote while he was a student at Dar al-'Ulum, Qutb puts forth the issue of the portraying poet. Qutb writes that the poet who "conveys the picture as it is is not considered an artist. Those who want the poet to be a painter who conveys only the picture as seen take him out from his first nature, the nature of the poet who depicts emotions or the scenes as he sees them and not as other eyes see them. Artistic portrayal attains the level of high art when it does not become frozen at sensual pictures; rather, it provides a way for imagination to work on these portraits."[73]

EMERGENCE OF A LITERARY CRITIC

Qutb's Early Career in Literary Criticism

Qutb's career as a poet gave way gradually to a career in literary criticism. Qutb's poetry became less visible beginning in 1939, although individual poems continued to appear in Cairo's main literary reviews until 1950. Qutb's reputation as a promising young literary critic had already been firmly established at Dar al-'Ulum with the appearance of his 1932 work *Muhimmat al-sha'ir fi al-hayah*.

Following his graduation from Dar al-'Ulum in 1933 with a B.A. degree in Arabic language and literature and a diploma in education, Qutb was appointed a teacher of Arabic in government schools with a salary of six Egyptian guineas. He taught at al-Da'udiyyah Preparatory School (1933–1935) and the schools of Dumyat (1935), Bani Sweif (1935–1936) and Halwan (1936–1940). He was then transferred to the supervision of general education in the Ministry of Education and the administration of translation and statistics (1940–1944). He worked as an inspector of elementary education in 1944 and in the Directorate General of Culture (1945–1948). On November 3, 1948, he was sent on a scholarship from the Ministry of Education to become acquainted with the fundamentals of curricula in the United States. He then returned to Egypt on August 23, 1950, as an assistant supervisor in technical research and projects (1950–1952). He submitted his resignation on October 18, 1952, protesting what he claimed to be non-Islamic governmental educational policies.[74]

Qutb's activities and associations both at Dar al-'Ulum and after his graduation indicate his determination to take an active part in the leading intellectual circles of Cairo. They also reveal his ambition to join the ranks of the leading literati of Cairo such as al-'Aqqad, Taha Hussayn, Mustafa Sadiq al-Rafi'i, Ahmad Amin, and Ibrahim 'Abd al-Qadir al-Mazini. His aspirations as a literary critic were given a boost when he joined the staff of *al-Ahram's* literary supplement around 1934. There he became involved in critical and sometimes controversial reviews of literary works, especially anthologies of literary figures such as al-'Aqqad, Ahmad Zaki Abu Shadi, Salih Jawdat, and Mahmud Abu al-Wafa, among others.[75]

Qutb's Literary Battle with the Apollo Group

Qutb's prominence as a controversial critic was very evident in the vigorous literary battle (ma'rakah adabiyyah) that erupted in 1934 following the publication in *al-Usbu'* of his analysis of the motives behind the heated critical debates between al-Mazini and 'Ali Mahmud Taha, Taha Hussayn and Ibrahim Naji, Taha Hussayn, and Ibrahim al-Misri, and al-'Aqqad and Ibrahim Naji. In his analysis, Qutb accused the older generation of literati, including al-Mazini, Taha Hussayn, and al-'Aqqad, of insincerity and undue harshness in their criticism of the younger generation of poets. This battle lasted from June to November of 1934 and involved other Cairene publications in addition to *al-Usbu'* such as *al-Balagh*, *al-Wadi*, *Apollo*, *al-Risalah*, *al-Majallah al-jadidah*, and *al-Jihad*.[76]

Qutb's allegiance to al-'Aqqad became very evident in the heat of the debates. He gradually began to focus his attacks on Ahmad Zaki Abu Shadi and the Apollo Society, which had been founded in 1932 to serve as a forum for such romantic poets as Abu Shadi, Ibrahim Naji, 'Ali Mahmud Taha, Hasan Kamil al-Sayrafi, Salih Jawdat, 'Abd al-'Aziz 'Atiq, Mustafa 'Abd al-Latif al-Saharti, and Mahmud Abu al-Wafa. Qutb focused his attacks on them in part in retaliation for Abu Shadi's and the Apollo Society's attacks on al-'Aqqad and his poetry in the *Apollo Review*.[77]

According to Abd al-'Aziz al-Dasuqi, the conflict between al-'Aqqad and his supporters on the one hand and the Apollo Society on the other hand had a political undertone. The Wafdist al-'Aqqad had nothing but contempt for Abu Shadi and his group because of their alleged collaboration with the unpopular dictatorial regime of Isma'il Sidqi and with the royal palace. These same factors also motivated Taha Hussayn to attack the Apollo poets during this period.[78] Qutb's hostility toward the poets of the Apollo group is apparent in his writings. He accused the group of trying to influence the integrity of the critical reviews he published in *al-Ahram*, especially those pertaining to the works of Mahmud Abu al-Wafa, 'Ali Mahmud Taha, and Ibrahim Naji.[79] Qutb described the animosity of the Apollo group, especially that of Ahmad Zaki Abu Shadi, as a manifestation of frustration at their inability to influence him or convince him to join their ranks and contribute to their monthly review. Qutb wrote that he repeatedly turned down offers from Abu Shadi to feature his works in his literary reviews and public lectures.[80]

Qutb also accused the Apollo Society of being excessively noisy and pretentious and lacking in literary, social and ethical qualities. He dubbed them "Mawkib al-'ajazah" (The Procession of the Handicapped) because, in his view, the major reason for their grouping together was a feeling of individual handicap and weakness despite their pretensions to soundness and maturity. Qutb described the members of the group as having no spiritual bond among them and accused them of knifing each other in the back (as seen in Abu Shadi's relationship with Ibrahim Naji and Salih Jawdat's relationship with Mukhtar al-Wakil).[81]

Qutb likened Abu Shadi's attacks on al-'Aqqad to a confrontation between unequals. On the one side was al-'Aqqad, the man whose distinguished manhood and philosophy of life were reflected in his prose and verse; on the other side was Abu Shadi, the gentle, smiling one who was satisfied with writing anthologies full of naked pictures and permissive tendencies (naza'at ibahiyah). Qutb criticized the Apollo Society's effort to elevate the status of the poets Khalil Mutran and 'Abd al-Rahman Shukri as innovators in contemporary Arabic poetry and not merely as a ploy by which they sought to strike back at al-'Aqqad.[82] Throughout the 1930s, Qutb remained a devout disciple of al-'Aqqad and the most vocal defender of al-'Aqqad's vision of poetry and criticism.

Qutb's Literary Battle with al-Rafi'i's Supporters

The next phase of Qutb's career was highlighted by heated debates between the supporters of al-'Aqqad and those of the neoclassicist Mustafa Sadiq al-Rafi'i. Qutb himself spearheaded the pro-'Aqqad attacks against al-Rafi'i in the Cairene monthly review *al-Risalah* from April to November 1938.[83] These debates culminated in a bitter decade-long battle between the two literary giants that had begun when al Rafi'i's style was harshly attacked by al-'Aqqad and al-Mazini in their controversial work *al-Diwan: Kitab fi al-naqd wa-al-adab* (The Diwan: A Book on Criticism and Literature) in 1921.[84] It seems, too, that personal jealousies between the two literati played an important role in the debate, especially following the publication of al-Rafi'i's work *I'jaz al-Qur'an* (Inimitability of the Qur'an) in 1926, which was described by the Wafdist leader Sa'd Zaghlul as follows: "It is like a revelation from the Rev-

elation or a firebrand from the light of the Qur'an." According to
pro-Rafi'i figures, al-'Aqqad became very jealous upon hearing that
Zaghlul, the man to whom he had dedicated his life in service of the
nationalist cause, had given his enemy, al-Rafi'i, such praise.[85]

The violent tone of the debates became even more evident with
the publication of al-Rafi'i's work *'Ala al-saffud* (On the Skewer) in
1929, in which al-'Aqqad was ridiculed and accused of plagiarism.
This conflict was further inflamed following the publication of al-
'Aqqad's anthology *Wahi al-arba'in* (Revelation of the Age of Forty)
in 1933, in which al-Rafi'i was accused of collaborating with Isma'il
Sidqi's dictatorial regime against the nationalist Wafdist forces.[86]

These debates are described by Qutb as a clash between old (al-
Rafi'i's group) and new (al-'Aqqad's group). The differences between
the two, according to Qutb, were not only linguistic or literary, but
also differences in mentality and outlook on life. The old school,
which embodied the old mentality ('aqliyah qadimah), saw Arabic
expressions and the means of their rendition as idols that were im-
bued with sacrosanctity (qadasah wa-hurmah). They were thus
treated as ends in themselves and not merely means of illustration.
Qutb added that it was therefore difficult for this school to use Arabic expressions, constructions, illustrations, and patterns in ways
that differ from ancient literature.[87]

On the other hand, according to Qutb, the new school held that
Arabic expressions and constructions were tools of illustration,
which may differ from one portrayal to another depending on the
intent, style, and temperament of the individual illustrator, as well
as on the characteristics of the nation to which the illustrator belongs. The old school, in Qutb's view, refused to allow new renditions of the language, even though Arabic was not the original
Egyptian language but rather the language of people who differed
from Egyptians in many traditions and customs, as well as in economics, politics, and environment. Qutb does acknowledge Egyptian religious and literary links with the Arabs but nevertheless
points out the differences in temperament, thought, emotions and
aspirations between the two peoples. These intellectual and psychological differences mean that the rendition and expression of the language will also differ. Qutb also emphasizes that the new renditions
of language do not imply a rejection of customary Arabic. Instead,
the new school sought to create usages and illustrations that reflected
the characteristic sentiments of the Egyptian people, some of which
were not common to the Arabs.[88]

The conflict in 1938 between the disciples of the two literati made clear the extent of Qutb's absolute devotion to his mentor al-'Aqqad, which brought upon Qutb the wrath and ridicule of al-Rafi'i's partisans as well as that of some other critics.[89] Qutb considered al-'Aqqad's poetical talent unsurpassed among Arabic-speaking poets. Even the title 'Amir al-Shu'ara (The Prince of Poets), which was given to al-'Aqqad by Taha Hussayn following the death of Ahmad Shawqi was not, in Qutb's view, sufficient recognition of al-'Aqqad's great literary talents.[90]

Qutb attempts to rebut the assertion that al-'Aqqad had benefited greatly from his association with the Wafd in his 1933 literary battle with al-Rafi'i. He states that al-'Aqqad's greatness was independent of his political connections. He argues that al-'Aqqad's severance of ties with the ruling Wafd Party (1938) showed that al-'Aqqad remained the all-powerful author regardless of the power of his enemies. According to Qutb, those who, like al-Rafi'i's forces, used religion to fight al-'Aqqad did not succeed, even though a religious weapon is more potent than a political one. Qutb asserts that al-'Aqqad's greatness was based on his stature "as a great natural force, as an expression of life's energy, and that within himself and his talents lay the seeds of greatness, the yeast of excellence, and the motives for revival, all of which were derived from his inexhaustible spiritual resources."[91]

Qutb admits that defending al-'Aqqad was a difficult task that brought upon him the wrath of influential people in government, including his superiors in the Ministry of Education. Those defending al-Rafi'i had a far easier task, since they had the reputation of being the defenders of a religion whose followers numbered in the millions in Egypt and the Arab world. Because of this, al-Rafi'i's defenders were able to win the popularity contest among ordinary readers and literati.[92]

The main features of Qutb's character began to emerge in the 1930s. The journalist 'Adel Hammuda wrote that "there is no doubt that he was audacious. . . . His words were sharp sometimes. His expressions were sticks of fire. . . . His pencil was a whip. The one who sees him does not believe that he is the same person who writes. . . . For with people he was milder than the breeze. . . . With the paper and the pencil, he was a hell which does not cool off."[93]

Ali Ahmad 'Amer, a contemporary of Qutb in the 1930s, wrote an article on July 25, 1934, focusing on Qutb and his accomplishments. 'Amer wrote:

I read his works thirteen years ago in *al-Hayat al-Jadidah* newspaper. Then I read his works as a poet and a writer in *al-Balagh*. Now I read his work here as a poet and a writer in *al-Ahram* and *al-Usbu'*. If we consider his works in the light of his age, we will call all the colleagues to a general contribution in which the writer of this chapter will be pleased to contribute his head so that we erect a statue for him in the size of form and we coronate him with this testimony: We the undersigned testify that our colleague Sayyid Qutb is one of those whose destinies exceeded their ages! However, we are in Egypt, the country of ingratitude.[94]

PERSPECTIVES ON SAYYID QUTB'S CAREER, 1906–1938

Contrasts in Qutb's Spiritual Outlook of the 1930s with That of the 1940s, 1950s, and 1960s

Qutb's upbringing in a traditional environment amid popular Sufi practices and belief in the spirits was, by his own admission, to a large extent responsible for the mystical outlook and strong belief in the world of spirits, which are evident in his *al-Shati' al-majhul* anthology and his *Muhimmat al-Sha'ir fi al-hayah*. Qutb was convinced that his quest for the infinite and the world of spirits helped him more than any other factor. He did not follow blindly in the footsteps of his mentor al-'Aqqad, who believed that reason ('aql) is the main guiding light in human and spiritual matters. Qutb's interest in the world of spirits helped him to chart an independent intellectual career which began in 1939 with his renewed interest in the Qur'an and which gradually led him away from literature and al-'Aqqad into the advocacy of the Islamic way in the late 1940s.[95]

Qutb's mystical outlook during this period stands in contrast to his Islamic outlook in the 1950s and 1960s. His mystical absorption in the infinite and his excessive pessimism about finite existence, which characterize much of his poetry at this time, contradict his later Islamic writings in which he describes finite existence as an abode of tribulation and work (dar ibtila' wa-'amal) that requires each believer to realize the way of Allah (manhaj Allah) in his own life and in the lives of others. Everlasting life, Qutb says, will depend on one's deeds on earth as judged in the Abode of Reckoning (Dar al-Hisab wa-al-Jaza'). According to Qutb's understanding of

Qur'anic teaching, one must accept this finite world (dar al-fana') and seek the everlasting abode (Dar al-Baqa'). The particularity of balance (khasiyat al tawazun) which he believed to characterize the Islamic conception (al-tasawwur al Islami) requires a person to live a balanced life.[96]

Qutb's espousal of cosmic unity (wahdat al-kawn) in his *Muhimmat al-sha'ir* to express the cosmic role of the poet also contradicts his later writings. According to this early published work of Qutb, the truth of cosmic unity or unity of existence is embedded in people's deepest natures, especially in those of poets and artists. Having felt the relationship that connects them with the highest ideal, the road that leads them to it, and the great headway the universe is making in its direction, poets and artists are able to lead humankind as a whole closer to that ideal. In the process, poets and artists experience the interdependence of all living things and the unity of all beings whether dead or alive.[97] Qutb's pan-cosmic philosophy centers around the notion that a poet should hold a philosophy derived from the poet's own personal feelings, in light of which the poet can explain life.[98]

In his later Islamic writings, however, Qutb says that it is impossible for any individual to give a comprehensive explanation for existence and the place of the individual in the universe, because knowledge of the Creator and his plans for his creatures is beyond human understanding and reason. Qutb thus belittled the philosophers' attempts to explain existence, asserting that only a realization of the Divine method (al-Manhaj al-Ilahi) on earth could lead to a comprehensive explanation of existence and humanity's proper place in it.[99]

Qutb's earliest philosophy, with its vague reference to the unity of the universe and its relationship to the highest ideal, stands in clear contrast to his later Islamic unitarian belief (tawhid), where a clear distinction is drawn between two separate existences, the existence of God and the existence of human beings. Qutb believes that a relationship exists between God and slaves (al-Ilah bi-al 'abid) and between Creator and creature (al-Khaliq bi-al makhluq).[100]

Qutb's earlier writings give repeated reference to the vaguely defined "highest ideal" (al-mathal al-a'la) but do not indicate any clear religious symbol. Rather, the highest ideal is a general reference to one's quest for the good (al-khayr) in the struggle between good and evil (al-sharr).[101] The highest ideal for which one strives is, according to Qutb, still in the future: "We believe that the 'highest ideal' of poetry and non-poetry lies in the future because the ideal (al-kamal) and what comes closer to it lie ahead, and it could be that we are closer today to this ideal than in previous eras."[102]

Qutb criticizes those poets who saw the highest ideal in the past but not in the present or the future: "We are obliged, according to their norms, to sanctify everything which relates to the past and to annihilate ourselves in it."[103] Furthermore, the notion of the highest ideal as set forth in Qutb's poetry stands in clear contrast to the highest ideal as he developed that concept later in his Islamic-oriented career. In Qutb's later thought, the highest ideal is the unique experience of the early Islamic Ummah in Medinah, which remains the beacon and the prototype for humankind, and which can be recreated only through human efforts similar to those of the earliest Muslims.[104]

Qutb's Secularist Literary Career

A partisan of the Islamic movement claims that al-'Aqqad was a negative factor in Qutb's life because he hampered Qutb's Islamic leanings from developing. As a result of al-'Aqqad's influence, it is argued, Qutb developed a deep interest in literature, criticism, and poetry for a period that exceeded a quarter of a century.[105]

This partisan claim is unsubstantiated. It does not take into account the fact that Qutb never forsook Islam during his "literary period" and that he remained loyal to his Arab Islamic heritage. A major share of the credit for this should in fact go to al-'Aqqad himself. While it is true that al-'Aqqad believed strongly that reason ('aql) was humanity's guiding light, he also was antimaterialistic in his outlook, firm in his opposition to materialistic ideologies such as Marxism, and a strong defender of Islam. Al-'Aqqad's influence on Qutb was great, and this, more than anything else, actually kept Qutb from espousing materialistic ideologies.[106]

In the 1920s and 1930s, Qutb was not religiously oriented. Instead, he ventured outside the religious frame of reference in his day-to-day life. Like the literati of his time, he was greatly influenced by liberal nationalist currents. His attitude toward religion at this stage was that of a Muslim secularist. The term *Muslim secularist* (in Sharabi's definition) "derives from the fact that this secularist was Muslim (hence to be differentiated from the Christian westernizing intellectuals) and that he was not religiously oriented (hence to be differentiated from the Muslim traditionalists and reformists)."[107]

Qutb saw the role of religion as that of reforming the individual's soul for the sake of society and preparing society for the life of the individual. Qutb believed that religion should not be injected into every discussion. In addition, he opposed those who passed religious judgments on others. According to Qutb, those who committed the greatest offense against religion were those who placed religion outside its own domain, comparing it with science or art, and who, as a result, harmed religion by raising doubts about its validity.[108] Whereas religion is based on the conviction of one's conscience (al-iqna' al-wijdani) and on intellectual research (al-bahth al-'aqli), most science is based on seeing, touching, and other sensory experience. In this light, according to Qutb, it is not wise to compare religion and science because many people, if given a choice between their senses and their religious feelings, would choose their senses.[109]

Likewise, it is not wise to compare religion and art, for religion is not an artistic method. Art, in Qutb's view, is a reflection of the human soul and its feeling and aspirations, which are not religious inclinations except in areas which pertain to the reform of the individual's soul for society and the reform of society for the individual. Through art, however, some people are overwhelmed by sentiments, thoughts, and hopes. Because of this, it would not be wise, Qutb claims, to force some people to choose between the way of art and the way of religion.[110]

Qutb's remarks about religion were made in response to partisans of al-Rafi'i, such as Muhammad Ahmad al-Ghamrawi, who attempted to portray al-'Aqqad and his followers, especially Qutb, as irreligious. Qutb accuses al-Rafi'i's supporters of falsely attempting to categorize the debate between the two schools into a battle between "the people of Paradise" (Ahl al-Jannah), that is, al-Rafi'i's group, and "the people of Hell," that is, al-'Aqqad's group. In response to their injection of religion into the debate, Qutb attacks them by saying: "Religion . . . Religion . . . This cry of the feeble and the weak who take refuge in religion every time the current overwhelms them." He concludes his remarks by saying: "Religion. Religion . . . , say it a hundred times. We are not the type, thank God, who are intimidated by these empty slogans. For we study and understand religion more than you do."[111]

Qutb's belief in the separation of religion and art (including literature) in the late 1930s is contradicted by his stand in the 1950s when he writes that literature, and all art in Muslim society, is derived from the Islamic conception of life (al-tasawwur al-Islami lilhayah). Islamic art is a "guided art" (fann muwajjah) by its very nature, because Islam opposes merely human conceptions and values. Islamic art, therefore, has a definite method that commits it in all its spheres.[112]

When comparing and contrasting Qutb's cultural orientation in the 1930s, when he was a secular Egyptian nationalist and a follower of al-'Aqqad's school of literature, with his orientation in 1939–1948, when he was a student of the Qur'an searching for an independent path, one finds drastic changes in his worldview. A case in point was his views concerning Arabs, Arabic language, and Islamic religion.

In January 1938, while discussing the "Psychological Indication of Arabic Utterances and Structures," Qutb pointed out the many differences that separate Egyptians from Arabs. He said:

> We should not feel guilty to declare openly that this language is not our native language. Rather it is the language of another people who differ from us in many traditions, customs, ideas, environment and economic and political factors . . . to the last thing in which two peoples differ. All that ties us to this people are religious connections and the literary heritage. These two aspects do not preoccupy the human soul with its branching trends. It is inevitable that there remains large gaps between our temperament and their temperament, our ideas and their ideas, our emotions and their emotions and our hopes and their hopes.[113]

A few months later in 1939, however, Qutb wrote a lengthy article to rebut Taha Hussayn's arguments that Egypt and Europe possess a common intellectual heritage. Qutb defended Egypt's Arabic links and saw Egypt as a connecting link between the Arab East and the Arab West and took issue with Hussayn's rejection of the intellectual unity between Egypt and the East, including Arab Muslim nations. In addition, Qutb criticized Hussayn's assertion that Islam did not change the Egyptian mentality. On the contrary, Qutb said, the masses had been affected profoundly by Islam itself which had instilled in them its pure Arabic spirit.[114] Later in 1947 Qutb became involved in pan-Arab activities, having become editor in chief of the pan-Arab review *al-'Alam al-'Arabi* (The Arab World), which appeared in Cairo in April 1947.[115]

CHAPTER 3

EMERGENCE OF THE STUDENT OF THE QUR'AN AND EARLY CHANGES, 1939–1947

My aim here is a purely and merely an artistic aim. I am not influenced by it but by the sense of an independent artistic critic. If the creativity of art ultimately meets with the sanctity of religion, then this is a result which I did not intend. However, it is a latent characteristic in the nature of this Qur'an at which the roads of search ultimately meet, even it the traveler did not take it into consideration while on the road. *(Sayyid Qutb, 1947)*

QUTB'S LITERARY CAREER, 1939–1947

Qutb's vigorous interest in literary criticism was evident in the dozens of articles that appeared in Cairo's leading literary reviews *al-Risalah* and *al-Thaqafah* during the years 1939–1947. These articles were collected in his work *Kutub wa-Shakhsiyat* (Books and Personalities), which was published in 1946.[1]

Critic Muhammad al-Nuwayhi, who was highly critical of Qutb's attempts to establish a theoretical basis for literary criticism, praises highly Qutb's talent in literary appreciation. He describes Qutb as a "man with pure artistic taste" who was instinctively able to convey to his readers the artistic enjoyment he derived from his analysis of a literary text.[2]

Qutb's career in literary criticism was highlighted by his work *al-Naqd al-Adabi: Usuluhu wa Manahijuhu* (Literary Criticism: Its Sources and Methods), which appeared in 1947. Al-Nuwayhi was extremely critical of this work,[3] but critic Muhammad Yusuf Najm describes it as reflecting a fine taste (dhawq murhaf), a deep original understanding (fahm 'amiq asil), and a comprehensive Arabic education.[4]

Qutb describes his critical method as comprehensive (manhaj takamuli), encompassing, and utilizing literary methods that include artistic, historical, and psychological analyses necessary to pass a comprehensive judgment on a literary work.[5] Qutb the literary critic is described by Najm as a self-made critic of al-'Aqqad's school who, unlike most Arab literary critics, paved his own way in the field without the knowledge of a foreign language or firsthand exposure to Western literary criticism. Qutb's exposure to Western literary criticism came through the Arabic translations of Western-educated writers such as Zaki Najib Mahmud, Muhammad 'Awad Muhammad, Muhammad Mandur, Mahmud al-Ghul, and Nazmi Khalil.[6] Qutb's exposure to Western literature also came through the translations of his mentor al-'Aqqad and Qutb's younger brother Muhammad.[7] Qutb's reliance on translated works in his comparative studies of poetical works was criticized by Badawi, who wrote that it is not fair to compare an original text with a translated text and then to pass an absolute judgment on the translated text as Qutb did.[8]

Sayyid Qutb waged many literary battles in the 1940s, including his battle with the literary critic Dr. Muhammad Mandur in 1943 on "whispered" poetry and prose as embodied in "al-Mahjari" (diaspora) literature. "Whispered" poetry, as defined by Mandur, comprises warm melodies that are derived from the inner soul but that are full of thought and feeling as seen in the poems of the diaspora literati Mika'il Nu'aymah and Nasib 'Arida.[9] Qutb rejected the "whispered" literature and preferred that "truth and not whispering" should be the standard in evaluating literary works. This literary battle developed into "violence, cruelty and defamation."[10]

Qutb's other controversial battles included his attack on the supporters of the book *Hadihih hiya al-aghlal* (These Are the Fetters) by 'Abd Allah al-Qusaimi. Qutb accused the author of plagiarism from the book *U'min bi-al-insan* (I Believe in Man) by Abd al-Mun'im Khallaf. The editor of *al-Muqtataf* magazine, Isma'il Mazhar, led the confrontation with Sayyid Qutb.[11]

Sayyid Qutb continued to distinguish himself in essay writing. One of his observers and friends, Sulaiman Fayyad, commented on the style of Sayyid Qutb at this juncture. Fayyad wrote:

Qutb's essays on the pages of *al-Risalah* "seemed to me as masterpieces of artistic prose in its most wonderful and clearest zeniths. . . . Qutb came to present another new style with the ability of Taha Hussayn in intonation and rhythm and al-'Aqqad's ability in logic and good division of long and short sentences."[12]

As a literary critic, Qutb figured prominently in the emergence of the Egyptian novelist and the 1988 Nobel Prize winner, Naguib Mahfouz, from obscurity. According to Mahfouz, the first two critics to review his works in *al-Risalah*, Sayyid Qutb and Anwar al-Ma'adawi, deserve the credit for bringing him into the limelight.[13] Qutb's enthusiastic analysis of Mahfouz's work can be seen in his review of *Khan al-Khalili* (1945), a novel about Egyptian society during World War II. Qutb said that the novel portrayed in depth and in a true, precise, and simple manner a living picture (surah hayyah) of the air-raids, fears, mentality, and surrounding conditions of the war years. According to Qutb, this novel ought to be singled out in the annals of modern Egyptian literature because it marked a decisive step (khatwah hasimah) toward a national literature with both a pure Egyptian spirit and an international aura. Qutb concluded his review as follows: "I hope that these words will not excite the vanities of the young author who I hope will be Egypt's writer of the long novel."[14]

In addition to his critical works, Qutb wrote short novels that included *al-Madinah al-mashurah* (The Bewitched City) in 1946, fashioned after *A Thousand and One Nights*, and *Ashwak* (Thorns) in 1947. It is generally believed that *Ashwak*, which is about two lovers whose affair comes to a painful end, reflects Qutb's own love affair in the 1940s. Qutb also wrote short stories which included *al-Kharif* (Autumn) in 1941, in which he dealt with the phenomenon of abstension from marriage, and *Ahya' wa-amwat* (The Living and the Dead) in 1944, which revolves around the issue of social solidarity and social differences.[15]

The first short novel, *The Bewitched City*, is a story of love and revenge in an Egyptian city in ancient times. In telling the events of the story, in the words of Shahrazad, Qutb dwells on the theme of social justice and the removal of class differences. We also see Qutb's continuous interest in what is beyond sensory reality and in the un-limited. Qutb writes, "This world is narrow, narrow, trifling, trifling, small, small. What is attained by the senses is a short duration of time, and what is attained by awareness is only a narrow horizon. Imagination and dreams take this limited human creature to the far-thest durations of time and the broadest boundaries. O! how wretched is the man who does not possess in this world except what his eyes behold!"[16] This thought pattern was evident in the poetry of Sayyid Qutb, and we also find it in his Islamic writings in which he justifies religious thought.

Qutb also coauthored many educational booklets in the 1940s. These include *Rawdat al-Tifl* (Child's Garden) in collaboration with Aminah al-Sa'id and Yousuf Murad (1947), *al-Jadid fi al-lughah al-'Arabiyah* (The New in the Arabic Language), and *al-Jadid fi al-mahfuzat* (The New in Memorized Materials), in collaboration with others from the Ministry of Education. The first episode in the se-ries *al-Qisas al-dini* (Religious Stories) in collaboration with 'Abd al-Hamid Jua al-Sahhar in 1947 had an unparalleled success in of-fering useful and beneficial instructions.[17] However, Qutb's fame as a poet waned during this time. In 1943 he was beset by doubts about the purpose of poetry, especially of "the poetry of psychological states" that no longer served his spiritual search for the absolute. As he preoccupied himself more in Islamic studies, he wrote less poetry, and his thinking diverged further from al-'Aqqad and his poetic and literary visions.

QUTB'S RENEWED INTEREST IN THE QUR'AN

Qutb's vigorous interest in literary criticism in the 1930s and 1940s branched into a new area of analysis in modern Arabic liter-ature, namely, the literary analysis of artistic imagery and portrayal in the Qur'an. In February and March 1939, Qutb's articles on the Qur'an appeared in Cairo's leading cultural and scientific monthly review, *al-Muqtataf*, in which Qutb pointed out inter alia the inim-itability (I'jaz) of the Qur'anic literary style and called for a com-prehensive study of the Qur'an as a literary text.

Qutb's interest in the Qur'an in 1939, albeit for literary purposes only, can be seen as the first major sign of the change that was to take place in his intellectual orientation and the beginning of his search for an Islamic ideology. According to Qutb himself, the

Qur'an, more than any other single factor, was instrumental in leading him out of the turbulence he experienced in his fruitless search for the infinite into a strong belief in the Islamic way of life.

Qutb's emergence as a serious student of the Qur'an was accompanied by his emergence as a moralist and as an anti-Western, antiestablishment intellectual. These mutually reinforcing developments were, like the Qur'anic teachings, crucially significant in the makeup of Qutb's ideology in the late 1940s, 1950s, and 1960s.

Qur'an of Childhood

Qutb's childhood memorization of the Qur'an did not give him a deep insight into its meaning and significance. Certain verses did, however, leave a deep impression on his imagination in the form of imagery or personal associations. For example, the imagery of a man praying at the edge of a cliff and on the verge of falling down from it was invoked whenever he read Qur'an 22:11: "*And among mankind is he who worshippeth Allah upon a narrow marge so that if good befalleth him he is content therewith, but if a trial befalleth him he falleth away utterly. He loseth both the world and the Hereafter.*"[18] Another strong impression was the image of a man breathing heavily with mouth wide open and tongue hanging out, which came to him whenever he read Qur'an 7:175–76: "*Recite unto them the tale of him to whom We gave Our revelations, but he sloughed them off, so Satan overtook him and he became of those who lead astray. Therefore his likeness is as the likeness of a dog; if thou attackest him he panteth with his tongue out, and if thou leavest him he panteth with his tongue out.*"[19]

According to Qutb, the pleasant, simplified, and exciting Qur'an of his childhood (Qur'an al-tufulah al-'adhib, al-muyassar, al-mushawwiq) was transformed into the difficult, complicated, and broken Qur'an of his youth (Qur'an al-shabab al-'asir, al-mumazzaq) as a result of his reading Qur'anic commentaries while attending institutions of learning in Cairo.[20] Furthermore, Qutb's secular-oriented life in Cairo in the 1920s and the 1930s led to a diminishing of his Islamic beliefs and to extreme doubt about his faith.[21] Even so, Qutb admits that "intermittently he felt a secret desire to take comfort in the Qur'an." "These moments," Qutb writes, "invigorated me like no other experience did and made me feel that he was indeed standing on firm grounds that had not been desecrated by mud."[22]

Literary Analysis of the Qur'an: The Beginning

By the late 1930s Qutb appears to have rediscovered his "beautiful and beloved Qur'an" (Qur'ani al-jamil al-habib), including its vivid and moving imagery. It occurred to him, as a result, to write about the imagery of the Qur'an from a purely artistic point of view.[23] At this stage Qutb firmly believed in the separation of religion and literature. He held that if the Qur'an were temporarily stripped of its religious sanctity and set aside as a book of legislation and political order, one would find in it a literary work of art, beauty, peculiar charm and abundant imagination, all of which were integral to its "artistic inimitability" (al-I'jaz al-fanni).[24]

Qutb justifies his literary analysis of the Qur'an on the grounds that the nation had reached a stage of development that permitted intellectual and psychological luxury. This was different from the stage of necessities in the infancy of the nation, when Muslims necessarily studied the Qur'an as a source of legislation for their daily lives.[25]

In his first attempt at Qur'anic literary analysis, Qutb focused on such artistic aspects as imagery, tales, dialogues, and expressions. He points out first the charm, narration, and imagination to be found in Qur'anic imagery. He marvels, for example, at the simile of the unbeliever and the thirsty man who is deceived by a mirage in the desert, or the simile of the unbeliever and the man who is deceived by darkness at sea, as seen in Qur'an 24:39–40: *"As for those who disbelieve, their deeds are as a mirage in a desert. The thirsty one supposeth it to be water till he cometh into it and findeth it naught, and findeth, in the place thereof, Allah, Who payeth him his due, and Allah is swift at reckoning. Or as a darkness on a vast, abysmal sea. There covereth him a wave, above which is a wave, above which is a cloud. Layer upon Layer of darkness. When he holdeth out his hand he scarce can see it. And he for whom Allah hath not appointed light, for him there is no light."*[26]

Likewise, Qutb marvels at the Qur'anic art of storytelling, with its artistic, psychological, and philosophical dimensions citing the tale of Maryam (Virgin Mary) in Qur'an 19:16–34 as a prime example that contains the dramatic elements of a narrative. He points to Maryam's dilemma upon being told by the Spirit of Allah that she is pregnant: *"She said: How can I have a son when no mortal hath touched me, neither have I been unchaste?"* Her labor pain, deep anxiety, and fear of the adverse reaction of those around her lead her to despair and to desire death: "*Oh, would that I had died ere this and had become a thing of naught, forgotten!*" Her fears were in fact confirmed when she received a hostile reception upon returning home with her baby: "*Oh sister of Aaron! thy father was not a wicked man nor was thy mother a harlot.*" Only divine intervention saved her from the wrath of her people, when the child in the cradle suddenly began to speak: "*Lo! I am the slave of Allah. He hath given me the Scripture and hath appointed me a Prophet. And hath made me blessed wheresoever I may be, and hath enjoined upon me prayer and alms giving so long as I remain alive.*"[27]

Qutb writes in the most glowing terms about artistic dialogue in the Qur'an, saying that it transcends imagination. In illustration, he cites several Qur'anic dialogues, including that between the dwellers of Heaven and Hell in Qur'an 7:44: "*And the dwellers of the Garden cry unto the dwellers of the Fire: We have found that which our Lord promised us (to be) the Truth. Have ye (too) found that which your Lord promised the Truth? They say: Yea, verily. And a crier in between them crieth: The curse of Allah is on evil-doers.*"[28]

Qutb then goes on to examine the artisitic expressions of the Qur'an, describing them as brief though paramount in precision and beauty. He cites Qur'an 81:18: "*And the morning when it breathes*" (wa-al-Subh idha tanaffas) as an example of a Qur'anic expression that invokes imageries of vitality and activity in a living creation.[29]

Qutb concludes his article with an attempt to place the artistic imagery of the Qur'an in one of the literary traditions of classicism, symbolism, realism, and romanticism. He suggests that Qur'anic imagery is akin to romanticism, terming it the "light kind of romanticism" that is devoid of constraints and artificiality and reflects Arab mentality and specifically Arabic forms of expression. For the Qur'an was addressed to the Arabs first and, in Qutb's view, it represents the highest stage of inimitability in Arab eloquence.[30]

In the five years following the publication of his preliminary articles on the artistic aspects of the Qur'an, Qutb maintained fluctuating literary interest in the subject but did not publish any new study. The more he read the Qur'an and realized its artistic inimitability, however, the more the idea of writing an expanded study of it appealed to him.[31]

Qutb also began to feel that Qur'anic portrayal (taswir) is not separable from the rest of the Qur'an, but rather forms the basis of expression (qaʿidat al-taʿbir) for all the Qur'anic purposes, save for the sections dealing with legislation.[32] It was upon Qutb's discovery of this underlying unity that he decided to resume his writing on Qur'anic imagery. In 1944 he published articles in Cairo's monthly review *al-Risalah* in which he called for the adoption of the Qur'anic artistic method of portrayal in modern literature so as to raise it to loftier horizons. Qutb also expressed astonishment at both ancient and modern Arabic literature for their failure to utilize the artistic method of the "First Book of the Arabs."[33]

This and similar articles were highlighted by the appearance of Qutb's two major works on the literary aspects of the Qur'an, *al-Taswir al-fanni fi al-Qur'an* (Artistic Portrayal in the Qur'an) and *Mashahid al-qiyamah fi al-Qur'an* (Scenes of Resurrection in the Qur'an) in Cairo in 1945 and 1947, respectively. Qutb's basic goal in these works was to restore the Qur'an "to our hearts" in a way similar to how the Arabs first received it and were charmed by it, to present it in such a way as to rid it of the baggage of linguistic, syntactical, juristic, historical, and mythical commentaries, and to bring out its artistic aspects and literary peculiarities and in the process reveal its beauty.[34]

Furthermore, Qutb explains that he attempted to present Qur'anic scenes as portrayed by the clear outward expression (zahir al-lafz al-wadih). He thus sought to avoid complicating them with unnecessary interpretations and discussions. Qutb adds that, in his own belief, the Arabs first received the artistic beauty of the Qur'an in such a manner as to deepen their feelings and shake their souls, and that the later Qur'anic commentators and interpreters complicated this response.[35]

It should be noted that Qutb's interest in the Qur'an at this stage was purely artistic (hadafi huna hadafun fanniyun khalisun mahid). In other words, Qutb professed to be influenced only by his sense of being an independent artistic critic (bi-hasat al-naqid al-fanni al-mustaqil). If the excellence of art and the sanctity of religion happened to coincide, he added, it would be purely unintentional and would not influence his beliefs (fa-idha iltaqat fi al-nihayah baraʿat al-fann bi-qadasat al-din, fa-tilka natijah lamm aqsudu ilayha wa-lamm ataʿaththaru biha).[36] Qutb's pre-occupation with the purely artistic features of the Qur'an at this stage, according to ʿAzm, was criticized by the general guide of the Muslim Brothers, Hassan al-Banna (1906–1949), for ignoring the religious aspects of the Qur'an.[37]

AL-TASWIR AL-FANNI FI AL-QUR'AN (1945)

It is beyond the scope of this chapter to examine in detail the content of *al-Taswir al-Fanni fi al-Qur'an*. Therefore, only the highlights and pertinent material will be discussed. This work is considered to be the foundation of Qutb's Qur'anic studies and to have had a great influence on his Qur'anic commentary, *Fi Zilal al-Qur'an*, which appeared in the 1950s and 1960s.[38]

Upon completing the writing of *al-Taswir*, Qutb states that he experienced the rebirth of the Qur'an within himself. He had already exprienced the Qur'an as being beautiful within himself, but the beauty had been composed of fragmented parts. Now, by contrast, the Qur'an appeared to him to be one united sentence based on a "special rule," with a wondrous coordination he had never dreamed possible.[39]

Qutb maintains throughout *al-Taswir* that the Qur'an has a unified artistic method of expression (tariqah muwahhadah fi al-ta'bir) used for all purposes, including demonstration and argumentation. Qutb introduces this main thesis by examining what he considers to be the charm of the Qur'an and its source. In doing so, he cites the story of Caliph 'Umar ibn al-Khattab, whose decision to become Muslim was greatly influenced by the charm of the Qur'an.[40] Qutb sees the sources of this charm in the beautiful, effective, expressive, and picturesque Qur'anic expressions found in the early Meccan chapters that, he says, bewitched the pagans into accepting Islam.[41]

Qutb also devotes some attention to the historical development of Qur'anic study and interpretation. In his view, Qur'anic study in the form of exegesis was initiated by some companions of the Prophet and was expanded greatly by the end of second century of the Islamic Lunar year, Hij-rah. Instead of studying the artistic beauty and its harmony with the religious beauty, however, later commentators immersed themselves deeply in the juristic, dialectical, grammatical, syntactical, historical, and other aspects of the Qur'an.[42]

Those commentators who studied the inimitability of the Qur'an, according to Qutb, did have the opportunity to examine its artistic method, but instead they occupied themselves in studies dealing with utterance and meaning (al-lafz wa-al-ma'na) and their relationship to rhetoric. Only two scholars, 'Abd al-Qahir al-Jurjani and, to a lesser extent, al-Zamakhshari, went beyond the confines of "utterance and meaning" to show awareness of Qur'anic artistic imagery. However, none dealt as Qutb himself does with the general characteristics that bring out the artistic merits of the Qur'an.[43]

Qutb then concentrates his discussion on Qur'anic artistic portrayal, pointing out that portrayal is the favorite device of the
Qur'anic style. In his view, this portrayal is full of color, motion, and
rhythm. Often description, dialogue, words, and expressions mag-
nify the imagery and make it lively and human. As an example of
mental meanings (ma'ani dhihniyah) reproduced in sensual image,
Qutb cites Qur'an 7:40, in which the impossibility of nonbelievers
entering Heaven is vividly likened to the impossibility of a camel entering a needle's eye: "*Lo! they who deny Our revelations and scorn
them, for them the gates of Heaven will not be opened nor will they
enter the Garden until the camel goeth through the needle's eye.
Thus do We require the guilty.*"[44]

Qutb then elaborates on the methods that form the basis of
Qur'anic portrayal, namely, "sensual dramatization" (al-takhyil al-
hissi) and "magnification" (tajsim). By the technique of sensual
dramatization, the Qur'an imparts to solid objects and natural phenomena a life akin to that of humans. A case in point is Qur'an
81:18: "*And the morning when it breathes.*" Here a human quality,
that is, breathing, is ascribed to the morning. Magnification (al-
tajsim), in Qutb's scheme, gives meanings and states, dealing with
ma'nawiyat (mores), magnified images and forms. The Qur'an applies this technique when it likens sins to loads (ahmal) that are carried on one's back and when it describes the suffering of sinners as
being thick (ghaliz) and the days of sinners as being heavy (thaqil).[45]

Qutb points out that anthropomorphic Qur'anic expressions such
as "The Hand of Allah is above their hands," "His Throne on the
water," and "He sat on the throne"—expressions that have aroused
heated dialectical theological debates in the past—are examples of
dramatization and magnification used for the simple purpose of clar-
ifying abstract meanings.[46]

The difficulty of separating the artistic and religious aspects of the
Qur'an is evident when Qutb examines the Qur'anic tale. Despite
his declared intent to deal only with the literary aspects of the
Qur'an, it is clear that Qutb gradually began to emphasize the religious rather than the artistic aspect. This was especially true when,
in writing about the purposes of dramatic narrative in the Qur'an,
Qutb devoted much space to a discussion of purely religious purposes. His outline of the major purposes includes the following: The
confirmation of the truth of the revelation of Allah's message, the
reaffirmation that true religion from Noah to Muhammad was from
Allah, the reiteration that Unitarianism (al-tawhid) is the basis of Ju-

daism, Christianity, and Islam and that the means utilized by the prophets and their experiences with their people were the same in the different monotheistic religions and that the religions of Muhammad and Ibrahim were the same. Other purposes of dramatic narrative in the Qur'an include the declarations that Allah supports and blesses his prophets and his sincere friends, that Satan is the enemy of the children of Adam, and that divine wisdom is infinitely greater than human wisdom.[47]

Qutb also points out the subordination of the narrative to the religious message. This subordination is apparent in the repetition of parts of tales in different chapters of the Qur'an. The tale of the prophet Moses, for example, appears in no less than twelve chapters. This subordination is also manifested in the variety with which the tales in the Qur'an are treated. Sometimes a tale is presented from the beginning of the story, as in the tales of the births of Jesus, Mary, and Moses. Sometimes a tale is taken up at a later stage of the story, as in the tales of Yusuf (Joseph), Ibrahim (Abraham), Da'ud (David), and Sulayman (Solomon). Some tales are detailed like those of Yusuf, Ibrahim, and Sulayman, while others are given only briefly, like those of Hud, Salih, Lut Shu'ayab, Zakariya, and Ayyub. Finally, the tale's subordination can be seen in the frequent incorporation of religious directives as prologues or epilogues to them.[48]

After the appearance of the book *al-Taswir al-fanni* (Artistic Portrayal in the Qur'an) in March 1945, a rising literary figure at Cairo University, Bint al-Shati', commented on it in the *al-Ahram* newspaper, writing that the book is "an attempt to research the beauty of the Qur'an which was preceded by works at the university." Sayyid Qutb responded to her: "Where are the university research papers in this direction?" He added: "If the purpose is to do research in the beauty of the Qur'an, then this is an old research. If the research is a special unprecedented study, reality says that what is written in *al-Ahram* is not true." Some point out that the person who supported Bint al-Shati' was her professor at Cairo University and later her husband Amin al-Khouli. Sayyid Qutb waged a violent and personal attack on Amin al-Khouli when the latter supervised and defended Muhammad Ahmad Khalaf Allah and his controversial university dissertation "The Art of the Story in the Qur'an" (1947), in which Khalaf Allah describes Qur'anic stories as artistic literary works that are devoid of investigatory historical exposition.[49]

Abdul-Mun'im Khallaf criticized Sayyid Qutb's assertions that artistic portrayal is the tool preferred in the style of the Qur'an. He presented Qur'anic verses that are devoid of artistic portrayal. Khallaf also criticized Qutb's attempt to connect artistic portrayal and the inimitability of the Qur'an. He viewed that Sayyid Qutb negates inimitability from Qur'anic verses which are devoid of portrayal. He accused Sayyid Qutb of undermining the role of the mind in firmly establishing the creed in the human individual. Sayyid Qutb responded accurately to all the points raised by Khallaf. The argument between them was constructive, "whereby it was criticism and guidance on the one hand and a response and clarification on the other hand."[50]

Even though the youthful novelist Naguib Mahfouz criticized some aspects of the book, his comments on the book of Sayyid Qutb were positive overall:

> From the aesthetic aspect, our age is the age of music, portrayal and the narrative. Here you are indicating to us forcefully and with inspiration that our beloved Book is the most sublime form of inspiration and creativity. . . . Your book came as the guide for the Arab reader and listener in our generation. It guides him to the places of feeling and domains of beauty. It manifests for him the secrets of enchantment and the charms of creativity. The Qur'an was in the heart and now it fills the heart, the eye, the ear and the mind and all of them.[51]

MASHAHID AL-QIYAMAH FI AL-QUR'AN (1947)

In his second major literary-oriented Qur'anic work, *Mashahid al-qiyamah fi al-Qur'an*, which appeared in 1947, Qutb applies the views articulated in *al-Taswir* to the Qur'anic chapters and verses dealing with the scenes of Resurrection (al-qiyamah).[52] In a long introduction to this work, Qutb surveys the development of the idea of the other world (al-'alam al-akhar) in human consciousness, beginning with the ancient Egyptians and continuing with the Persians, Greeks, Romans, Hindus, Jews, and Christians.

In Qutb's view, the Qur'anic portrayal of the "other world" is unprecedented because of its deep impact on the mind, the comprehensiveness of its imagery, and the purity of its conception.[53] According to Qutb, the idea of the "other world" in the Qur'an is as simple and clear as the Islamic system of belief itself. It deals with death, resurrection, happiness, and suffering. Those who believe and do good deeds are bound for heaven and happiness, while those who do not are bound for hell and suffering.

Qutb finds in each resurrection scene a symmetry between the parts of the scene, the expressions used, and the underlying rhythm and music.[54] In the rest of the book, Qutb presents the Qur'anic verses that deal with the resurrection scenes and analyzes them according to the principles enunciated in *al-Taswir.* Thus the scene of Resurrection in Qur'an 81:1–14 is given as follows:

When the sun is overthrown,
And when the stars fall,
And when the hills are moved,
And when the camels big with young are abandoned,
And when the wild beasts are herded together,
And when the seas rise,
And when souls are reunited,
And when the girl-child that was buried alive is asked,
For what sin she was slain.
And when the pages are laid open,
And when the sky is torn away,
And when hell is lighted,
And when the garden is brought nigh,
(Then) every soul will know what it had made ready.

Qutb describes this scene as portraying a total overthrow of everything familiar and a comprehensive revolution of all existing entities. Participating in this overthrow and revolution are the heavenly bodies, the beasts, domesticated birds, human souls, and so on. The opening scene is a calamitous movement which turns everything upside down, excites the calm, and frightens the secure. The music and rhythm that underlie the scene are breathlessly rapid, reflecting the calamity.[55]

REASONS FOR QUTB'S INTEREST IN THE QUR'AN

Renewed Interest in Islamic Studies among the Literati

Qutb's renewed interest in the Qur'an in 1939 and thereafter should be seen within the larger context of the renewed interest of

liberal literati in Islamics in the 1930s and l940s. This period saw
the proliferation of Islamic works, especially Islamic history and biography, on the Egyptian literary scene. In these works can be seen
a search for ideals and values drawn from Arabic Islamic history
and tradition, which was inspired by resentment against Western
hegemony in Egypt and the Arab world and a gradual loss of faith
in the popular appeal of liberal nationalist parliamentary ideals.

For example, the one-time bastion of secular liberal ideas and
Pharaohnism, the weekly *al-Siyasah* (Politics) of Muhammad Hussayn
Haykal, changed its orientation during this period, adopting an Islamic
tone and topics. Haykal himself wrote a biography of the Prophet
(1935) and argued that "the Egyptian cultural soil was inhospitable to
any but Muslim-inspired ideals and values." Likewise, in 1942, Qutb's
mentor, al-'Aqqad, wrote a biography of the Prophet, which was followed by similar works on the Caliph 'Umar (1942), the Caliph Abu
Bakr (1943), the Prophet's wife 'A'ishah (1943), the Caliph 'Ali (1944),
and 'Ali's son al-Hussayn (1944), among others. In fact, all the senior
literati including Haykal, Taha Hussayn, al-'Aqqad, Tawfiq al-Hakim,
and Ahmad Amin concentrated their efforts on Islamic biographies and
history.[56] Qutb, however, chose an independent path by concentrating
on a new area in modern Arabic literature, namely, the literary analysis of the Qur'an.

Thus the literary atmosphere in Cairo was conducive to Islamic-
oriented writings. The more prominent literati took the lead and the
younger generation, including Qutb, followed.

Personal Reasons: The Death of Qutb's Mother

Qutb's study of the Qur'an was not merely an "intellectual and
psychological luxury," as he termed the literary analyses he pursued
in his first Qur'anic study, but was apparently a psychological and
spiritual necessity. As mentioned earlier, Qutb admitted that during
his secular life in Cairo in the 1930s and 1940s he felt a persistent
secret desire to take comfort in the Qur'an because it gave him the
feeling of standing on firm ground. The Qur'an was a comforting
refuge from the pain of the environment in which he lived. Qutb's
unhappiness in Cairo was reflected in his poetry of the heart in the
1930s, and it continued to manifest itself in his prose and verse of
the 1940s when he described himself as that fugitive young man, a
lover of the impossible, who seeks what he cannot find and is bored
with all that he attains.[57]

The death of Qutb's mother, Fatimah, in October 1940 was a major blow that partially explains Qutb's increased interest in the Qur'an at that period. Fatimah's influence on Qutb was enormous in instilling in him a deep sense of mission that remained with him until his execution in 1966. Upon her death he writes, "Mother, who will narrate to me the tales of my childhood in which you portray me as if I were of a unique texture (nasij farid) which made me think that I was great and required to live up to this greatness?" He writes further, "Mother . . . to whom do I ascend the step of life and who will celebrate when I am ascending? . . . Maybe many will re-joice . . . but your celebration is unique because it is the rejoicing of the skillful cultivator who realizes the fruits of his cultivation and efforts."[58]

Fatimah's death was also devastating because Sayyid was not mar-ried and Fatimah had been a major source of emotional support for him. Since the death of his father (ca. 1933), Fatimah had also shared with him the responsibility of raising his brother Muham-mad and his sisters Hamidah and Aminah. Qutb writes again: "Only today have I felt the heavy burden because as long as you lived I was strengthened by you. But now that you are gone I am alone and weak."[59]

The impact of Fatimah's death on her children can be seen in *al-Atyaf al-arba'ah* (The Four Phantoms), which was written by her children in 1945. In their joint dedication, Hamidah, Aminah, Muhammad, and Sayyid write, "After we had lost our father and migrated from our home to Cairo we have lived like strangers. How-ever, your death had left us alienated. We have become lost plants without roots and perplexed phantoms without a dwelling."[60] Qutb describes himself and his brother and sisters as strangers without a mother.[61]

Personal Reasons: Shattered Love Affair

Another event that partially explains Qutb's increasing interest in the Qur'an was an unsuccessful love affair (around 1942 or 1943) that is depicted in his prose and verse. Following his mother's death, it appears that Qutb sought to fill the void in his life through mar-riage, and consequently he fell in love and was engaged. Problems developed that led to the breakup of the engagement, however. Deeply shattered, Qutb was never again seriously involved with a woman. It is generally believed that Qutb's novel *Ashwak* (Thorns), which appeared in Cairo in 1947, reflects this disastrous affair.[62] Qutb dedicates his work "to the one who plunged into the thorns with me, bled as I bled, became miserable as I became miserable, and went her own way as I went mine both wounded after the battle."[63]

The impact of this affair is evident in Qutb's prose and verse in the early 1940s. His unhappiness is evident in his poem entitled "Hilm al-Hayah" (The Dream of Life), in which he laments the lost dream that idealized his love and gave meaning to his life:[64]

O, dream which kindled
A tumultuous flame burning in my blood,
Whenever the palm of my hand touches her hand
Ecstasy touches my heart and my mouth!

Where are you now O, secret of my life?
Where are you now O, meaning of my existence?
Where are you O, the inspiration of my hymn and my prayer?
Where? In a remote valley of silence.

In another poem, entitled "Nida' al-Kharif" (The Call of Autumn), Qutb calls on his love to return to their love nest, because the days of their lives are running out without hope or reunion. The renewal of their love, Qutb says, will invigorate their lives:[65]

Come, our days are about to end,
Come, our breaths are about to cool,
Without hope, no meeting and no date.

So return, here is the nest calling us;
Let us not O, sister destroy it with our hands;
Come, let us spend the rest of our lifetime,

Two comrades in good and evil,
Two allies in wealth and in poverty.

Later the poet refers to his love as a "forbidden fruit" (al-fakihah al-muharramah), which leaves him suspended between heaven and earth. For he hates and loves life for her sake and runs aimlessly, only to return to seek life from her. He describes his idealized love as a myth, a child, a snake, a gazelle, a saint, a nun. He concludes by saying: "Oh Fate (qadar), Why did you put her in my way and make her a forbidden fruit? I hear, Oh Fate, your severe and mocking judgment."[66]

A year later, in 1944, Qutb was still pondering his sadness and his shattered love. He wrote that he did not grieve the girl he loved, but the youngster within himself who was full of excitement and idealized love but was no longer there.[67]

Personal Reasons: Qutb's Health

Another development that partially explains Qutb's renewed interest in the Qur'an at this time was his poor health. Although it cannot be proven that Qutb had suffered from poor health since early youth, there is evidence of ill health in his writings from September 1940.[68] In November 1945, Qutb reports that he was ill for four months.[69] In July 1946, Qutb remarks sarcastically that he had consumed half of the medicine in Hulwan's pharmacy.[70] He was also reported hospitalized during his stay in the United States (1948–1950). In January 1952, he was reported to have serious eye problems. In the same month, he was reported generally ill. It was also reported that one of his lungs was removed.[71]

It has been suggested that Qutb's health deteriorated in the aftermath of his parents' death. The attendant anxiety, responsibility for his brother and two sisters, and the frustrations of his career could well have contributed to the development of the stomach, lung, and heart ailments that were to become more noticeable and serious in the 1950s and 1960s after having been exacerbated by his imprisonment between 1954 and 1964. It is certainly not unlikely that a man afflicted with sickness and other personal problems, without the comfort of a mother or wife, would turn to his religion for refuge. In Qutb's case, it was the Qur'an that increasingly became his refuge.

EARLY SIGNS OF CHANGES IN QUTB'S ORIENTATION

Despite the fact that Qutb was stressing the purely artistic or literary goal of his Qur'anic studies, one should not underestimate the long-lasting spiritual effect of his deep submergence in the Qur'an, especially at a time when he was experiencing personal crisis and his society was passing through unprecedented turmoil resulting from the social, political, and economic dislocations of World War II in

1939–1945. In a conversation with the Indian Muslim scholar Abul Hassan 'Ali Nadvi in 1951, Qutb acknowledged that his literary analysis of the Qur'an gradually led him to take a deeper interest in its religious message, which eventually influenced him and guided him to faith.[72]

One can therefore observe in this period some changes in Qutb's attitude toward poetry and the infinite. By late 1943, he had begun to have doubts about poetry of the psychological states, that is, sub-jective poetry of the heart, which he had been composing and cham-pioning since the beginning of his literary career. Qutb still believed in it, seeing it as exemplifying the highest ideal of modern poetry, but now he saw it as being limited in its horizons (mahdud al-afaq) and not in itself sufficient to fulfill his need for the infinite. He writes:

> I want to be set free and become an integral atom of nature which does not feel an independent entity for itself. I want to feel nei-ther the intention and the purpose, nor the limited actual states. I hate "awareness" because it is a kind of finiteness. I disavow my poetry and the poetry of the others. I fear that the wave which in-undates me is nothing but an ambiguous feeling which is incapable of being expressed in the limited language of human beings.[73]

Qutb's continual but fruitless search for the infinite (al-ghayr mah-dud, al-taliq) finally comes to a triumphant conclusion: "There is an only consolation. There is God (al-Ilah) whose existence has no be-ginning and for His extension no end. God who is free from all fet-ters. I love you! I love you because you are 'the infinite': the only one in this existence. I love you because you are the only hope for the human heart when it is unable to stand the limits."[74]

The Emergence of Qur'anic Ideology

From all available data, it appears that the article entitled "Madaris lil-sakht" (Schools for Indignation), which appeared in late September 1946, was the first that Qutb wrote to articulate a Qur'anic ideology.[75] At this juncture he was working on his second literary-oriented Qur'anic work, *Mashahid al-qiyamah fi al-Qur'an*.

In "Madaris lil-sakht," Qutb expresses indignation at Egyptian political and social conditions and disagreement with Egyptians who were hopeless and pathetic, resigning themselves to asking God to take care of their problems. In support of his argument, Qutb quotes

Qur'an 3:104, which has traditionally served as a motto of the Islamic movement, in which Allah calls on his people to be active in the spread of his message: *"and there may spring from you a nation who invite to goodness, and enjoin right conduct and forbid indecency."*[76]

He also quotes Qur'an 5:79 to criticize those people who were indifferent: *"They restrained not one another from the wickedness they did. Verily evil was what they used to do."* Further, in the same article Qutb employs Qur'anic phraseology: "They swallow fire into their bellies" (maya'kuluna fi butunihim illa al-nar) to describe privileged Egyptians who were exploiting the people. This phraseology is derived from Qur'an 4:10: *"Lo! Those who devour the wealth of orphans wrongfully, they do but swallow fire into their bellies and they will be exposed to burning flame."*[77]

Qutb's Call for Spiritual Leadership

Concrete religious ideas and symbolism began to emerge in Qutb's writing early in 1947. In January, very much alienated from the prevailing system, Qutb writes that the nation was in need of spiritual energy and leadership (taqah wa-qiyadah ruhiyah). In his view, political awakening will not last unless it is augmented by spiritual leadership similar to that of Jamal al-Din al-Afghani, which fueled three national revivals: the 'Urabi nationalist movement, Mustafa Kamil's resistance to the British, and Sa'd Zaghlul's revolt for independence.[78]

The absence of this spiritual element, says Qutb, explains both the lowering standard of political life and the moral decay of individuals and groups in society. What is needed, Qutb adds, is a leadership that creates great personalities, as was created by al-Afghani, and which orients individuals and groups from temporal to higher needs.[79]

Closely related to Qutb's view of the spiritual leadership of al-Afghani was his vision of Muslim history. The greatest moment of Muslim history, according to Qutb, was the period of pristine Islam, namely, that of the Prophet and the rightly guided caliphs, which Qutb refers to as "the first towering flow" (al-madd al-'ali al-awwal) that has never been equaled in human history. Strengthened by the great spiritual stock derived from the high ideals of Islam, the Muslims of that time overran the aging Persian and Byzantine empires, reaching China to the east and the Atlantic to the west, not for imperialistic purposes but for the spread of the "High Idea" and to liberate people from despotism, exploitation, and errors, restoring their human dignity and giving them equality.[80]

According to Qutb, the first setback of the true spirit of Islam was at the hands of Mu'awiyah ibn Abi Sufyan, 'Amr ibn al-'As, and his brothers (the Umayyads), who restored tribalism and used means to justify ends. Since their time there has been an ebb and flow of Islamic spirit, but it would never again achieve the intensity of the "first towering flow."[81]

The most recent resurgence of the spirit of Islam, Qutb says, came at the hands of Jamal al-Din al-Afghani at a time when the Muslim world had reached spiritual and moral decline, weakness, and bankruptcy.[82] Qutb's view of Muslim history at this point in his life (January 1947) was similar to views expressed by Islamists including the Muslim Brothers.[83] Two years later, these same views of Qutb would be reiterated in an expanded version in his work on social justice in Islam.

CHAPTER 4

THE ALIENATION OF SAYYID QUTB, 1939–1947

EMERGENCE OF A MORALIST

Sayyid Qutb's emergence as a serious student of the Qur'an, 1939–1947, was accompanied by his emergence as a stern moralist, an anti-Western thinker, and an anti-political, anti–literary establishment intellectual. These mutually reinforcing developments were, like the Qur'anic teachings, crucially significant in the makeup of Qutb's ideology in the late 1940s, 1950s and 1960s. The emergence of Qutb as a stern moralist should not be seen merely as a development of the 1940s. Moralism had been ingrained in him by his upbringing and environment. Qutb had been brought up in a rural environment, which he refers to as "conservative and clean." As an adult, he maintains that he led a serious life that allowed no time for play. He also believed that poetry and art had preserved his imagination from pollution. Qutb was always proud of his rural origin, holding the opinion that rural people were more authentic, with more fortitude, and a purer conscience than the urban people of Cairo.[1]

On the other hand, Qutb was alleged to have held views in the 1930s that were considered immoral. Mahmud 'Abd al-Halim, a member of the Muslim Brothers, writes that he read an article by Qutb in the late 1930s in which Qutb calls on people to strip themselves naked and live accordingly. 'Abd al-Halim was so angered by this article that he wrote a rebuttal and sought the General Guide al-Banna's approval to publish it. Al-Banna counseled against it, however, on the grounds that it would only give Qutb's ideas more prominence. By ignoring Qutb's ideas, al-Banna reasoned, they would be forgotten. As a result, 'Abd al-Halim did not publish his rebuttal.[2] In the context of the many articles that Qutb wrote, his "bohemian ideas," if they indeed existed, should not be seen as integral to his thought. The article in question could well have been written out of frustration, or as a ploy to gather attention, rather than out of genuine belief.

None of Qutb's ethical views that were expressed in his prose and verse of the 1930s occupied as significant a part of his literary output or ideology as they did in the 1940s. This development of Qutb's ethical views should be seen in light of the ravaging impact of World War II upon Egyptian society resulting from the large presence of foreign troops on Egyptian soil.

The effects of World War II fostered an atmosphere in Egyptian society that was seen by many, including Qutb, as contributing to the decay of public morality and institutions. The deep impact of these effects upon Qutb can be seen clearly in his later Islamic writings. For example, in his *Ma'rakat al-Islam wa-al-ra'smaliyyah* (The Battle of Islam and Capitalism), Qutb reminds his readers of the treatment accorded the Egyptians by the Allied soldiers during World War II. He accuses the soldiers of crushing Egyptians with their cars like dogs and of trampling Egyptian dignity and honor. Qutb also recalls the soldiers' looks of disdain at the Egyptian police and army officers.[3]

Qutb's Ethical Standards and Views of Singing

According to Qutb, the essence of ethics is not represented by the acts of those who avoid evil for fear of the suffering of the day of reckoning, or by the acts of those who avoid crime for fear of the penal code.[4] Rather, the essence of ethics is represented by men who possess true manhood and its virtues, which include fortitude, courage in helping others, compassion, confidence with dignity, affection, and responsibility, and by women who possess sound womanhood and its virtues, which include shyness, mercy, and sacrifice. It is represented further by virtues common to men and women alike, namely, sensitivity of conscience, exaltedness of self, purity of feelings, and clean speech. Any attempt to destroy these virtues is, according to Qutb, an evil act that should be resisted because it entails the destruction of character and society.[5]

With these ethical standards as his guide, Qutb began in 1940 to articulate his criticism publicly of what appeared to him to be moral decay in Egyptian society. He started by criticizing what he termed the "sick singing" (al-ghina' al-marid), that is, the songs that were broadcast on Egyptian radio. He asserts in his writings that such songs destroyed Egyptian social structure and personal character because they corrupted the virtues of men and women. In his view, these songs reflected popular taste (al-dhawq al-baladi) and hence lacked any trace of intellectual, ethical, and social education. An educated listener, therefore, could not find anything in such music that met his higher standards and refined emotions.[6]

Earlier, Qutb writes that these songs were more dangerous than any "fifth column." He calls them a poison running through the essence of the nation and suggests that severe public pressure should be applied to discredit them.[7] He also suggests the institution of censorship of music and singing in the broadcasting service, clubs, and record companies by a committee made up of educated people well versed in the arts and who possessed excellent taste. This committee would be empowered to prevent, if necessary, the broadcasting of songs, the production of records and tapes, and the showing of films. Qutb also calls for laws that would penalize those who sing forbidden songs.[8]

In addition, Qutb advocated forming groups to combat the "sick singing" which destroys Egypt's pride, manhood and femininity, excites its instincts, and anesthetizes its nerves like narcotics. These groups would function like any other group combating disease and narcotics. They would spread the message and resist the commercial influence of vested interests by way of newspapers and broadcasting and would apply public pressure to discredit harmful songs in all clubs and societies.[9]

Qutb states that the type of singing he advocates would not necessarily entail ethical, social, or nationalist themes. He prefers songs with dignified humor and biting criticism, which portray refined human emotions and introduce the senses to the thrills of the universe, the secrets of the self, and the beauty of nature.[10] Qutb's public criticism of singing and songs will become an integral part of his Islamic ideology in the late 1940s, 1950s, and 1960s.

Campaign against Public Bathers

Qutb was also highly critical of the behavior of public bathers on Alexandria's beaches. Commenting on some women clad in swimsuits wandering aimlessly on the beaches, he writes that these "naked" women were cheap meat (Lahm rakhis): "Cheap. Many of these naked bodies lose even the value of the expensive meat. I do not doubt now that clothes are a product of Eve. For concealment and secrecy are the source of attractiveness and desire."[11]

Qutb describes the lifestyle of those on the beaches as being permissive: "Here quick friendships thrive: acquainting one with another begins in the forenoon and everything is accomplished by night. Next morning all are dispersed and friendships are terminated as if nothing had happened. Then they all begin looking for something new."[12]

He compares the parading of girls on the beaches to the parading of slave girls in the slave market. For both are exhibitions on which the eyes are fixed and from which sick thoughts creep. He points out, furthermore, that the dignities of these girls are being usurped in these bleak days in the name of "modernism."[13]

Criticism of the Younger Generation

Qutb was also critical of the ethical standards and way of life of the younger generation.[14] He is critical, for example, of the younger generation's lack of interest in serious books. "Why should they read a serious book," Qutb writes, "when they have cheap magazines and obscene films which flatter their instincts and appeal to the more contemptible parts in them?"[15]

Qutb blames the mass media, including radio, films, and the press, for contributing to the deterioration of Egyptian moral standards. He calls sarcastically for the whip (al-sut) to correct the situation, and in the process shows some affinity with "the puritan Wahhabis" and the Saudis' strict observance of moral standards.[16] He writes, "Over there in the Nejd, poets who flirt with love poetry are whipped. Over here in Egypt they clap for those who guide boys and girls toward immorality (da'arah) and train them on shamelessness (mujun). God have mercy on you oh Muhammad ibn 'Abd al-Wahhab! and God favor you oh 'Abd al-'Aziz ibn Sa'ud. We need only one day and one night in Egypt to whip those fools in the broadcasting service, the cinema studios and in all Egyptian magazines."[17]

EMERGENCE OF AN ANTI-WESTERN INTELLECTUAL

Criticism of Western Civilization

Qutb's attitudes toward Western culture and civilization (East versus West) began to emerge publicly in the 1930s, mirroring the general intellectual trend of the 1920s and 1930s when many Egyptians were in the process of searching for cultural identity and political independence. Thus, shortly after his graduation from Dar al-'Ulum in 1933, Qutb warns his fellow countrymen against blind imitation (taqlid) of Western civilization. He accuses the West of going astray because of its blind, one-sided devotion to everything connected with speed (sur'ah).[18]

Qutb explains that the Western world's addiction to speed had made steam, the telephone, and the telegraph obsolete, and the airplane, radio, television, and moving pictures paramount. He terms this addiction to speed "a strange psychological phenomenon" that swept away with it literature and the arts as well. Art and literature thus became passing glimpses (lamahat khatifah) and quick observations (mulahazat sari'ah), with no place for in-depth study or precise analysis.[19]

Qutb attributes the financial, political, literary, and social crises that afflicted people around the world to their addiction to speed. This phenomenon, he states, blinds people to their surroundings, making them see only what lies in front of them. As a result, they do not stop to consider where they are heading. Instead, they keep committing the same errors until they break down completely. According to Qutb, this breakdown is the source of worldwide crisis.[20]

Qutb criticizes those who call for the imitation of the West at a time when the West itself does not know where it is heading. He attributes this imitative phenomenon, which he says was observed earlier by Ibn Khaldun (1332–1406 A.D.), to the tendency of the conquered to imitate their conquerors, the former believing that the latter possess qualities that make them superior. But even though imitation is understandable and natural, it is not sound. Therefore, the East should take heed and not follow the West without contemplation and thinking.[21]

Qutb emphasizes the notion that "vitality," which is beneficial for both individual and society, is to be preferred over "haste." The East, according to Qutb, should adopt vitality and should also preserve its conviction, depth, spaciousness, and enchantment. The East should not be excessive in its imitation of the West, especially since the latter, intoxicated with its achievement, continues to stumble and run impulsively.[22]

On another occasion, in 1934, Qutb accuses the West of being both consciously and unconsciously biased against the East and Islam, singling out in particular the Orientalists for their failure to understand the spirit and spiritual forces of Islam. He adds that all the Orientalists are to be excused for not penetrating deeply into the meaning of Islam and for not understanding the deep psychological motivations of Easterners because the faculty of reason (al-'aql) on which they depend is not enough to understand such motives and tendencies.[23]

Qutb's views on the cultural direction of Egypt and the conflict of East and West were highlighted in a lengthy article published in April 1939 in the journal of his alma mater, *Sahifat Dar al-'Ulum*, to rebut sections of Taha Hussayn's controversial work *Mustaqbal al-Thaqafah fi Misr* (The Future of Culture in Egypt), which appeared in Cairo in 1938. In his two-volume work, Hussayn asserts that Egypt and Europe have a common intellectual heritage, argues for the adoption of comparable European patterns of education, and calls on the state to assume control over all education. He says too that al-Azhar must accept the leadership of the state and come to terms with modern ideas. Moreover, Egypt should acknowledge its leadership of the Arab world and attempt to coordinate its educational programs with Arab needs.

Qutb's Positive Reaction to *The Future of Culture in Egypt*

Qutb's overall reaction to Hussayn's work is very positive. Qutb considers Hussayn's work the first work in Egypt's post-independence era to lay out a detailed policy for all stages of theoretical education, beginning with the primary grades and ending with the university. Hussayn's book also deals with the education of society, the duties of the state, and such cultural activities as the theatre, radio, journalism, research, and literature.[24]

Qutb generally agrees with Hussayn's premise that the interdependence of educational and national interests makes it necessary to promote educational policies that would ensure common national loyalties. Overall governmental control of education is therefore absolutely necessary for ensuring common national goals in both private and public schools, in addition to making education available to every Egyptian child regardless of his or her family's financial status.[25]

Qutb agrees with Hussayn that the Ministry of Education lacked consistent educational policies because of partisanship and internal power struggles and that the overhaul and decentralization of the department were therefore necessary.[26] Qutb further agrees with Hussayn that the graduates of al-Azhar should not be allowed to teach Arabic in the public schools unless the government takes an active role in supervising Arabic language instruction at al-Azhar. Failure to do so would undermine the natural unity of mentality among the educated, and would instill in the children reactionary principles that would conflict with the secular education they were pursuing.[27]

Qutb adds that the Arabic language college at al-Azhar should be eliminated. If this is not done, then Qutb believes that the government must actively supervise the college to prevent its graduates from molding the children of the nation however they wish.[28]

Qutb's Negative Reaction to *The Future of Culture in Egypt*

Qutb strongly disagrees, however, with some of Hussayn's arguments. He takes issue particularly with Hussayn's view that Egypt and Europe have shared a common intellectual heritage since the time of the Pharaohs and that Egypt is a Western, not an Eastern, nation.[29] Qutb criticizes Hussayn's categorization of the world into two cultural spheres: the East, represented by China, Japan, India and Indonesia; and the West, represented by France, England, the rest of Europe and America.

Hussayn, Qutb says, ignores a third cultural category: the East as symbolized by Egypt's role as a connecting link between the Arab East and the Arab West.[30] To bring this third cultural category into focus, according to Qutb, would have changed Hussayn's argument significantly. The choice would then become a clear one between Egypt's Arabic and Western cultural links.[31]

Qutb rejects Hussayn's assertion that Egypt is a Western nation that traces its roots back to the interaction of Egyptian and Greek minds in ancient history. According to Qutb, the Greek presence in Egypt did not necessarily imply a positive (or a negative) interaction of mind. By the same token, the Egyptian resistance to Persian invasion did not necessarily involve a rejection of the Persian mind. The Greek colonies founded by the Pharaohs for the purpose of settling the Greek mercenaries to uphold their unpopular regimes were much disdained by the Egyptians. Qutb maintains that Egyptian preoccupations in relation to their oppressors throughout history were first directed toward achieving freedom and sovereignty, not toward any kind of "meeting of minds."[32]

Qutb also takes issue with Hussayn's rejection of the intellectual unity between Egypt and the East, including Arab Muslim nations. Qutb disagrees with Hussayn's assertion that language and religion do not create unity, citing the enmity between the Muslim Umayyad state in Spain and the Muslim Abbasid state in Iraq as an example.[33] Qutb seeks to explain that the differences between the Umayyads and the Abbasids were strictly political. The scientific and literary output of the two groups clearly indicates their intellectual unity. Qutb believed that, as dean of the College of Literature at Egyptian University, Taha Hussayn should have been aware of this fact.[34]

Qutb also refutes the sweeping generalizations Hussayn makes in rejecting the idea that Egypt is part of the East because the mentality of Egypt differs from those of India and China. According to Qutb, each nation has its own mentality and culture. One cannot therefore lump together such diverse peoples and cultures as Egypt, India, and China and hope to arrive at an intelligent classification. Mentalities of nations may grow closer (or further apart), but they can never become one. In support of this, Qutb points to the many dissimilarities that exist among Western nations as manifested, for example, in the differences between the school curricula of England, France, and Germany, the literatures of England and America, and the systems of government of Germany and Italy on the one hand, and those of England, France, and the United States on the other.[35]

Qutb also criticizes Hussayn's claim that Islam did not change the Egyptian mentality because it had been supposedly blended with Greek philosophy and thus become compatible with the Greek elements that made up the Egyptian mentality. While acknowledging that Greek philosophy had an influence on Islam, Qutb asserts that only the educated elite had been affected by it. By contrast, Qutb explains, the masses had been affected profoundly by Islam itself, which had instilled in them its pure Arab spirit.[36]

Qutb rejects the idea that religion imprints the masses with its philosophy and logic, asserting instead that the prime influence of religion is its spiritual system. By spiritual system Qutb means preaching, admonition, law, and the social, economic, and political system elaborated in the Torah and the Qur'an.[37] Qutb takes issue with Hussayn's arguments that since Christianity did not change the mentality of Europeans when it spread throughout Europe, neither did Islam change the Egyptian mentality when it spread in Egypt, especially since the Qur'an had been sent to confirm the Gospel. Qutb answers Hussayn by saying that while religions might agree on certain issues, they differ in the nature of their mentalities.

A comparative study of the Qur'an and the New Testament clearly reveals, according to Qutb, significantly different views on the nature of God, the relation between God, and the prophets and the teachings of prophets. Whereas the Qur'an and the Torah both contain religious, social, economic, and political statutes, the Gospel lacks them almost completely.[38]

Qutb quotes extensively from Christ's teachings in the Gospel of Matthew (chapter 5, verses 21–41) to illustrate that Christianity as enunciated by Christ is spiritually oriented and has little to do with the enactment of laws, statutes, or religious duties.[39] Thus, when Christianity spread in Europe, it left a spiritual and ethical legacy but did not lay down the kind of foundation of legislation, economics, and politics that the Qur'an was able to lay in Egypt. Qutb adds that secular European thought was altered very little by Christianity and that this secular thought continued to dominate European affairs, while Egyptian thought came under the influence of the Qur'an and became the focus of Qur'anic legislation and its political-economic-social system. This subjugation of Egyptian thought to the Qur'anic mentality can be clearly seen in current Egyptian law, which although drawing greatly on Roman canon and French law, was also influenced by Islamic law.[40]

Hussayn's assertion that Greek influence over the nations of the Mediterranean area, including Egypt, forged an intellectual and cultural unity among them is rejected by Qutb because regardless of the extent of the ties that may have bound these peoples together, highly significant differences still existed between them. It was inevitable, according to Qutb, given the geographical, political, and economic differences between the European countries and Egypt, that intellectual differences among them would persist. These differences are reflected in, for example, the differences in educational curricula, at least in terms of their theoretical basis, between Egypt and the nations of Europe.[41] Qutb also rejects Hussayn's claim that Egypt's adoption of European civilization in the modern age is rooted in the harmony of the Egyptian and European minds, a harmony that was interrupted by five centuries of Turkish rule. Qutb asserts that the emulation of the more advanced European civilization by Eastern nations such as Japan, China, Iran, Turkey, Egypt, and Syria is simply inevitable. Like the Europeans who had emulated Islamic civilization when the latter was more highly developed, so Egyptians and other peoples now emulate Europe. The pattern of world relations, Qutb maintains, is based on mutual needs.[42]

Qutb argues that the greatest proof that the Egyptian and European mentalities are different is the clash between the materialistic European civilization that Egyptians emulate and the system of beliefs, traditions, and consciousness that lie in the Egyptian mind and soul. Qutb adds that it will take a long time before Egyptians will feel at ease with and accept this civilization like Westerners.[43]

Western civilization, according to Qutb, is in continuous conflict with humanity because technical inventions and their vestiges, which are a product of the conscious mind, have surpassed the unconscious and have thus created an unbalanced situation that can be rectified only by striking a balance between the external world (environment) and the inner self.[44]

If it is necessary to emulate European civilization and maintain Egyptian character, then civilization, Qutb maintains, must be dissected into two elements: thaqafah (culture) and madaniyyah (civilization).[45] In this model, *thaqafah* is defined comprehensively to include religion, art, ethical norms, traditions, and myths. These elements must be preserved, but they must also be renewed as much as the natural evolutionary process requires.[46] *Madaniyyah*, on the other hand, is to include sciences and applied arts. These, according to Qutb, can be adopted outright from Europe.[47]

Qutb acknowledges that differentiating between thaqafah and madaniyyah is not easy and that a great effort at the social and ethical levels would be necessary to maintain the desired balance. He cites Japan as the prime example of a country that was able to maintain its culture while adopting the latest in European "civilization."[48] This idea of differentiating the cultural and the scientific and then adopting the latter wholesale becomes paramount in Qutb's *Social Justice in Islam* (al-'Adalah al-Ijtima'Iyah Fi al-Islam), where he totally rejects the borrowing of cultural aspects of the West but accepts without hesitation the wholesale adoption of Western pure sciences and their applied results.[49]

Hussayn's ridicule of those who attempt to prove materialism of the West and spiritualism of the East is also attacked by Qutb, who insists that there is a clear difference between the two worlds. Qutb agrees with the Egyptian scholar and litterateur Ahmad Amin's comparison of materialism and spiritualism.[50] According to Amin, belief in materialism rests on the notion that matter constitutes the universe and that all phenomena, including those of the brain, are due to material factors. This is in contrast to spiritualism, the belief dominant in the East, that holds matter alone is incapable of explaining all phenomena, thus implying the existence of a nonmaterial world as well. While holding, as materialism does, that the brain is a "thinking machine," spiritualism rejects the materialist idea that the human mind, which feels its own personality and freedom of will, can be a result of matter that does not sense or feel.[51]

Qutb states that the materialistic outlook of the West is evident in some of its religious theories, such as the "temporal theory of God." According to this theory, which is based on Darwinian natural science, philosophy, life, and progress are a product of the cosmos, which is made possible by a special compound in the heart of the cosmos known as God.[52] Eastern theories, according to Qutb, do not allow God to become a mere property or part of the cosmos because they always view God as larger and different from the cosmos.[53]

Qutb's rebuttal of *The Future of Culture in Egypt* was received warmly by many Egyptians. Two months after his article appeared, the Muslim Brothers requested and received permission to reprint it in their newspaper, the political weekly *al-Nadhir* (Herald) (f. 1938), where it was published on June 9, 1939. This first contact between Qutb and the Brothers did not go beyond the courtesy of having his article appear in their weekly. Later, in 1939, Qutb reprinted his rebuttal of Taha Hussayn in a booklet entitled *Naqd Kitab mustaqbal al-thaqafah* (Criticism of *The Future of Culture in Egypt*).[54]

Qutb's Attacks on the West and on France

By the mid 1940s, Qutb became fiercely anti-Western. In 1944, he attacked Western civilization and hailed its demise. In his view, the West has failed and it is now the turn of the East to take over the leadership of the world and create by the power of its spirituality a new civilization.[55] Qutb also calls on the Arabs not to trust the West, because the West has neither conscience nor honor. He writes: "Before we trust European or American conscience we have to remember France and events in Syria and Lebanon, England and the abominable days of February 4 (1942), and Truman's support for the Zionists."[56] Whereas Qutb's criticism in the 1930s was predominantly cultural, his stance in the 1940s became increasingly political, focusing his attacks on individual Western countries, namely France, England, and the United States, in light of what he perceived as Western suppression of Arab nationalist aspirations in Egypt and the Arab world.

Qutb calls the moral decay of society a mihnah (tribulation), an integral part of the tribulation of humanity that resulted from the adoption of the materialistic civilization of Europe. He writes: "How I hate and despise this European civilization and eulogize humanity which is being tricked by its lustre, noise, and sensual enjoyment in which the soul suffocates and the conscience dies down (yakhfut), while instincts and senses become intoxicated, quarrelsome and excited."[57]

Qutb focused his attack on France's suppression of the nationalist movements in Syria, Morocco, Tunisia, and Algeria. The history of the French presence in the East, he says, is nothing but "savage barbarism" and "pools of blood." The Napoleonic invasion of Egypt and the bloody occupation of Cairo, the 1925 bombardment of Damascus, the suppression of the nationalists in Morocco, and French attempts to force Christianity on Moroccan Muslims only attest to the true evil nature of France.[58]

Qutb also attacked the Egyptians who were glorifying France. He said those Egyptians who at one time lived in France were few. They were permitted by immoral France (Faransa al-da'irah) to satisfy their extreme, animalistic pleasures and to quench their sensual desires. When they returned to Egypt, he says, they found some remnants of tradition and some obstacles, and they did not like the so-called reactionary nature of the East. In the meantime, they continued to long for the "immoral" memory of France, its pleasures and desires.[59]

Qutb's Attacks on Britain

On February 4, 1942, the British imposed a Wafdist cabinet on the king by force of arms. At the end of 1945, when the details of that incident became known to the public, Qutb reacted angrily. He accused the existing political parties of being aqzam (midgets). "Where are you, oh Mustafa Kamil? Where are you to teach them how to repel the shame that was committed against the nation on February 4, as you had repelled the oppression that gripped Egypt on the day of Denshawai?"[60]

According to Qutb, following the Denshawai incident in 1906 the British consul Lord Cromer was forced to leave his post. By contrast, the British Ambassador Sir Miles Lampson, who played a leading role in the February 4 incident, remained his country's representative to the Egyptian court. The difference between Mustafa Kamil and the politicians, according to Qutb, is the difference between someone who was not interested in governing and did not trust anyone's conscience and people who trusted and believed British conscience and honor.[61]

Qutb attacks the myth of the so-called political conscience of Britain and those politicians who, in spite of past experiences, still believed it. Qutb calls on the Arab nation to take matters into its own hands and not to rely on diplomacy in light of Zionist immigration to Palestine.[62]

The Day of Evacuation (Yawm al-Jala'), February 21, 1946, witnessed widespread national strikes and demonstrations by workers and students who were demanding Britain's evacuation and Egypt's total independence. It resulted in bloody clashes which left 20 dead and 150 wounded. Commenting on the casualties, Qutb writes that blood is the down payment ('arabun) for freedom and that martyrdom is the price of dignity.[63] The innocent blood that was shed, Qutb writes, refutes those leaders and politicians in Egypt and the Arab world who stood behind Britain in its difficulties (i.e., during the war years) without securing a British pledge of evacuation. Instead, they trusted the honor of Britain's so-called political conscience. According to Qutb, a forty-eight-hour Egyptian revolt to disrupt communications during the decisive battle of al-'Alamayn (1942) would have been enough to change the results of the war, but Egypt did not revolt, because it trusted Britain's conscience.[64]

Qutb adds that the true intentions of the West were now apparent. They were apparent in Egypt in the February 4 incident and the bloodshed of the Day of Evacuation. They were apparent in French suppression of the nationalists in Syria, in Truman's demands for the opening of Palestine to 100,000 Jews, and in Britain's suppression of the Muslims of Indonesia. The British, Americans, French, and Dutch were waging war against Easterners in general and against Muslim countries in particular. Qutb concludes that belief in this Western threat must be engraved in the consciousness of all Easterners, whether Indian, Indonesian, Egyptian, Syrian, Lebanese, Iraqi, Hijazi, Najdi, Palestinian, Algerian, Tunisian, Moroccan, or other.[65]

Qutb's Attacks on the United States

Qutb's attacks on the United States became more pronounced in 1946 as a result of President Truman's policies supporting Jewish immigration to Palestine. At last the "conscience of the United States" has been uncovered, writes Qutb. The Palestinian problem has shown that this "conscience" gambles with the fate and rights of humans in order to buy a few votes in the election.[66] Americans, Qutb writes, are no different from any other Westerners with a "rotten conscience" (damir muta'affin). Their conscience is all derived from the same source, namely, the materialistic civilization that has no heart or conscience, and which hears nothing but the sounds of machines. Qutb writes, "How I hate and despise those Westerners! All without exception: the British, the French, the Dutch and now the Americans who were at one time trusted by many. . . . And I do not hate or despise these alone. I hate and despise just as much those Egyptians and Arabs who continue to trust Western conscience."[67]

EMERGENCE OF AN ANTI-ESTABLISHMENT INTELLECTUAL

Qutb's Call for Social Justice

By the mid-1940s, Qutb, the longtime supporter of the Wafd and the Sa'dist parties, had become very disillusioned with the prevailing political system. In mid-1945, he accused the existing parties of being indifferent to the problem of social justice (al-'adalah al-ijtima'iyah). According to Qutb, there was an absence of planned constructive policy geared toward the realization of social justice and the rejuvenation of Egyptian society. What was needed, in Qutb's view, were new parties with a constructive mentality and with comprehensive social programs for correcting the unequal distribution of wealth and promoting social justice in their educational policies.[68]

By the mid-1940s, Qutb's concern with social justice had become paramount in his writings, including his autobiographical work *Tifl min al-Qaryah* (Child from the Village), which appeared in Cairo in

1946. Qutb vividly describes the wretched conditions of the migrant workers who used to toil on his family's land. These and similar childhood memories haunted him in his adult life in Cairo and gave him the feeling that justice did not reign in the country. If there were just laws in the "valley," according to Qutb, they would have taken him to prison instead of the many whom the law considered thieves and criminals. Two years later, in 1948, the theme of social justice was to headline Qutb's Islamic ideology.

Qutb's Attacks on the Establishment

By September 1946, Qutb was attacking various sectors of the establishment. He became very critical of the privileged upper classes, calling them "aristocrats." He accused them of not speaking the language of the people, of not even physically resembling the Egyptians, and of being as imperialist as the British. He asserted that these privileged ones were aristocrats in name only, being heir to no noble descent or traditions. On the contrary, they were the children of slave girls and emancipated ones, a caste that served the British occupation so well.[69]

At about the same time, Qutb was expressing indignation at those sectors of the establishment that included writers, politicians, and the mass media. He attacked writers and journalists, the so-called opinion leaders and spiritual fathers of the people, whose pens and consciences were put at the disposal of politicians instead of the people.[70] He expressed outrage at those politicians who promised programs for social reform, intellectual revival, and the purification of the administrative apparatus of government only to renege on their promises upon assuming power. He criticized the pashas and the privileged of society, the aristocrats, for exploiting the people and for their snobbish attitudes toward the *fellahs* (peasants) and the masses. He also attacked the ordinary people (abna' al-sha'b) who, upon becoming part of the establishment, reneged on their support of free education.[71]

Qutb expressed indignation at the radio station that wasted people's money on broadcasting to every home, whether people wanted it or not, material that was more appropriate for brothels, clubs, and cinemas than for families. He also attacked the "immoral press," the so-called successful press, because it appealed to animalistic instincts and did the same job as managers of brothels. In Qutb's view, this press was killing the fortitude, honor and strength of the people who, as a result, were not concerned with the nation-alist cause or with independence.[72]

EMERGENCE OF THE ANTI–LITERARY ESTABLISHMENT INTELLECTUAL

Qutb's Departure from the Orbit of al-'Aqqad

The tremendous influence of al-'Aqqad on Sayyid Qutb in the 1930s is well known. Qutb was weary of imitating al-'Aqqad and thus tried to chart an independent literary career. Qutb's quest for the infinite and the world of spirits helped him to take an independent path in 1939 with his renewed interest in the Qur'an and its literary analysis. His fear that his personality would disappear seems to have been finally overcome by 1944, when he declared that he had done so. He said that he could now envision the milestones (ma'alim) and horizons of his own path, even though he would continue to benefit from al-'Aqqad and his expertise.[73]

Al-'Aqqad's reaction to Qutb's works on the Qur'an and literature, which began to appear in 1945, was muted, however. Al-'Aqqad did not write a single word in favor of or against Qutb's works. Al-'Aqqad's indifference toward one of his most dedicated and loyal students left Qutb greatly embittered for several years.[74] Undoubtedly, al-'Aqqad's behavior also helped drive a wedge between the two and to speed Qutb's departure from al-'Aqqad's orbit.

This development also coincided with Qutb's changing views of poetry, which began to crystallize in 1946 and culminated in his rejection of al-'Aqqad's vision of poetry in 1948.[75] At that time, Qutb claimed that when al-'Aqqad's school of poetry attempted practical application of this vision, the attempt failed because its poetic energy lacked warmth and feelings.[76] In Qutb's view, al-'Aqqad's school failed to differentiate between al-fikrah (idea) and al-ihsas (feeling) in poetry, having preoccupied itself with the former at the expense of the latter. Feeling, according to Qutb, gives life to an idea and becomes an integral part of the poet and the poetry. Without it the poetical idea remains only an abstraction that does not touch the heart.[77]

As an illustration of poetry that is full of feelings, Qutb cites the lyric poetry of Rabindranath Tagore (1861–1941) of India.[78] A scholar and a student of Tagore, Humayun Kabir, describes Tagore's poetry as follows:

It is born out of an amalgam of the rich classical heritage of ancient India, the spacious way, of the Moghal court, the simple ver-
ities of the life of the common people of Bengal and the restless
energy and intellectual vigour of modern Europe. He is an inher-
itor of all times and all cultures. It is this combination of many
different strands and themes that gives to his poetry its resilience,
universality and infinite appeal.[79]

Kabir further describes Tagore's poetry as being a "fusion of feeling, imagery and music." Another important aspect of Tagore's poetry, Kabir writes, is "the fusion of nature and man in an indissoluble
unity . . . which remained one of the most characteristic traits of
Tagore's poetry throughout his life."[80]

Egyptians' interest in Tagore's poetry had become evident by the
late 1940s when translations of his poems began to be studied by
literati such as Qutb. Interest in Tagore continued in the 1950s, cul-
minating in the centennial celebration of Tagore's birth in 1961 with
the appearance of two state-sponsored anthologies: *Taghur fi al-
dhikra al-Mi'awiyah li-miladih* (The Centennial Celebration of
Tagore's Birth, Cairo: 1961) and *Taghur lamahat min hayatihi wa-
fannih* (Tagore: Glances from His Life and Art, Cairo: 1961).

Qutb's Attacks on Senior Literati

According to Qutb, the war years drove a wedge between the senior and junior literati because of deep differences in their outlooks
on the nation, society, and humanity.[81] Instead of focusing on national problems during the war years, the senior literati became in
the mass media a tool of propaganda for the Allied cause that resulted in their material enrichment.[82]

In the postwar period, Qutb asserts, the senior literati became a
tool of partisan politics instead of devoting themselves to the national cause. Furthermore, according to Qutb, instead of leading the
call for social justice in a society whose development in Qutb's view
had not yet transcended the feudal stage, some of the senior literati
either were silent or reacted hysterically by equating social justice
with communism.[83]

The majority of senior literati, Qutb asserts, were more concerned
with their own material welfare and luxury than with the millions
of hungry and naked Egyptians. Whereas the prewar era saw the
literati express themselves in "clean" (nazif) literary or scientific

press and books, the years during the war and afterward witnessed a reversal in which the literati lost their literary conscience and adopted an immoral lifestyle.[84]

The 1940s: An Age of Pessimism

Qutb's alienation from the literary and political establishment undoubtedly contributed to his decision to give up literature altogether. However, one should remember that Qutb lived at a time when the younger generation of writers felt alienated from the political status quo. This partially explains the phenomenon of pessimism that was common among the younger generation of writers. Naguib Mahfouz vividly describes the dilemma of his generation when he points out that young writers in the 1940s were faced with a psychological crisis characterized by extreme pessimism and the feeling that nothing in the world was worthwhile.

There was a belief that every effort exerted in literature was a waste for both writer and society and that such effort should instead be channeled into more fruitful work. There was also a general agreement that writing and publishing were frivolous ('abath). This was the same crisis, says Mahfouz, that led young writers like 'Adil Kamil and Ahmad Zaki Makhluf to give up writing permanently. According to Mahfouz, this phenomenon reflected the prevailing political crisis of the time.[85]

This decade of pessimism is another key to understanding Qutb's decision to give up literature and to focus, instead, on promoting the Islamic way of life.

IN SEARCH OF SOCIAL JUSTICE: THE EMERGENCE OF AN INDEPENDENT ISLAMIC IDEOLOGUE, 1947–1948

> Capital only reaches the disgracefully swollen propor-
> tions which we see today; it is amassed by swindling,
> usury, oppression of the workers, monopolies or ex-
> ploitation of the needs of the community, robbing,
> plundering and pillaging, and by all semi-criminal meth-
> ods of contemporary exploitation. *(Sayyid Qutb, 1949)*

QUTB'S NATIONALIST AND PAN-ARAB VIEWS

Qutb's Islamic commitment, apart from his interest in the Qur'an, the quoting of Qur'anic verses, and the use of Islamic slogans, was not as yet crystallized. Indeed, in much of his writings at the time he does not appear as an Islamic ideologue, but rather as an Egyptian nationalist, a pan-Easterner or pan-Arab, and an anti-Western.

His attacks on America included angry remarks about Western civilization in general. In the process he quotes a British cardinal, whom he calls an inaudible (khafit) human voice amid the noise of machines. The cardinal was asking the world to return to God and His principles, which are based on charity and justice, so that freedom could become a reality resulting in peace and security for all.[1]

Qutb concludes by calling the Palestine problem a problem for all Arabs and Easterners because it represents the struggle between the resurgent (nahid) East and the savage (mutawahhish) West, and between God's Shari'ah (revealed Islamic law) and the shari'ah of the wilderness of beasts.[2]

In February 1947, in a tirade against the British and their sympathizers in Egypt, whom he calls slaves, Qutb calls on all Egyptians to shout in unison: " 'Ummuna misr. 'Ammuna al-Sharq. Abuna al-Nil . . . al-mawt lil-isti'mar wa-al-wayl lil-musta'mirin" (Egypt is our motherland. The East is our uncle. The Nile is our father. Death to imperialism and woe to the colonialists).[3]

Qutb, the pan-Arabist, in many articles he wrote, attacked French, British, and American policies toward the Arabs. His concern with the liberation movements in the Arab world was apparent in his active participation in the Convention of the Arab Maghrib (Mu'tamar al-Maghrib al-'Arabi) held in Cairo on February 15–22, 1947, which led to the creation of the Bureau of the Arab Maghrib (Maktab al-Maghrib al-'Arabi) in Cairo to coordinate nationalist activities in Morocco. Qutb gave the closing address at the convention.[4]

Qutb's pan-Arabism also figures prominently in the appearance of the Cairene pan-Arab monthly *al-'Alam al-'Arabi* (The Arab World) in April 1947 under his editorial leadership. Qutb's tenure in this publication lasted until July of the same year, when he resigned unexpectedly for undisclosed reasons that he described as private principles (mabadi' khasah).[5]

The purpose of publishing the journal was to acquaint the Arab world, every place on earth where Arabic was spoken, with itself; its past, present, and future, its potential, obstacles to its progress, and ways to overcome them. Qutb adds that the Arab world did fulfill its message to humanity at one time, but is now required to do it again because the Western world has failed in its message due to its bloodletting, lack of conscience, and hedonism.[6]

Qutb does not, however, clarify here what he means by "the message," even though one can discern that he means Islam. He goes on to state that the Arab world must project power (quwwah) in every direction. This is the power that subdues matter, but does not surrender to it; utilizes the machine, but does not become subservient to it; and rises to new heights and strength in order to spread right guidance (al-huda), light (al-nur), and knowledge (al-'irfan) to all humanity, irrespective of race or color.[7]

Qutb further clarifies the program that is being promoted by the pan-Arab monthly:

> In brief our program is to make the newspaper of Arab countries available to all readers of Arabic. We want to study the conditions of education, journalism, literature, art, science, sociology and economics in all Arab countries. We want to present true and honest pictures about each of these domains, to take note of areas of shortage and perfection in them and to be honest to the past, enthusiastic for the future and to deal with the present situation without contrivance or pretense. Every Arab country will have its share and there will be a representative from each. The writers of the entire Arab world will meet on the pages of this magazine; writers from the Nile valley, Palestine, Lebanon, Syria, Iraq, Saudi Arabia, Yemen, Tripoli, Algeria, Tunisia, Morocco, Indonesia and the diaspora . . . and every area on the earth where Arabic is spoken. After all, we pledge before God and people to present to readers clean journalism, clean ideas, clean pictures, clean entertainment, and clean humor.[8]

QUTB'S ATTITUDE TOWARD THE ISLAMIC GROUPS

Commenting on groups that were involved in the call to Islam (jama'at tad'u da'awat Islamiyah), Qutb maintains that they were spiritually weak, depleted, quiescent, and not strong enough to revive the sunken and decayed generation.[9] Does Qutb include the Muslim Brothers in his wholesale condemnation of Islamic groups at this stage? He certainly does not single them out as an exception to criticism. At this time, Qutb was an independent thinker not associated with any political or religious groups, with the exception of his brief association from October 1947 to April 1948 with Muhammad Hilmi al-Miniyawi, a founding member of the Society of Muslim Brothers and owner of Dar al-Kitab al-'Arabi press in Cairo, who helped Qutb and other Egyptian intellectuals publish and print the weekly journal *al-Fikr al-Jadid* (New Thought), which will be discussed shortly.[10]

Attorney al-Damardash al-'Iqali, a prominent member in the Muslim Brothers movement and a friend and a relative of Sayyid Qutb, comments on Qutb's position toward Hassan al-Banna and the Muslim Brothers movement in the 1940s. Al-'Iqali stated, "Sayyid Qutb used to come to his village and visit his nephew who belonged to the Muslim Brothers. A large number of his nephew's companions were followers of Hassan al-Banna. . . . Sayyid Qutb would begin a violent quarrel that would not end until we interfered and put an end to it. . . . Sayyid Qutb remained extremely inimical to the Muslim Brothers and their leader Hassan al-Banna, until he traveled to America on a scholarship from the Ministry of Education."[11]

QUTB'S COMMITMENT TO ISLAM AND SOCIAL JUSTICE

Al-Fikr al-Jadid (Modern Thought) (1947–1948)

It appears that by the beginning of fall in 1947 Qutb's interest in Islam was becoming deeper than the mere articulation of Islamic slogans. In October 1947, Sayyid Qutb and eight other Egyptian intellectuals—Sadiq Ibrahim 'Arjun, Muhammad Al-Ghazali, Fayid al-'Amrusi, 'Imad al-Din 'Abd al-Hamid, Muhammad Qutb, Naguib Mahfouz, 'Abd Mun'im Shumays and 'Abd al-Hamid Juda al-Sahhar—began to set up a journal entitled *al-Fikr al-Jadid* (The New Thought).[12] The journal was officially registered in the name of Muhammad Hilmi al-Miniyawi because Qutb and his colleagues, as public employees, were forbidden by law to be publishers. Qutb, however, was the chief editor who directed the journal's policies. In doing so, he claimed he was independent of any Egyptian party or group.[13]

According to J. Heyworth-Dunne, "Qutb and his colleagues at *al-Fikr al-Jadid* were approached several times by representatives of the Ikhwan (Society of Muslim Brothers) on the instructions of Hassan al-Banna with a view of being won over on the grounds that their work was exactly what the Ikhwan wanted," but Qutb refused their solicitations.[14] At this stage, Qutb did not believe that any Islamic group fulfilled his own vision of the spiritual leadership and energy necessary to rekindle life in Egyptian society.

Only twelve issues of this illustrated, thirty-six-page weekly appeared (between January 1948 and March 1948). Publication came to a halt partly as a result of the restrictions imposed by the martial law which accompanied Egypt's entry into the 1948 Palestine War.[15] In addition, Qutb claimed that the journal had met with a great deal of opposition from capitalists, government authorities, ultraconservative religious figures, and communists.[16] Heyworth-Dunne relates that when Qutb and his colleagues refused to join the Ikhwan, *al-Fikr al-Jadid* was boycotted.[17]

The major factor that led to the appearance of *al-Fikr al-Jadid* was, according to Qutb, the deteriorating social condition of the country which was causing the spread of communist ideas among the educated and the workers. *Al-Fikr al-Jadid* was an attempt by educated Egyptians to present alternative solutions to the problems of society. Qutb and his colleagues saw a need to base social justice on the comprehensive Islamic way of life. They believed that Islam was the only system that could stand against the communist current, because Islam offered social justice that was spiritually superior to that offered by communism.[18]

The group also believed that Islam must be understood correctly and its principles must be applied in a modern spirit (ruh 'asriyah). If, instead, Islam was understood with a rigid mentality, it would not realize its goals in society. This new interpretation of Islam, however, also had to agree with Islam as it was understood by the Prophet Muhammad, Caliph Abu Bakr and Caliph 'Umar if it was to solve social problems in a practical and realistic manner and in true accord with both the spirit of Islam and the contemporary human situation.[19]

Al-Fikr al-Jadid therefore came into being as a result of this group's determination to spread their ideas and offer practical Islamic solutions to the problems of the modern age. According to Heyworth-Dunne, the journal "promised to be one of the most interesting experiments of modern times, as it offered some real contributions by suggesting methods which could be employed for the solution of some of the acute social problems facing the Egyptians today."[20] Problems addressed by the journal included individual ownership and the distribution of wealth in Egypt, relations between landowners and tenants and peasants, and relations between employers and employees. In the opening editorial of the new publication, Qutb writes:

> We are still in the stage of feudalism and serfdom! We today only ask to elevate ten millions of this deprived people to the rank of the animal and the beast. The beast finds sufficient food and water but those people do not. What we ask is to elevate another eight million to the lowest ranks of humanity whereby they eat, drink,

dress and dwell. And those are the ones who make gold for the affluent people! This is what we ask today. As for tomorrow, only God knows it, and the wheel of life turns![21]

What Qutb and his colleagues, in their agitation for social justice, most desired was to articulate the views of the underprivileged masses who lived in an inequitable society dominated by the large landowning ruling classes. Qutb's role in *al-Fikr al-Jadid* is described by Heyworth-Dunne as follows:

> He and his agents collected a number of detailed reports on the living conditions of their compatriots and published these with photographs. He has examined the extreme poverty of four or five million fellahin and has described their way of life to the Egyptians. His courageous approach in this journal puts him in the forefront of those who are advocating a system whereby large estates should be reasonably diminished in size, and the land distributed amongst the completely landless, in order to eliminate destitution. He also advocates legislation regulating the relations between capital and labor, so that workers can get a fairer deal. He believes in encouraging the system of cooperative societies.[22]

Sayyid Qutb wrote that the educated youths "became alerted to this magazine which presented a new idea. They extended their support to it. So tens of university and high school youths volunteered to sell the magazine and spread it among their acquaintances. Little by little the place where the magazine was published became a forum for meetings to discuss social problems. Prominent men of law, Islamic religious law, and sociology, such as 'Abdul-Qawi Ahmad, the former minister; Muhammad Saleh, Dean of the Law School; Sheikh Muhammad 'Arafah, director of preaching and guidance at al-Azhar; and Sheikh Muhammad Abu Zahra, Professor of Shari'ah (Islamic religious law) at the Law School, began voluntarily to write in it."[23]

Qutb's 1948 agitation for social justice in the pages of *al-Fikr al-Jadid* caused an uproar among vested interest groups in the country, including the royal palace. The displeasure of the palace, probably more than any other single factor, quickened the demise of the weekly when the palace instituted martial law on May 13, 1948. According to partisan sources, the palace had become very impatient with Qutb and had ordered the prime minister, Mahmud Fahmi al-Nuqrashi, to arrest him. But al-Nuqrashi, an associate of Qutb in the Wafd and Sa'dist parties, managed to salvage the situation by ordering Qutb's superior at the Ministry of Education to send him abroad on an educational mission, and so in the fall of 1948, Qutb left Egypt for the United States to study English and the American educational curricula.[24]

Social Justice in Islam (1949)

Qutb's agitation for social justice did not end with the demise of *al-Fikr al-Jadid*. On the contrary, Qutb began writing his first major Islamic work dealing with social justice, *al-'Adalah al-Ijtima'iyyah Fi al-Islam* (Social Justice in Islam), and completed it before his departure for the United States. He entrusted the final draft of the work to his brother Muhammad and left the country in November 1948. In April 1949 the book was published, but it was immediately confiscated due to the controversial content of its dedication page. It is said that the government censors had believed Qutb to be dedicating his book to the Muslim Brothers, which was then an outlawed organization. Qutb writes in his dedication: "To the youngsters whom I see in my fantasy coming to restore this religion anew like when it first began . . . fighting for the cause of Allah by killing and getting killed, believing in the bottom of their hearts that the glory belongs to Allah, to his Prophet and to the believers. . . . To those youngsters whom I do not doubt for a moment will be revived by the strong spirit of Islam . . . in the very near future."[25] The book was allowed to go on sale only after the dedication had been deleted.[26]

Qutb did not, in fact, dedicate his book to the Muslim Brothers, however. At this stage Qutb was still independent.[27] The wording of the dedication to the 1951 and subsequent editions of the book was changed to reflect Qutb's later close association with the Muslim Brothers. Thus his words in the first edition, "the youngsters whom I see in my fantasy coming to restore this religion anew," were changed in later editions to read "to the youngsters whom I used to see in my fantasy coming but have found them in real life existing."[28]

Those using Qutb's *al-'Adalah* should therefore keep in mind the many editions in which the book was published and the changes that were made in them. The first edition and its 1953 English translation represent Qutb's thought before he was aligned with the Muslim Brothers, which is not, of course, always the same as his later thought. For example, a new chapter was added to the 1964 Cairo edition to reflect Qutb's Islamic thought in the aftermath of his ten-year imprisonment (1954–1964).[29]

The appearance of Qutb's work on Islamic social justice in 1949 was hailed as a landmark by the various Islamic groups in Egypt and the Arab world. It was also judged significant by the Western world. Shortly after the work's publication, the Committee on Near Eastern Studies of the American Council of Learned Societies entrusted the Arabist John B. Hardie with the task of translating the 1949 edition. His translation appeared in 1953 under the title *Social Justice in Islam*.

Some Features of *al-'Adalah*

The deep interest in the Qur'an which manifests itself in Qutb's articles and books between 1939 and 1947 is apparent in *al-'Adalah*. Qutb used at least 284 verses from the Qur'an to support his ideas, thus making the Qur'an his major source. Unlike his earlier works, in which Qur'anic verses were utilized to illustrate artistic and literary beauty in the Qur'an, Qutb's works during this time now used Qur'anic verses to articulate various aspects of Islamic social justice and Qutb's discontent with the existing conditions in Egypt.

The articulation of Qur'anic ideology in Qutb's thought, at this early stage of his Islamic career, is significant. Henceforth and without exception, all Qutb's Islamic writings are grounded in and justified by quotations from the Qur'an. In his call for the establishment of an Islamic way of life, Qutb uses the Qur'an as an unequivocal guide ordained by Allah. This guidance is all-encompassing and not limited to human or spiritual activities. In Qutb's writings in the late 1950s and 1960s, especially in the revised portions of his Qur'anic commentary and his controversial work *Ma'alim* (Milestones)—which, inter alia, led to his execution—quotations from the Qur'an assume a crucial role because they validate and justify Islamic revolution against the Jahili (pagan) way of life on earth.[30]

Further, Qutb's emergence in 1948 as a champion of the Islamic way, and his total alienation from the status quo, should be seen within the context of the general public outrage at Egyptian and Arab performance in the disastrous Palestine War. The decision of the Egyptian government to intervene in May 1948 gave it "some short-term relief from the ceaseless round of strikes and riots, and for a time a rigid censorship was able to conceal the disastrous course of the war."[31] Censorship, however, could not hide the utter defeat of the Arab forces. There were also scandals over inferior army equipment, and "king and government were blamed for treacherously letting down the army that developed an intense feeling of shame . . . and the ground was immensely fertile for the growth of a resistance movement."[32]

Qutb's Controversial Thought of the 1960s: The Roots

One finds in *al-ʿAdalah* the seeds of Qutb's controversial thought of the 1960s. For example, when discussing the Islamic political system, Qutb asserts that obedience on the part of the ruled is "derived from obedience to Allah and the Messenger." The ruler, on the other hand, "is to be obeyed only by virtue of holding his position through the law of Allah and His Messenger. . . . If he departs from the law, he is no longer entitled to obedience, and his orders need no longer to obeyed."[33] Qutb's arguments as well as his other controversial thought would lead the Nasser regime in 1965–1966 to accuse Qutb of being a Kharijite, an early Islamic dissident takfir (excommunicating) group who disavowed Caliph ʿAli's army at the battle of Siffin, demanding, inter alia, that obedience to the ruler was conditioned by the latter's observance of the laws of Allah.[34]

In his *Maʿalim* (1964), Qutb writes that Islam knows only two types of society, the Islamic and the Jahili.[35] In the first society, Islam is applied fully, while in the second, it is not.[36] Although in his work on social justice he does not use the term 'al-Jahili', Qutb does charge Egyptian society with being un-Islamic. He writes:

> Islamic society today is not Islamic in any true sense (laysa Islamiyan bi-halin min al-ahwal). We have already quoted a verse from the Qur'an which cannot in any way be honestly applied today: "*Whoever does not judge by what Allah has revealed is an unbeliever.*" In our modern society we do not judge by what Allah has revealed; the basis of our economic life is usury; our laws permit rather than punish oppression; the poor tax is not obligatory, and is not spent in the requisite ways.[37]

Qutb's Ideology in *al-'Adalah al-Ijtima'Iyyah Fi al-Islam*

In his opening remarks, Qutb reminds Muslims not to follow blindly in the footsteps of capitalism and communism. Muslims must return to their own heritage. Qutb writes in *al-'Adalah* that Muslims should not resort to French legislation to derive their laws, or to communist ideas to adopt their social order, without first examining what can be supplied from the Islamic legislation that was the foundation of their first Muslim society. However, according to Qutb, this does not mean that Muslims avoid the intellectual, spiritual, and social ways of the rest of the world, for the spirit of Islam rejects such an avoidance and is a message for the whole world. Qutb adds that "our summons is to return to our own stored-up resources, to become familiar with their ideas, and to proclaim their value and permanent worth, before we have recourse to an untimely servility which will deprive us of the historical background of our life, and through which our individuality will be lost to the point that we will become mere hangers-on to the progress of mankind."[38]

Islamic Theory of the Universe and Social Justice

In order to understand social justice in Islam, Qutb holds that one must first examine the Islamic theory of the universe, life, and humankind. This Islamic universal theory or philosophy cannot be found in Ibn Sina (Avicenna), Ibn Rushd (Averroes), or any of those known as Muslim philosophers, because the philosophy that they teach is no more than a shadow of Greek philosophy. Instead, this universal theory and philosophy should be sought in Islam itself, in "the Qur'an, and the Traditions, the life of the Prophet, and his everyday customs."[39]

It is from the Islamic sources that one learns that creation, which was produced deliberately by a single, absolute and comprehensive Will, forms an all-embracing unity in which each individual part is in harmonious order with the other parts. Humanity is an essential unity because individuals are as atoms, dependent upon and related to the world and one another. In this universal scheme, the body and soul are one, and values of life are material as well as spiritual. In this theory, Islamic social justice is therefore "essentially an all-embracing justice," which takes account of the body and soul and not merely the material and economic factors. It holds that humankind is essentially one body, the members of which are mutually responsible and interdependent. In Qutb's words: "This comprehensive view will serve to explain the regulations on individual possession, on the poor-tax, on the law of inheritance; on the rules for estates, on politics, on commercial transactions. In a word, it will explain all the regulations prescribed by Islam for individuals, societies, nations, and races."[40]

Foundations of Social Justice

The foundations of social justice in Islam, according to Qutb, include freedom of conscience, complete equality of all human beings, and social solidarity. On freedom of conscience (al-taharrur al-wijdani), he writes: "When the conscience is freed from the instinct of servitude to and worship of any of the servants of Allah; when it is filled with the knowledge that it can of itself gain complete access to Allah then it cannot be disturbed by any feeling of fear of life, or fear of its livelihood, or fear for its (position)."[41]

The human mind is then released from "the tyranny of the values of social standing and wealth; it is saved from the humiliation of need and beggary, and it can rise superior to its desires and its bodily appetites." Without this freedom of conscience, Qutb writes, "human nature cannot prevail against the force of humiliation, submissiveness and servility, nor can it lay claim to its rightful share in social justice when it has attained it." He terms this freedom as one of the "cornerstones for the building of social justice in Islam."[42]

On the complete equality of human beings, Qutb believes that Islamic teaching adamantly supports equality because of the oneness of human origin and growth: "When it is thus denied that one individual can be intrinsically superior to another, it follows that there can be no race and no class which is superior by reason of its origin or its nature."[43] In regard to equality, Qutb writes that "Islam was freed from the conflict of tribal, racial and religious loyalties, and thus it achieved an equality which civilization in the West has not gained to this day." He adds that this Western civilization "permits the American conscience to acquiesce in the disappearance of the Red Indian race, a disappearance which is being organized in the sight and hearing of the government. It permits also Field-Marshal Smuts in South Africa to introduce racial laws which discriminate against Indians."[44]

As for social solidarity (al-takaful al-ijtima'i), Qutb writes, "Islam sets the principle of individual responsibility against that of individual freedom; and beside them both it sets the principle of social responsibility, which makes demands alike on the individual and on society." In this social solidarity one finds the responsibilities which exist "between a man and his soul, between a man and his immediate family, between the individual and society, between one community and other communities, and between one nation and the various other nations."[45]

Thus each individual is charged with the care of society and with the duty of putting an end to whatever evil-doing he or she may find. The community, on the other hand, is responsible for taking care of its poor and needy. Qutb quotes the Prophet, who says: "The likeness of the Believers in their mutual love and mercy and relationship is that of the body, when one member is afflicted, all the rest of the body joins with it to suffer feverish sleeplessness."[46]

In Qutb's view, the best examples of social solidarity and of the general method of Islamic social justice are the poor-tax (al-zakah) and voluntary almsgiving (al-sadaqah), which serve as indispensable cornerstones of true religion. According to Qutb, the poor-tax is an "obligatory claim on the property of the wealthy in favor of the poor," which the government can exact by law.[47] Voluntary almsgiving, however, is left to the conscience of the individual Muslim. The rewards of almsgiving as a means of purification for one's character and for one's property are tremendous, because "Paradise is the worthy recompense of those who expend freely in alms."[48]

The Islamic Political System

Having discussed the general teaching of Islam on social justice, Qutb now turns to the Islamic political solution system. An Islamic political system that has a bearing on social justice "rests on the basis of justice on the part of the rulers, obedience on the part of the ruled, and consultation between ruler and ruled."[49]

Under this system, the ruler must be impartial, not influenced by any relationship, be it a hateful or loving relationship. The ruler derives authority from observance of the religious law, not from religion itself. According to Qutb, "he [the ruler] occupies his post by the complete and absolute free choice of all Muslims who are not bound to elect him by any compact with his predecessor, nor likewise is there any necessity for the position to be hereditary in the family. When the Muslim community is no longer satisfied with him, his office must lapse."[50]

Furthermore, there must be consultation (shura) between the ruler and the ruled, which Qutb explains "is one of the fundamentals of Islamic politics, although no specific method of administering it has even been laid down." According to Qutb, the Prophet and caliphs consulted with their community in worldly affairs.[51]

The Islamic Economic System

Qutb turns next to a discussion of the economic system in Islam, which is considered "the most essential part of any discussion of social justice."[52] In regard to the right of individual possession (al-mulkiyah al-fardiyah), "the fundamental principle is that property belongs to the community in general, individual possession is a stewardship which carries with it conditions and limitations. Some property is held in common, and thus no individual has any right to possess. A proportion of all property is a due which must be paid to the community (al-zakah). Thus possession in the sense of profitable use of property is impossible except by the authority of the law."[53]

According to Qutb, the recognized methods of gaining the right of acquisition in Islam are the following: hunting as a means of livelihood, irrigating wasteland that has no owner for at least three years, the production of minerals or mining, raiding against nonbelievers, working for a wage, assigning ownership of a piece of land that has no owner or lies in waste, and acquiring money to sustain life through the poor-tax.[54]

Absolute freedom is not granted in the case of passing on possessions (but gifts and presents are free from all restraint). Thus inheritance and bequest are subject to regulations under Islamic law. For example, a man can have the same share as two women, and an heir from the paternal side takes precedence over one from the maternal side, and a full brother takes precedence over a half-brother. In addition, inheritance does not pass to a single individual but rather to a multitude of children and relatives.[55]

As regards the ways of increasing property, there is no absolute freedom in Islam. Here Qutb is very critical of his society: "Capital only reaches the disgracefully swollen proportions which we see today when it is amassed by swindling, by usury, by oppression of the workers, by monopolies or exploitation of the needs of the community, by robbing, plundering, despoiling and pillaging and by all the other semi-criminal methods of contemporary exploitation."[56]

Thus Islam forbids dishonesty in business because it defiles the conscience, injures others, and represents a gain without effort (which is therefore un-Islamic). Islam does not recognize monopolies, because monopolies inflict hardship and distress on people and lessen the flow of supplies to the public. Islam is also opposed to usury, considering it even more shameful than adultery. It is likewise opposed to both niggardliness and wastefulness (luxury) in personal spending.[57]

Moreover, Qutb writes that Islam disapproves of the existence of class distinction in a community where some live on a standard of luxury and others on a standard of hardship. For this and other related reasons "the poor-tax (zakah) is prescribed as a compulsory duty on property; it is as much the right of those who receive it as it is the duty of those who pay it." When the poor-tax is not adequate to meet the needs of the people, according to Qutb, additional legal methods are available to the ruler.[58]

Qutb's View of Muslim History

Qutb moves on to a lengthy discussion of the historical reality of justice in Islam and the spirit of Islam. This discussion provides a clear picture of Qutb's view of Muslim history, parts of which he had presented earlier in 1947.

According to Qutb, as long as Muslims adhered to Islam (including its political and economic systems), they manifested no weakness and no tendency to abdicate their control of life. When they deviated from their religion, however, weakness overtook them. Thus, during the life of the Prophet and his two companions Abu Bakr and 'Umar as well as during the caliphate of 'Ali, Muslims were true to the Islamic way and were strong. But when the caliphate became a tyrannical monarchy under the Umayyads, the Islamic way was abandoned and Muslims grew weak. Qutb asserts that these changes came from "an unfortunate mischance," which was a result of the transfer of control into the hands of the Umayyads, "first in an indirect way in the reign of Caliph 'Uthman, and latterly quite openly in the reign of Mu'awiyah."[59]

Qutb asserts that "if the life of 'Umar had lasted several years longer, or if 'Ali had been the third Caliph, or even if 'Uthman had become Caliph when he was twenty years younger, then the course of Islamic history would have been changed very considerably."[60] According to Qutb, 'Umar would have conducted social and economic programs that would have restored economic and social equity to the Islamic world, and civil war would have been averted or at least postponed for a long time. If 'Ali had succeeded 'Umar, he would have guided the people in 'Umar's policy and so under 'Ali's rule as well the emerging Islamic state would have avoided rebellion or civil war.[61]

Qutb holds that in spite of the "first internal disaster," that is, the subjugation of the Muslims by the tyrannical monarchy of the Umayyads, the spirit of Islam continued to manifest itself in "charity and benevolence, mutual help and responsibility, tolerance and freedom of conscience and human equality, payment of the poor-tax and the alms."[62] Because of the inner force and vitality of this spirit, it was able to survive the many setbacks and disasters which befell Islam, such as the rise of the 'Abbasid state and its reliance on new converts opposed to the true spirit of Islam, the destructive raids of the Tartars, the downfall of the Arabs in al-Andalus, and the disaster of the Crusades.[63]

"The final overthrow of Islam," Qutb writes, "took place only in the present age, when Europe conquered the world, and when the dark shadow of colonization spread over the whole Islamic world, East and West alike." He adds: "Europe mustered its forces to extinguish the spirit of Islam, it revived the inheritance of the Crusaders' hatred, and it employed all the materialistic and intellectual powers at its disposal. With these it sought to break down the internal resistance of the Islamic community and to divorce it gradually over a long period from the teachings and the heritage of its religious faith."[64]

The Renewal of Islamic Life

Having discussed the theoretical bases of social justice in Islam and Muslim society as it evolved in the course of history, Qutb now turns to the preaching of the renewal of an Islamic life which is governed by the spirit and law of Islam.

He warns fellow Muslims against renewing their life by borrowing Western ways of thought, life and custom, for "such an experiment can only result in the suffocation of that very form of life which it seeks to revive."[65] However, in the case of the "pure sciences and their applied results of all kinds," Qutb writes that "we must not hesitate to utilize all things in the sphere of material life. Our use of them should be unhampered and unconditional, unhesitating and unimpeded."[66] Qutb acknowledges that the study of science cannot be separated from the method of Western thought. He also believes that the applied results of science might in time produce new ways of life inimical to Islam. He emphasizes, however, that "there is no possibility of living in isolation from science and its products, though the harm that it does may be greater than the good." He adds that "there is no such thing in life as an unmixed blessing or unalloyed evil. We must hold to the guiding principle that all material consequences of science do not essentially affect our universal philosophy of life and custom."[67]

In regard to "constitutional enactments which will ensure a sound form of Islamic life and which will guarantee social justice to all," Qutb writes that "we must utilize all possible and permissible means which fall within the general principles and the broad foundations of Islam."[68] He encourages his fellow Muslims not to be afraid "to use all the discoveries which man has made in the way of social legislation and systems," as long as these do not conflict with the principles of Islam and its theory of life and mankind.[69]

Furthermore, according to Qutb, the two legal principles of "public interest" (al-Masalih al-Mursalah), legislating on the basis of public interest or benefit in matters for which there are no Qur'anic texts and "blocking of means" (Sadd al-Dhara'i'), obstructing the means to illegitimate ends by prohibiting acts that would otherwise appear permissible by Qur'anic precepts give the ruler wide powers to ensure the general welfare of society, including a comprehensive social justice.[70] The application of these two principles can, in Qutb's view, lead to the expropriation of excessive wealth from bloated capitalists, the removal of extreme poverty by providing work and adequate wages to the able-bodied and social security to the disabled, and the availability of medical and educational care to every individual.[71] Other laws can likewise be promulgated to ensure equity in Islamic society, such as laws governing the poor-tax, the mutual solidarity of society, general taxation, public resources, cooperatives and usury, bequests, gambling, prostitution and alcohol.[72]

Islam versus Communism and Capitalism

In the concluding pages of his book, Qutb compares the Islamic way with the ways of communism and capitalism. He writes that these two latter systems do not differ, for "both philosophies depend on the preponderance of a materialistic doctrine of life. But while Russia has already become communist, Europe and America are as yet merely going the same way, and will ultimately arrive at the same position, barring the occurrence of any unforeseen happenings."[73]

Thus the struggle is not between East and West, but rather between Islam on the one hand and the two camps of East and West on the other. Qutb writes that "we are indeed at a crossroads, we may join the march at the tail of the Western caravan which calls itself Democracy; if we do so we shall eventually join up with the Eastern caravan which is known to the West as Communism. Or we may return to Islam and make it fully effective in the field of our own, spiritual, intellectual, social, and economic life." Qutb adds that "the world . . . is today more than ever in need of us to offer it our faith and our social system, our practical and spiritual theory of life. . . . Conditions today are favorable because of the birth of two great new Islamic blocs in Indonesia and Pakistan, and because of the awakening of the Arab world, both in East and West."[74]

PERSPECTIVES ON SAYYID QUTB'S THOUGHT, 1939–1948

By the mid-1930s there was a widespread reaction in Egypt against rampant Westernization. In addition, the liberal national establishment had failed to achieve the independence of the Nile valley and find a solution to society's pressing problems. The reaction to this situation ranged from the proliferation of Muslim clubs and societies to the articulation of anti-Western views, the promotion of pan-Eastern ideas, and an increased interest in Islamics among liberal literati. Qutb's writings reflected the "East versus West" theme, especially in his rebuttal of Taha Husayn's work on the future of culture in Egypt. In addition, in 1939, Qutb began to take a serious interest in the Qur'an, albeit for literary purposes.

World War II and the economic, political, and social dislocations it caused further alienated one-time adherents of liberal nationalist ideals like Qutb. The war's adverse effects are very much reflected in Qutb's writing in the years 1939–1945. Many drastic changes began to take place in Qutb's outlook during this time. Also, during the seven-year period preceding the July 1952 military revolt, Egypt was dominated by a sense of anger, grief, and despair at the established order. This state of mind was only exacerbated by the Egyptian defeat in the 1948 Palestine War and is reflected in the intellectual activity of the time, including that of Qutb. During this period, Qutb became totally alienated from the establishment. As a result, he chose to forsake literature permanently for the Islamic da'wah (propagation, or call).

Another factor of great significance in Qutb's change of outlook was his upbringing. His early life in Musha was crucial, because at this stage Qutb mastered the traditional culture, that is, Arabic and the memorization of the Qur'an. Moreover, traditional Islamic values were firmly implanted in his mind. This early experience revived later to haunt him, eventually bringing him back to Islam from his uncertain secular world. The impact of traditional life on the mind of Qutb the adib (literate) is reflected in the large space he devotes in his childhood biography (1946) to this Islamic upbringing, the customs and manners of the villagers, and popular religious practices.

When Qutb moved to Cairo in his teens, he experienced life in a modern and urban social structure very different from the rural settings in which he grew up. As a result, he became a product of two conflicting worlds, traditional and modern, with two outlooks. When one considers Qutb's transformation from secularist adib to an independent Islamic ideologue, one must not assume that Qutb possessed at one time a vigorous rationalist spirit that he later abandoned. Qutb's earliest literary works, especially his poetry, clearly indicate subjective and spiritual orientations. He attributes much of this spiritualism to his early upbringing.

In 1939, when Qutb became interested in the Qur'an and its artistic aspects, the more traditional component of his outlook began to reassert itself gradually, even though his modern outlook continued to exert itself prominently as seen in his work on social justice in Islam, where he calls for the outright adoption of Western technology regardless of the consequences. It can also be seen in his call for Muslims not to be afraid of using any human-made social legislation and systems, as long as they do not conflict with the principles of Islam.

Qutb's interest in the Qur'an was not merely as "intellectual and psychological luxury" but was apparently a psychological and spiritual necessity. The Qur'an was a comforting refuge from the pain of the environment in which he lived. His unhappiness in Cairo was very much evident in his poetry and prose in the 1930s and 1940s. Furthermore, the death of Qutb's mother, his shattered love affair, and his poor health in the 1940s, together with his alienation from the status quo, prompted him to turn increasingly toward his religion for his personal needs and for answers to his nation's ills.

Qutb's emergence as a student of the Qur'an and his articulation of Qur'anic ideology beginning in 1946 is significant. Henceforth all Qutb's Islamic writings were grounded on and justified by quotations from the Qur'an. These quotations assume a crucial role in the 1960s when Qutb, in his controversial *Ma'alim* (Milestones) in 1964, validates and justifies Islamic revolution against the Jahili (pagan) way of life that exists throughout the world, including the so-called Muslim countries like Egypt, on Qur'anic grounds. The early signs of this takfir (excommunicating) trend in Qutb's thought, as seen earlier in this chapter, appeared in his first major Islamic work on social justice in Islam in 1949. In addition, Qutb's articulation of Qur'anic ideology and his interpretation of Islamic history suggest that he was developing a worldview in both *al-Fikr al-Jadid* and in *al-'Adalah*, which was similar to that of the Muslim Brothers even though he did not join their ranks until early in 1953.

It was also noted earlier that Qutb's emergence as a serious student of the Qur'an in 1939–1947 was accompanied by his emergence as a stern moralist as well as an anti-Western and anti-establishment intellectual. These mutually reinforcing developments were, like the Qur'anic ideology, crucially significant in the makeup of Qutb's ideology during his stay in the United States in 1948–1950, and in the 1950s and 1960s.

Qutb's Experiences and Impressions in America, 1948–1950, and His Return, 1950–1952

In the 1950 issue of *Cache La Poudre* (Bear's Claw), the Year Book of the Colorado College of Education (in Greeley), are to be found the photographs of the 45 members of the college's international club. . . . Among the four with Arabic names is the Egyptian Sayyid Qutb who, mustachioed and immaculately attired in jacket and tie, stares out from the page with a benign, self assured smile. Few of the students at the college would have been aware that their colleague was in fact an Egyptian nationalist thinker with strong Islamist leanings, who had recently completed a noteworthy treatise on the subject of social justice in Islam. Certainly none could have imagined that, seventeen years after the Year Book photo-shot, their colleague would be executed in his homeland. *(John Calvert, 2000)*

QUTB'S JOURNEY TO AMERICA

Qutb's campaigns against the socioeconomic situation in the country and his demand for social justice on the pages of *al-Fikr al-Jadid*

(New Thought) and other magazines in the years 1945–1948 caused
an uproar among groups that had vested interests in the country, including the royal palace. According to partisan sources, the palace
became impatient with Qutb and ordered his arrest. However, Prime
Minister Mahmoud Fahmi al-Nuqrashi was a former colleague of
Qutb in the al-Wafd and Sa'dist parties and was able to remedy the
situation. He issued an order to Qutb's superiors in the Ministry of
Education to send him abroad on an educational scholarship. So in
November 1948, Qutb left Egypt for the United States to study the
principles of education and curricula, including American curricula.[1]

'Adel Hammuda wrote, "The matter with this visit arouses puzzle-
ment and anxiety and puts many questions and exclamation marks.
An important question is inevitable: Why the United States in particular at that period? Britain has more priority, is nearer, and every-
one who wants to get acquainted with Western methods of curricula
and education goes to it."[2]

According to Salah 'Abd al-Fattah al-Khalidi, "Qutb was not restricted in his scholarship to a certain university or special theoretical materials for studying. Also, this scholarship was not restricted
to a certain time. He was given the freedom to choose the field of
his study, and when and where to study. . . . Didn't we say that the
purpose was to get him out of Egypt, and other than that does not
concern the officials?"[3] Paul Berman's claim that Qutb had acquired
a master's degree from the University of Northern Colorado at Greeley is baseless.[4] Zafar Bangash's assertion that Qutb "could have
gone on to study for his doctoral thesis, but decided instead to return to Egypt and devote his life to the Islamic movement"[5] is un-
true. As John Calvert clearly points out, Qutb's study mission did
not require him to earn college credits.[6]

Qutb's Experiences aboard the Ship

Early in November 1948, Qutb left Egypt, heading for the United
States on a ship that took him from Alexandria to New York. The
aim of this visit was to study English before Qutb began his tour to
American institutions to examine the principles of education and the
curricula.

Qutb wrote from San Francisco about his impressions when he
was on board the ship while it was crossing the Mediterranean and
the Atlantic Ocean:

While I was in the midst of the Ocean and the ship was passing like wind on the surface of the huge sea, the breeze was gentle, night was quiet and the moon had a silvery glistening, I was not aware of how I felt . . . and how to say, except one expression which glided on my tongue at that moment and which flashed in my soul like the flashing of the torch. . . . One expression in which I felt all welled in my mind at that moment of sanctity, transparency and glorification: the music of existence (Musiqa al-wujud) . . . some musical pieces have a sense of that music. I sensed that in the few musical pieces of Mozart in particular. I felt that sometimes in the poetry of Tagor.[7]

Calvert writes that Qutb's experience with "Musiqa al-wujud" had heightened within him "a sense of destiny and moral purpose. Qutb's thoughts gravitated to the overwhelming majesty of the Divine Reality and to the music of God's creation. As never before, he came to comprehend his life as unfolding within the largess of God's providence."[8]

Qutb left us an image of his other experiences while he was on board the ship. It includes his steadfastness before sexual temptations and his organizing a collective prayer for Muslims on board the ship as a reaction to an evangelist attempt to convert them. The seamen of the ship, its cooks, and its servants—most of them were Muslim Nubians (from Nubia, a region in southern Egypt and northern Sudan)—participated in performing the rituals of the prayer. Qutb delivered the Friday sermon for them.[9]

QUTB'S NEGATIVE REACTION TO AMERICAN SOCIETY

During Qutb's stay in the United States, he moved from New York to the capital Washington, DC, to Greeley and Denver, Colorado, and to San Francisco, Palo Alto, and San Diego, California. He stayed for many months in Greeley. His writings from the United Stated that appeared in the two Cairene magazines *al-Risalah* and *al-Kitab* in 1949 and 1950, as well as his letters to his friends expressed a negative reaction toward Western civilization. These writings shed more light on his position vis-à-vis life.

On his experience as a student of English language at the International Center for Teaching Languages in Washington, DC, Qutb wrote to his friend from Dar al-'Ulum, Mohammad Jabr, on February 12, 1949:

> My job at the International Center for Teaching Languages was changed from being merely a student who learns the language into a teacher who teaches them how to study the language. My method succeeded somewhat in modifying their methods in many instances. America is the biggest lie known by the world. We can benefit from America in the pure scientific scholarships: mechanics, electricity, chemistry, agriculture . . . and the like. However, when we attempt to benefit from America in theoretical studies including methods of teaching, I think we commit the most serious mistake. We are driven behind the American way. Nevertheless, I do not like to make hasty judgments. Maybe there are things which hitherto I do not know.[10]

Qutb told his friend Mohammad Jabr, in addition, that even though the standard of living in the United States was high, he was able to live a comfortable life, to eat well, and to dress well. While an ordinary student could live a comfortable life on $180 per month, Qutb said that he needed from $250 to $280 to live a comfortable life suited to his educational mission both as a student and as a visitor. Qutb traveled from Egypt to the United States first class because of his job ranking.[11]

From Denver, Qutb writes that during his first year in the "workshop" of "the New World" (when he moved from New York to Washington to Denver) he did not see, except in rare moments, a human face with a look that radiated the meaning of humanity. Instead, Qutb writes, he found harried crowds (jumu' rakidah) resembling an excited herd (qati' ha'ij) that knew only lust and money. He describes love (al-hubb) in America as merely a body that lusts after another body, or hungry animal that craves another animal, with no time for spiritual longings, high aspirations, or even the flirtation (al-ghazal) that normally precedes "the final step." He adds that nature had bestowed on America many blessings, including natural and human beauty, but no one understood or felt this beauty except as animals and beasts.[12]

An American young woman at the Teachers' College in Greeley, Colorado, told Qutb during a discussion of social life in America: "The issue of sexual relations is a purely biological issue. You—the Orientals—complicate this simple issue by introducing the ethical element in it. The horse and the mare, the bull and the cow, the ram and the goat and the rooster and the hen do not think of this story of ethics while they are mating. So their life is easy, simple and comfortable!" In addition, Qutb relates how one of the female teachers at the International Center for Teaching the Languages at Wilson Teachers' College in Washington, DC, was giving a lesson on the traditions of American society to a group of Latin American students. At the end of the lesson, she asked a student from Guatemala about his observations on American society. He told her: "I have noticed that young girls who are fourteen years old and boys who are fifteen years old engage in complete sexual relations . . . and this is a very early age to engage in these relations." She responded with zeal: "Our life on earth is very short. We do not have time to waste more than fourteen years." Qutb adds, "I have chosen these two models exactly from hundreds of examples which I saw there. These models are from two female teachers. The influence of the female teachers in spreading such implications is wider than the influence of any other person."[13]

Sayyid Qutb comments further:

With this absolute licentiousness—or because of this absolute licentiousness—cheap licensed natural sexual relations no longer satisfy sexual inclinations. So sexual abnormality spread by inclination to the other sex whether in the world of boys or in the world of girls. Alfred Kinsey's report on "Sexual Behavior of Men and Women" contains accurate and amazing statistics on this abnormality. I remember—to the extent allowed by difference and the ethics of writing—a personal observation at one of the hotels of Washington, D.C. An Egyptian colleague of mine and I were lodging at this hotel—two days after our arrival in the United States. The black escalator operator felt at ease with us because we were nearer to his skin color and because we did not despise colored people. So he used to offer his "services" in "entertainment" to us. He used to mention "samples" of this entertainment including the different "abnormalities." During the offer, he told us that often "a pair" of boys or girls are in a room. Then both of them ask him to bring a bottle of Coca Cola to them without changing their posture when he entered the room! We were disgusted and surprised, so we told him: Don't they feel ashamed? In turn he was astonished because of our disgust, amazement and our inquiry about shame. He responded: "Why? They satisfy their private inclinations

and enjoy themselves." I knew later—from many observations—
that American society does not disapprove of any person's satisfy-
ing his pleasure in the way that appeals to him as long as there is
not coercion . . . and subsequently there is no crime . . . even in
what the law—on paper—still considers a crime.[14]

Sayyid Qutb severely criticized the status of the church in American society:

If the church is a place for worship in the Christian world—with
variance—the church in America is a place for everything except
worship. It is difficult for you to distinguish between the church
and any other place for fun and entertainment or what they call
in their language "Good time, fun." Most of those who frequent
churches consider it a necessary social tradition, a place for meeting and geniality and for having "a good time."[15]

Qutb describes further his firsthand experience with church in
America. He writes:

After the religious service in the church ended, and young men and
young women from the members participated in the hymns while
the others prayed, we entered by a side door to the dancing arena
adjoining the "prayer" hall. They are connected by a door. The
pastor sat at his desk. Then he came to "the gramophone" to
choose music for the dancing that suits that atmosphere and to
encourage those who were sitting from both sexes to participate
in dancing. And he chose a very famous American song called
"But, Baby it is Cold Outside!" This song includes a dialogue between a young man and a young woman returning from their
evening party. The young man detains her in his house and she
tells him to let her go home. It is late at night and her mother is
waiting for her. Whenever she uses a pretext he answers with that
"refrain" (But, Baby it is cold outside . . .).[16]

Qutb spent several months in 1949 studying education and curricula at Colorado State College of Education, now the University of
Northern Colorado, in Greeley, Colorado. Qutb described the city of
Greeley, which is located about 100 miles north of Denver, as "beautiful." Qutb wrote that one can imagine that Greeley "grew like plants
in a dreamy garden. Every house looks as if it is a plant in a garden,

and every street looks as if it is a path in a garden." On the other hand, he criticized Americans because they did not enjoy this natural beauty. They were mostly interested in "developing the garden and organizing it in the same way the store owner organizes his store, and the factory owner his factory. Behind this, there is no relishing of beauty and enjoying beauty. . . . It is the mechanism of organizing and putting into order, and not the spirit of good taste and beauty!"[17]

According to National Public Radio (NPR) journalist Robert Siegel, "Greeley in the middle of the 20th century was a very conservative town, where alcohol was illegal. It was a planned community, founded by utopian idealists looking to make a garden out of the dry plains north of Denver using irrigation. The founding fathers of Greeley were by all reports temperate, religious and peaceful people."[18]

At Colorado State College of Education, Qutb attended an eight-week summer session in which he audited a course in English composition. According to John Calvert, who researched Qutb's stay in Greeley, "the course appears to have led to a breakthrough in Qutb's knowledge of English, for, as he says in a published letter, it was during his Colorado stay that he began to be comfortable in the language, a real lesson for a man who hitherto had been dependent upon Arabic translations of foreign works." For the fall term, Qutb audited courses in education and oral interpretation. Calvert concludes that "the terms of Qutb's study mission did not require that he secure college credit for the courses which he attended."[19]

Qutb severely criticized the brutality of athletic life in America.

Football, boxing and wrestling are tantamount to hitting in the belly, breaking arms and legs with all violence and fierceness and the crowds shouting, each encouraging his team: smash his head, break his neck, crush his ribs, knead him into dough. . . . This scene leaves no doubt concerning the primitive feelings which are fascinated by muscular strength.[20]

Qutb, likewise, criticized American music. He said that

jazz music was created by the negroes to satisfy their primitive inclinations and their desire in noise on the one hand, and to arouse the vital dispositions on the other hand. The louder the din of instruments and voices becomes and whizzes in the ears to an unbearable degree, the more excited the crowds become.[21]

In a letter to his friend, critic Anwar al-Ma'adawi, Sayyid Qutb wrote from Colorado toward the end of December: "Here is alienation, the real alienation, the alienation of the soul and the thought, the alienation of the spirit and the body, here in that huge workshop which they call the New World. I know now the extent of propaganda with which America inundates the world and in which the Egyptians who came to America then returned contribute. . . . They don't find a subjective value for themselves. Thus they exaggerate in magnifying America hoping they derive a subjective value from it."[22]

These and other of Qutb's negative impressions of the United States and the American way of life during his stay appeared in a series of articles entitled "Amrika al-lati ra'ayt: fi mizan al-qiyyam al-insaniyah" (America That I Have Seen: In the Scale of Human Values), which were published in the review *al-Risalah* upon Qutb's return to Egypt in November and December 1951. They appeared also in works published during his imprisonment, 1954–1964, namely, *al-Islam wa-mushkilat al-hadarah* (Islam and the Problem of Civilization), *Fi-Zilal al-Qur'an* (In the Shade of the Qur'an), and *Ma'alim fi al-tariq* (Milestones on the Road). In addition, Qutb's criticism of American foreign policy, including the Marshall Plan and American involvement in the Korean War, both of which coincided with his stay in the United States, is also very prominent in his book *al-Salam al-'alami wa-al-Islam* (Islam and Universal Peace), especially in the last chapter entitled "Wa-al-'an" (And Now), which, according to Yusuf al-'Azm, was deleted by government censors from editions appearing after 1954.[23]

Sayyid Qutb's negative attitude toward the United States, its society and culture, and his sweeping generalizations did not come all of a sudden. When Qutb arrived in the United States in 1948, he already had many preconceived ideas about the United States and Western civilization. Throughout his travels in the United States, whether in New York, Washington, DC, Colorado, or California, Qutb was looking for things to reinforce the ideas he had already formed about American society and its values. What Qutb saw and what he perceived in his travels reinforced his preconceived ideas about the moral decay of Western civilization, including American society, which he had already written about prior to his arrival in the United States in late 1948.

As Robert Siegel points out, "America in 1949 was not a natural place for Qutb. He was a man of color, and the United States was still largely segregated. He was an Arab. American public opinion favored Israel, which had come into existence just a year before."[24]

Paul Berman adds that when Qutb arrived in the United States, Qutb considered himself "a devout and perhaps even a radical Islamist, which means that everything about the United States was bound to rub him wrong—the national mood, habits, materialism, racism, vices, pastimes, business practices, and sexual freedom, not to mention America's larger politics and policies."[25]

Qutb maintains that the positive aspects of America lie in the area of applied science, in the domain of scientific research, and in the sphere of organizing and improving the production and administration of everything that needs minds and muscles. Here American ingenuity is prominent. Qutb concludes by stating that his criticism does not imply that Americans lack all virtues. Americans do have "virtues of production and organization but not virtues of human and social leadership, virtues of mind and hand but not virtues of taste and feelings."[26]

QUTB'S CHANGING ATTITUDE TOWARD LITERATURE AND WRITING

Qutb's stay in the United States reinforced his earlier belief that the Islamic way of life was man's only salvation from the abyss of godless capitalism. During his stay in America, Qutb also began giving more serious thought to abandoning his literary career and concentrating instead on a career that would involve him in the Islamic movement. Thus in a letter dated March 6, 1950, to his friend the literary critic Anwar al-Ma'adawi, Qutb writes: "You are looking forward to seeing me return in order that I take my place in literary criticism! I am afraid to tell you that this will not happen. It would be better if a new literary critic were to emerge; for I am planning to devote the rest of my life to a comprehensive social program that will involve the lives and efforts of many."[27]

Qutb's stay in America, furthermore, appears to have strengthened his conviction that writing is not worthwhile unless it has practical application. The articulation of an idea is not enough by itself; it must have deep conviction behind it, and it must be expressed in action. Qutb writes from Colorado Springs that an idea (al-fikrah) does not live in the soul of individuals and generations unless it becomes a system of belief ('aqidah). Only then does the idea become believable and the person who believes in it come to embody this conviction. The warmth of faith belongs to the one who gives life to ideas and opens the windows of souls and hearts to them. This is why Qutb writes that the words of the prophets and saints live, while the words of philosophers and thinkers have died.[28]

From California, Qutb commented on the potential of Egyptians by criticizing "the selfish, sick and ignorant bunch who are the masters of its destiny who do not render it a service. They do not exploit the treasures of the country whether the natural treasurers of the land or the human treasures. Through ignorance, illiteracy and poverty . . . in order that a handful of Pashas and bellies enjoy an extravagance which the Middle Ages did not know."[29]

Following a two-year stay in the United States, Qutb became very homesick and longed to return to his homeland. This longing is evident in his poem "Nida' al-Gharib" (Invocation of the Stranger), composed in San Francisco:[30]

Oh, You whose banks are remote,
Here is your beloved lad,
Wandering has become long for him,
When will the stranger return?

When will his steps touch
That dusty surface?
When will he smell its fragrance
Like scented daisy?

Your visions in his eyes
Flutter like dreams,
I wonder if your heart beat with passion for him
Throughout the days

Your passing nights
Are like the genius breeze,
Which changed into scented
And dewy memories

Their fragrance have wings,
Their wishes flutter
In an exhausted world
Embroidered by songs

There where his steps
Are scattered on the road,
They still have life,
They utter the call of the drowned!

O, land restore to you
This lonely stranger,
His love is dedicated to you,
Restore your beloved lad

Jonathan Raban offers the following commentary concerning Qutb's stay in America and his homesickness:

Like many homesick people living outside their language in an abrasive foreign culture, Qutb aggrandized his loneliness into heroic solitude. Walking the streets of Greeley, he was the secret, lone agent of God's will. In *Milestones* (Qutb's controversial Jihadist manifesto), there is a passage that is unmistakably a portrait of Qutb in America: "the Believer from his height looks down at the people drowning in dirt and mud. He may be the only one; yet he is not dejected or grieved, nor does his heart desire that he takes off his neat and immaculate garments and join the crowd." Being able to look down on people drowning in dirt and mud makes you feel taller.[31]

QUTB'S CHANGING ATTITUDE TOWARD HASSAN AL-BANNA AND THE MUSLIM BROTHERS

According to partisan sources, it was also in America that Qutb's attitude toward the Islamic movement in Egypt began to change following the assassination of Hassan al-Banna in February 1949. It is said in these accounts that when Qutb was in America he noticed great jubilation among Americans at the news of al-Banna's death. It was only then that Qutb realized the threat al-Banna had posed to the West, and Qutb regretted not getting in closer contact with him.

Regarding his changing attitudes toward Hassan al-Banna and the Muslim Brothers while in America, Sayyid Qutb wrote:

My attention was very much drawn to the extreme interest in the Brothers shown by American newspapers as well as the British newspapers which used to reach America, and their gloating and obvious placidity over dissolving the Muslim Brothers group, hitting it and killing their leader. At the same time a book of mine, *Social Justice in Islam*, was published in 1949 and in which I put this sentence as a dedication: "To the youngsters whom I see in my fantasy coming to restore this religion anew as it began fighting for the cause of Allah by killing and getting killed . . . etc." The Brothers in Egypt understood that I meant them by this dedication. The matter was not like that. However, on their part, they adopted the book. They considered its author as their friend and they began to be interested in him. So when I returned at the end of 1950, some of their young men began to visit me and to talk to me about the book.[32]

It is also reported that, upon Qutb's return to Egypt in August 1950, a delegation comprising some of the younger members of the Muslim Brothers was waiting to welcome Qutb at Cairo's airport. This unexpectedly warm reception left a deep impression on him, and henceforth cordial relations were to develop between Qutb and these young men.

QUTB'S RETURN TO EGYPT AND INDEPENDENT ISLAMIC INTELLECTUAL CAREER, 1950–1952

After his return to Egypt and for most of 1950–1951, Qutb took an independent path in his work, calling people to Islam and to agitation against the conditions existing in the country. This period in Egypt's history is characterized by J.C.B. Richmond as "a period of intense frustration for the Egyptian people. . . . Financial and sexual scandals touching the king became the staple of Cairo gossip. Stories of faulty weapons supplied to the army in Palestine under contracts which had been profitable to the king and his courtiers were widely circulated. So were stories of the rigging of the Alexandria cotton market for the profit of Wafdist Ministers."[33]

Qutb wrote articles which appeared in Cairo's leading publications, including *al-Risalah*, and in publications connected with the Muslim Brothers, especially *al-Da'wah* of Salih al-'Ashmawi, a prominent member of the Brothers' Guidance Council (Maktab al-Irshad). Qutb's agitation and outspoken criticism of the Egyptian established order and his attacks on the West in the 1940s and early

1950s, according to al-'Azm, led some Egyptian writers to dub him the "Mirabeau of the Egyptian revolution of 1952,"[34] in reference to Comte de Mirabeau (1747–1791), the great orator of the French Revolution who was instrumental in arousing the masses against feudalism and tyranny.

The Battle of Islam and Capitalism (1951)

In this period, Qutb began writing his *Ma'rakat al-Islam wa-al-ra'smaliyah* (The Battle of Islam and Capitalism), which appeared in February 1951.[35] In this work, Qutb wages with revolutionary zeal an assault on the status quo. In the opening pages, he warns that the bad social conditions that the people of Egypt were experiencing could not continue, because they were contrary to the spirit of civilization, religion, and the simplest sound economic principles. He charges that these conditions hampered economic, social, and human growth.[36]

Qutb challenges the exploiting tyrants, professional men of religion and hired writers and journalists who were accusing those calling for reform of being "communists," or "outlaws," or a "danger to public security and order." The voices of the millions with empty stomachs and the reality that they represent, Qutb warns, cannot be silenced.[37]

Qutb argues that prevailing social conditions were paralyzing the nation's efforts to work and produce, and preventing adequate utilization of human and natural resources, because the state represented the forces of capitalism and not the needy masses. Furthermore, these social conditions were denying human dignity and destroying human rights, as could be seen in the miserable state of millions of peasants and others. Their condition made a mockery of the parliamentary system's credo that "the nation is the source of power." It was a myth, according to Qutb, that constitutions and parliaments governed Egypt when in reality feudalism and slavery prevailed in the country.[38]

The existing social conditions, in Qutb's view, were corrupting character and conscience, causing corruption to proliferate in society and the state, and leading to individual and national decay. Excessive wealth had created a class of rich parasites who lived off the efforts of the hungry and the naked and who were preoccupied with lust, hedonism, and immoral behavior. Qutb attacks the religious hierarchy in Egypt for having been indifferent to these conditions rather than adopting a proper Muslim stand against them.[39]

Current social conditions, writes Qutb, render the notions of "equality of opportunity" and "justice between effort and its reward" a myth leading to anxiety and restlessness among individuals and groups. Furthermore, these social conditions were forcing people, especially the younger generation, into the arms of communism because they saw it as their only salvation from the existing miseries. Qutb accuses these conditions of having been, on the whole, contrary to the spirit of Islam. To those among the religious elite who were attempting to legitimize the status quo by reference to religion, Qutb quotes Qur'an 2:79: "*Therefore woe be unto those who write the Scripture with their hands and then say, 'This is from Allah,' that they may purchase a small gain therewith.*" Qutb claims that the country was at a crossroad, with three viable alternatives from which to choose: socialism, communism, and Islam. Only with a long-range organized struggle would one of these alternatives emerge victorious to save the country.[40]

Globally, the two major blocs, communist and capitalist, should be rejected, states Qutb, in favor of a third: the Islamic bloc that stretches from the Atlantic to the Pacific. Qutb rejects the importation of ready-made solutions from communism and capitalism, asking his countrymen to seek in Islam their solutions for such problems such as the inequitable distribution of property and wealth and unequal opportunity.[41]

Islam must rule; it must not be confined merely to places of worship, to hearts, or to conscience like Christianity. The system of belief is not in itself valuable; it must be translated into a "Shari'ah," an all-encompassing law which governs personal, penal, civil, and commercial affairs. Islam must govern because Islam itself decides "that there is no Islam without rule (hukm) and no Muslims without Islam in accordance with Qur'an 5:44: '*Whoso judgeth not by that which Allah hath revealed: such are wrong-doers.*'"[42]

Qutb attempts to allay possible suspicions regarding Islamic rule by emphasizing that Islam does not mean a retreat from civilization into the primitive rule of the desert Arabs. Neither does it mean that the Shari'ah will be limited to medieval rulers, or that power will be in the hands of the shaykhs and dervishes, or that the government will be despotic, or that textual sources of the religion will be obscure. If Islam rules, it will not, as many fear, confine women to the harem, nor will it be fanatical in its treatment of minorities.[43]

Qutb reiterates these ideas more forcefully and with much controversy during his ten-year imprisonment in 1954–1964, as seen in his work *Mile-stones*, which appeared in 1964.

Islam and Universal Peace (1951)

Qutb's second major Islamic work to appear following his return from the United States dealt with Islam's posture toward world peace. It appeared in October 1951. Qutb's views of peace were articulated in reaction to the turmoil in global politics, which had been exacerbated by the Berlin Blockade crisis of 1948, the victory of Mao Tse-tung's forces in China in 1949, and the outbreak of war in Korea in June 1950, which led to military confrontation between the United States and China. The intensification of the cold war between the Western states and the Soviet bloc further polarized the international political atmosphere. A British scholar, Isaiah Berlin, notes that by 1950 "the mild, sober, pensive mood of post–World War II years began to give way to the anxiety, and at times acute depression, of what seemed a new pre-war period."[44]

According to Qutb, the Islamic view of world peace and international politics had not been fully expressed. He wrote: "As humanity at present is deeply concerned about the problem of world peace, one should ask whether Islam has a constructive opinion on this matter, and what are the solutions it provides. This book is meant to answer this question in detail."[45]

In Islam, Qutb defines peace as "harmony in the universe and the laws of life, while war is the result of such violations of harmony such as injustice, despotism and corruption." Peace, he adds, must imply freedom, justice, and security for all people. If there are violations of this harmony, however, including the rejection of God's supremacy, then they must be resisted.[46]

In order to achieve world peace, Qutb held that Islam requires peace of conscience in the individual, peace at home, and peace in society. Peace of conscience in the individual is attained as a result of Islam's promotion of a balanced life in the individual's spiritual and physical quests, its acknowledgment of the fallibility of the individual and his or her redemption, its encouragement of a direct relationship between the individual and God, and its guaranteeing of the individual's security and sustenance.[47]

Peace at home is achieved as a result of living out the Islamic codes of conduct and laws that strengthen the family system. The institution of marriage, the promotion of chastity in the family, the prohibition of adultery, and the mutual support of family members all lead to peace at home. Peace in society is achieved by appealing to the individual's conscience and humanitarian feelings, by suggesting rules to govern the Muslim personal and social behavior, by promoting cooperation and solidarity among members of society, and by entrusting Muslims with the welfare of humanity. Peace in society is advanced, furthermore, by the legislative and judicial systems of Islam, which help guarantee legal rights, justice, security, material necessities, and social equilibrium.[48]

Social peace is further enhanced by the unique nature of Islamic law, which according to Qutb, is unequaled in human history. In Islam, "God is the Supreme legislator and He has no reason to favor an individual or a class as all belong to Him equally." Thus, there can be no class conflict or discontent "when Islamic laws are fully implemented in the political and economic spheres."[49]

According to Qutb, Muslims have a responsibility for achieving peace within themselves, at home, in society, and on earth. "It is a peace based on recognizing God's oneness and omnipotence, on instituting justice, equality and liberty, and on achieving social equilibrium and cooperation." World peace, Qutb maintains, can be achieved only if peace of conscience, peace in the home, and peace in society are first realized.[50]

The struggle to establish the sovereignty of God on earth, that is, "jihad," Qutb writes, "is a means to achieve a universal change by establishing peace of conscience, domestic peace, national peace and international peace." This universal peace must be based on universal Islamic justice. "The most serious injustice is luring people from the worship of God and forcing them to deify those rulers who empower themselves to legalize what God has prohibited and to prohibit what God has allowed."[51]

Qutb clarifies further the ways to establish universal justice, peace, and Islamic rule through jihad:

> Islam ordains that men persevere in their efforts to establish the Word of God on earth . . . and . . . seeks to destroy all injustice, irrespective of its perpetrator's race, creed or nationality. . . . When dealing with its enemies Islam takes one of three courses: they may adopt the religion, or pay tribute or fight. . . . If the enemy rejects the religion and also refuses to pay tribute, Muslims must declare war (jihad) on those who obdurately stand between men and

Islam's righteous and peaceful principles. If the enemies are defeated they are obliged to pay the tribute in return for which they become wards of the Islamic State and are entitled to protection and the same rights and obligations as those the Muslims enjoy.[52]

One can detect in the above-mentioned quote further development of Qutb's controversial thought of the 1960s. In his later writing, Qutb maintains that the transformation from Jahili society to Islamic society was thwarted by tyrants who refused to acknowledge the rule of Allah on this earth (al-Hakimiyyah) and by people who deified those tyrants rather than Allah. As we shall see, jihad becomes the central focus in Qutb's controversial thought during his imprisonment, as seen in his controversial work *Milestones*.

According to Qutb, Islamic international relations are based on "unqualified tolerance towards all human beings . . . and the absence of the prejudicies which are prevalent in all man-made political systems." Qutb adds that "humanity shall continue to suffer increasing injury at the hands of atheists, beguiled and misled by corrupted civilizations, unless man follows the Islamic system which leads people to justice, discipline and peace."[53]

In the last chapter of his book, entitled "And Now . . . ," Qutb presents his views of world politics in light of his stay in the United States, the outbreak of the Korean War, and the continued confrontation between the capitalist and the communist camps. This controversial chapter appeared in the first edition. Beginning with the third edition (1954), however, the chapter was deleted, reappearing only in an unidentified edition in 1967. Al-'Azm notes this deletion and suggests that the outspoken anti-American tone of the chapter led to its censorship.[54]

Qutb states in "And Now . . ." that anyone living in the United States between the 1948 Berlin crisis and the outbreak of the Korean War in 1950 could have clearly discerned that the United States was preparing for war. The full mobilization of its people and resources, the tone of press, radio, and cinema, even activities in the universities and institutions indicated that the nation was mobilizing for war.[55]

Qutb felt that the Korean War occurred because of the American capitalists' dire need to reverse stagnant postwar economic conditions in the United States and Europe. The Marshall Plan, devised by Truman's administration in 1947 to reconstruct Europe, was an attempt to reverse the situation by opening European markets to

American surplus goods. The intended result of the plan was increased industrial activity and a solution to unemployment.[56]

But this plan, says Qutb, did not bring about a solution, because five million Americans were still unemployed. Instead, the Marshall Plan only helped European recovery at a time when a potential market for American products, mainland China, had been cut off with the victory there of communist forces under Mao Tse-Tung in 1949. Although the Korean War had managed to decrease American unemployment by two million, Qutb maintains that it did not solve the economic problems. Hence American capitalists held the expectation that a large-scale war, which would eliminate unemployment and guarantee huge profits, was inevitable. War, according to Qutb, was therefore an economic necessity as well as a means of halting the advance of international communism. Sooner or later, Europe would have to follow America's example for the same reasons.[57]

Qutb maintains that the world was at a crossroad, with the capitalist and communist camps competing for the world's human, economic, and geographical resources. Under the leadership of America, the capitalist bloc was attempting to pressure other nations to join them by scaring capitalists and feudalists, especially in Arab countries, with the specter of communist expansion, using political, economic, and sometimes military pressure against countries that were directly or indirectly under colonial rule and by using economic inducements such as the Economic Assistance and Point Four programs. The capitalist bloc, according to Qutb, did not care about the masses; it cared only about those who ruled and exploited the masses.[58]

The communist bloc, on the other hand, did address the deprived masses, and the masses were ready to react favorably to any call promising salvation from social and economic conditions. The communist bloc, however, was as much opposed to every true Islamic call and Islamic social justice as the capitalist bloc. The communist countries, likewise, showed hostility toward Arabs during the Palestine conflict: Russia was hostile in the United Nations Security Council deliberations, and arms from the communist bloc were used against Arabs in Palestine. Qutb saw a need, however, for the existence of the communist bloc as a counter-balance to the capitalist bloc, and vice versa. A decisive victory by either of the "materialistic camps" would have been a serious blow, in Qutb's view, to the cause of international peace and to people uncommitted to either bloc.[59]

Qutb's road to salvation is the adoption of the Islamic way of life and the emergence of an Islamic bloc from Morocco to Indonesia, with a population of 300 million and resources unequaled in petroleum and other raw materials. This third bloc, which commands strategic importance in world communications, would consist of Shari'ah-based Muslim nations. These nations could serve as a buffer, in Qutb's view, between the two other blocs, thus preventing them from initiating war.[60]

Qutb's call for a third, nonaligned Islamic bloc reflected the newly independent nation of Egypt's desire to chart an independent path in regional and world politics. Indeed, Egypt in 1951 declined a British invitation to ally itself with the Western bloc, and in October 1951 the Egyptian parliament abrogated the 1936 Anglo-Egyptian Treaty. However, Qutb's Islamic concept of the "third bloc" differed from the concept adopted later by Egyptian leaders such as Nasser. For Nasser, the third bloc (as envisioned in the 1955 Bandung Asian-African Conference) comprised twenty-nine countries of diverse cultures and social systems, such as Indonesia, Egypt, Afghanistan, Iran, Yemen, Burma, Ceylon, India, China, Laos, Ethiopia, and the Gold Coast. These countries, which represented half the world's population, shared a common vision of world peace which entailed neutrality, the avoidance of alliances with the superpowers, and the freedom to receive aid or purchase arms from either bloc.[61]

Qutb's Agitation in *al-Risalah*, 1951–1952

Qutb wrote prolifically in various periodicals, including *al-Risalah* of Ahmad Hassan al-Zayyat, who began to give front-page prominence to Qutb's articles. In these articles, Qutb reiterated his criticism of the status quo and continued to advocate the Islamic way and the necessity of establishing an Islamic bloc. Qutb also attacked America and the West in these articles.

Qutb denounced al-Azhar's religious establishment for its failure to fulfill its "constructive and creative message," namely, an Islamic renaissance and the resurrection of the "Islamic idea." According to Qutb, Islam has a specific and all-encompassing idea about life, which extends to every aspect of human endeavor. Al-Azhar's task was to extract this all-encompassing idea, develop it with studies and research, prepare it for practical application in the light of present realities and, finally, to propagate it.[62]

Qutb's independent Islamic intellectual career was still evident in September 1951, when he wrote that the Islamic da'wah (call) was not the exclusive domain of the Muslim Brothers or other Islamic groups. Rather, the Islamic call emanated from the conscience of the Muslim nation: It emanated from the government of Pakistan, which was calling for an Islamic economic conference to regulate the economies of the Muslim world on an Islamic basis; it emanated from the Iranian religious leader Ayat Allah Kashani, who was demanding that the British leave Iran and the Muslim world altogether, and who was encouraging Iranians to demonstrate in support of Egypt's cause (British evacuation); it emanated from 'Alal al-Fasi and Muhammad Hassan al-Wazzani of Morocco, who spearheaded popular resistance to French occupation; and it emanated from Ahmad Hussayn, leader of Egypt's Socialist Party (formerly Young Egypt), who in May 1951 sent a warm letter via his newspaper, *al-Ishtirakiyah* (Socialism), to Ayat Allah Kashani and to Iranian Prime Minister Musaddaq calling upon them to end the oil monopoly in Iran and nationalize Iranian oil.[63]

QUTB'S CONTACTS WITH THE MUSLIM BROTHERS, 1951–1952

It appears that Qutb was gradually drawn into the Muslim Brothers' orbit in 1951 and 1952 when he began to contribute regularly to their publications, including *al-Da'wah* (The Call, f. 1951) of Salih al-'Ashmawi, who was a deputy of Hassan al-Banna and who became the chief contender for the Brothers' top post after al-Banna's assassination in 1949, and *al-Muslimun* (The Muslims, f. 1951) of Sa'id Ramadan, another prominent member of the Brothers.

The exact dates of Qutb's formal affiliation with the Brothers are unclear. However, from all available data it appears that his affiliation grew in stages: first, as a contributing writer to the Brothers' publications; second, as an admirer and friend of the movement in the aftermath of the Brothers' guerrilla war against the British in the Suez Canal area late in 1951; and third, as a member and then as a leading ideologue of the Brothers in the aftermath of the 1952 Free Officers revolt, that is, in the early months of 1953.

Qutb's serious interest in the Brothers (and vice versa) in 1951–1952 came at a time when the organization was going through a serious overhaul of top leadership and was rebuilding itself in accordance with the visions of the new leaders. Indeed, the Brothers had come a long way since the disastrous events of 1948 when, as a result of the government's fear of their increased strength in the aftermath of Egypt's defeat in the Palestine War and the Brothers' alleged terrorism and conspiracy to overthrow the government, Sa'dist Prime Minister Nuqrashi's cabinet dissolved the society.[64]

Nuqrashi's assassination in December 1948, allegedly at the hands of a Muslim Brother, had brought down on the Brothers the wrath of the new Sa'dist prime minister, Ibrahim 'Abd al-Hadi, who subjected the Brothers to persecution but took no action when the political police assassinated Hassan al-Banna in February 1949. By the time 'Abd al-Hadi had submitted his resignation in July 1949, several thousand Brothers were in prison. Although technically outlawed, the society managed to continue to operate as an organization both inside and outside the prisons under the leadership of al-Banna's deputy, Salih al-'Ashmawi.[65]

The Brothers' fortunes began to improve following the January 1950 victory of the Wafd Party in the elections. Some imprisoned members were released. In March 1951, the court found the charges against the Brothers, especially the most serious charge, that of criminal conspiracy to overthrow the government, to be unfounded. When martial law in Egypt ended on May 1, 1952, the society's central committee, Maktab al-Irshad, met and officially declared the existence of the society. In September 1951, the Council of State recommended releasing the society's assets and property, which was carried out in December. This gave the Brothers further legitimacy.[66]

In October 1951, an outsider, lawyer Hassan Isma'il al-Hudaybi, was selected to replace the deceased al-Banna as the General Guide of the society. This was done to avoid any internal divisions and also to project a positive image of the society. Al-Hudaybi, however, immediately began to reshuffle the leadership, "which invariably replaced venerable old members with relative neophytes in the Society." These changes were seen by old members as "unduly hasty and imperious, presumptuous, and offensive."[67] Salih 'Ashmawi, the aspirant to the post of the General Guide, emerged as al-Hudaybi's chief antagonist. The friction between these two men would eventually lead to a serious break in the Brothers' ranks and the expulsion of 'Ashmawi and his supporters from the society in December 1953.[68]

Qutb's Writings in *al-Muslimun*, 1951–1952

Qutb's contacts with the Muslim Brothers were further strengthened when the monthly Islamic review *al-Muslimun* of Sa'id Ramadan made its appearance in November 1951. Qutb became a regular contributor to the periodical, writing on subjects such as Islamic history, the Qur'an and Islamic society, until his arrest in late 1954. Qutb's popular commentary *Fi Zilal al-Qur'an* (In the Shade of the Qur'an) originated in this review.

In an article entitled "Fi al-tarikh, fikra wa-minhaj" (In History: An Idea and a Method) that appeared in the November and December 1951 issues of this journal, Qutb's negative views of Western interpretations of Islamic history were apparent in his call for the rewriting of that history. His point was that the European view of Europe as the center of the world, the predominance in Europe of a materialistic and experimental mentality, and the lack of appreciation in Europe for the spiritual and the transcendental, which are, in Qutb's view, essential ingredients of Islamic belief, made European study of Islamic history prone to serious distortion.

It is difficult, Qutb believed, for someone to study Islamic life without having an awareness of the spirit behind the Islamic system of belief, an awareness of the Islamic notion of the universe, life, and humanity, or an awareness of the Muslim's fulfillment of needs in the light of the Muslim system of belief. Non-Arabs in general and non-Muslims in particular are thus not qualified, according to Qutb, to rewrite Islamic history, because they do not understand the Islamic system of belief.[69]

In the third issue of *al-Muslimun*, Qutb started a series of articles entitled "Fi Zilal al-Qur'an" (In the Shades of the Qur'an), which came to an end with the ninth issue in July 1952. The series proved to be so popular that Dar Ihya' al-Kutub al-'Arabiyyah publishing house in Cairo contracted Qutb in 1952 to write a thirty-part Qur'anic commentary with the same title which Qutb completed in prison in 1959. Prison authorities allowed Qutb to continue his work on the commentary and to fulfill his contract obligation to the publishing house. This permission was given because the publisher successfully challenged the government in the courts for the losses it had suffered as a result of the imprisonment of Qutb, whose Qur'anic commentary was very popular in 1954. The government formed a censorship committee, however, to screen Qutb's writing. Upon his completion of the commentary in 1959, Qutb began major revisions of the earlier sections to reflect his Islamic conception in the light of the destruction of the Muslim Brothers Society in 1954 as well as Qutb's experience in Nasser's prisons. Qutb completed revising the first thirteen parts which appeared in the third edition of his commentary in 1961.

Fi Zilal al-Qur'an is not a commentary in the traditional sense. Instead, it is a free expression of the author's feelings while reading Qur'anic verses. It is a "commentary of the heart" very similar in approach to Qutb's subjective poetry of the heart and subjective prose. In his commentary, Qutb avoids the grammatical, dialectical, and legal discourse which characterizes traditional commentaries and which, in his words, "conceals the Qur'an from my soul and my soul from the Qur'an." Rather, the author's reflections and impressions while reading and living "in the shade of the Qur'an" fill him with spiritual, social, and humanistic inspirations, leading him, in addition, to freely express his feelings about the Qur'an's "wondrous" artistic beauty and its coordination of expression and portrayal.[70]

Qutb's Agitation in *al-Da'wah*, 1951–1952

Like his other writings which appeared after his return from the United States, Qutb's articles in *al-Da'wah* were highly critical of the conditions existing in Egypt, especially the British occupation. His criticism intensified in the aftermath of the unilateral abrogation of the Anglo-Egyptian Treaty of 1936 and the Sudan Condominium of 1899 by the Nahas (Wafd) cabinet on October 8, 1951. Qutb joined other nationalist forces in demanding the full mobilization of the people for armed struggle against British occupation, including the formation of Kata'ib al-fida' (Sacrifice Battalions) to serve as guerrilla forces against the British.[71]

Qutb's attitude toward the Muslim Brothers began to crystallize in November 1951, when he singled them out as the only group in Egypt who were actually carrying arms and fighting the British. In his view, the spirit of Islam and the Islamic system of belief were the prime movers behind the Brothers' willingness to sacrifice in accordance with Qur'an 9:111: "*Lo Allah hath bought from the believers their lives and their wealth because the Garden will be theirs: They shall fight in the way of Allah and shall slay and be slain. It is a promise which is binding in him in the Torah and the Gospel and the Qur'an. Who fulfilleth his covenant better than Allah?*"[72]

Richard P. Mitchell points out that the training of guerrilla battalions (Kata'ib al-tahrir), which was underway in November in universities and schools, was spearheaded by the Muslim Brothers. By December, several hundred Brothers were in the Suez Canal area participating in the fighting, and on January 14, 1952, a mass funeral was held for the first "martyr" of the battalions, 'Umar Shahin of the Muslim Brothers. In January, doubt and anger were popularly expressed through agitation and demonstration, at the government's insincerity in abrogating the treaty, in light of its failure to take serious measures to mobilize Egyptians against the British presence.[73]

Qutb's attacks on the Egyptian government's inaction continued throughout November and December 1951. In November, Qutb expressed an increased confidence in the Islamic system of belief. According to Qutb, struggle and jihad require a spirit of self-sacrifice emanating from a system of belief. Real victory would not be achieved until the masses were purified under a spiritual leadership that would educate them comprehensively. Qutb expressed his opposition to the involvement of "immoral" film stars and radio services in the struggle against the British.[74]

In December, Qutb accused the Wafdist government of improvising the abrogation of the treaty and of hampering the efforts of the liberation battalions, despite the desire of the people to fight. He charged the cabinet with having the mentality of the "feudalists, capitalists and the vested interests in the export and import business."[75]

Qutb's fiery articles on the status quo and especially against the Wafd cabinet led to the confiscation of two issues of *al-Da'wah* in January 1952. In the first case, the January 8, 1952, issue, the weekly was released for sale only after Qutb's article "nur wa-nar" (Light and Fire) was deleted.[76] Another issue, no. 49, was also confiscated and Qutb's article was likewise deleted.[77]

Qutb's Relations with the Muslim Brothers on the Eve of the 1952 Revolution

It appears that as early as January 1952 Qutb was not yet affiliated with the Muslim Brothers. Early in the month, Qutb said that his relation with the Brothers was based on friendship, trust, and cooperation. He referred to himself as a friend of the Islamic movement when he demanded that the General Guide of the Muslim Brothers, whom he considered the sole official spokesman of the movement, should clarify in precise Islamic terms and programs the society's official stand in regard to the fighting in the Canal Zone.[78]

Mitchell points out that the rank and file of the Brothers, including Salih 'Ashmawi and his newspaper *al-Da'wah*, had joined the call for armed struggle, and indeed the Brothers were spearheading guerrilla warfare against the British. Confusion had arisen, however, as to the official position of the leadership in the light of al-Hudaybi's apparent silence. Therefore, some activists, like Qutb, were demanding that al-Hudaybi take a clear stand in regard to the fighting.[79]

In March and April 1952, Qutb vigorously attacked those Egyptians who were advocating nationalism and communism, branding them as faqaqi' (bubbles). He accused those espousing the nationalist creed of being out of touch with the trend toward international unity and of playing into the hands of "imperialism by tearing up the Muslim nation into narrow national entities." Qutb, the long-time supporter of the 1919 popular uprising under the leadership of Zaghlul and the Wafd Party, as seen in his early literary writings, had now begun to take a different view of the nationalist uprising and its leadership. He termed the leaders of the 1919 revolt as "miserable" and "bubble-like," accusing them of having narrow horizons because they isolated themselves from the Islamic idea and the international trend toward conglomeration (the Islamic bloc). The Muslim world was suffering, he said, because "imperialism" managed to implant the narrow ideology of nationalism in order to serve its own purposes.[80]

Qutb made these attacks in conjunction with his and the Muslim Brothers' campaign for pan-Islamic unity and the creation of a viable Islamic bloc, which they had initiated in 1951 and which continued until the July 1952 Revolution. The bond between the Muslim Brothers and Qutb was further strengthened when the publishing house connected with the Brothers, Dar al-Ikhwan lil-Sihafah wa-al-Tiba'ah, sponsored the publication of Qutb's second printing of *Ma'rakat al-Islam wa-al-ra'smaliyah* and the third printing of *al-'Adalah al-Ijtima'iyah fi al-Islam* by April 1952.[81]

On the eve of the Free Officers revolution, Qutb's promotion of the ideas of the Muslim Brothers became evident. He writes that in view of the Ministry of Education's inability to solve the nation's educational ills, the only viable solutions were nongovernmental, like those advanced by the Muslim Brothers.[82]

Following the July 1952 Revolution, and more specifically early in 1953, Qutb emerged as one of the leaders of the society in charge of Qism Nashr al-Da'wah (the Propagation of Message Section). Qutb's common cause with the Muslim Brothers on a variety of subjects and his stature as a highly respected independent and progressive Muslim intellectual undoubtedly contributed greatly to his close association with the Brothers. According to a partisan source, it was Salih 'Ashmawi, the editor of *al-Da'wah*, who invited Qutb to become a member. A strong friendship had developed between the two after Qutb's return from the United States and his regular contributions to 'Ashmawi's newspaper in 1951 and 1952.[83] However, it was al-Hudaybi, the General Guide of the Muslim Brothers, who successfully managed to recruit Qutb to the society to head the powerful Propagation of the Message Section, Qism Nashr al-Da'wah, early in 1953.

EMERGENCE OF A RADICAL ISLAMIST, 1952–1964

> One line of thinking proposes that America's tragedy on September 11th was born in the prisons in Egypt. Human rights advocates in Cairo argue that torture created an appetite for revenge, first in Sayyid Qutb and later in his acolytes, including Ayman al-Zawahiri. . . . Egypt's prisons became a factory for producing militants whose need for retribution—they called it "justice"—was all consuming. *(Lawrence Wright, 2002)*

RELATIONS BETWEEN THE MUSLIM BROTHERS, QUTB AND THE FREE OFFICERS, 1952–1954

Sayyid Qutb's career from 1952 onward followed the same turbulent path that the Society of Muslim Brothers followed in Egypt in the aftermath of the revolution on July 23, 1952. With the swift overthrow of King Faruq and the long association of the Free Officers with the Brothers, it was not surprising that the Brothers came to regard the July 1952 Revolution as "our revolution."[1] In the first days of the revolution, the executive arm of the Free Officers, the Revolutionary Command Council (RCC), made certain goodwill gestures toward the Brothers, including the opening of the investigation of the unresolved case of the murder of Hassan al-Banna; the abolition of the secret police of the Ministry of Interior; the arrest of many of the enemies of the Brothers including the much feared and hated Muhammad al-Jazzar, who was notorious for his harassment and torture of the Brothers in 1948–1949; the appointment of Rashad Muhanna, who was closely associated with the Brothers, to the Regency Council responsible for the infant monarch; and the release of Brothers from prisons.[2] At this time, Sayyid Qutb was in close association with the Brothers but not a member of the society.

Friction between the RCC and the Muslim Brothers, however, began to surface in the early months of the revolution when it became apparent that the Muslim Brothers' pronouncements on the need to establish government in Egypt on the basis of Islam were neither to the liking of the leading military officers in the RCC nor in their long-range plans for Egypt.[3] In September 1952, the RCC rejected two cabinet nominees from among the Brothers because these nominations were conditioned with the demand that the Guidance Council of the Brothers should have the right to veto any legislation introduced by the new regime to ensure its Islamic orientation, which was flatly rejected by the RCC.[4] Thus when one of the Brothers, Shaykh Hassan al-Baquri, accepted the post of Minister of Islamic Waqf, he was dismissed from the society.[5] A month later, Rashad Muhanna was dismissed from the Regency Council, inter alia, for his strongly held views on the need to set up an Islamic state. Likewise, Free Officers who were connected with the Brothers were purged from the RCC.[6]

In January 1953, the Egyptian government abolished all existing parties except the Muslim Brothers, who were classified as a religious grouping. However, in the same month, the government founded its own mass movement, the Liberation Rally (Hay'at al-tahrir), to replace the abolished parties, a move that was seen by the Brothers as challenging them on their own ground by offering a rival social welfare and educational program to the masses.[7]

SAYYID QUTB AND THE FREE OFFICERS, 1952–1953

Qutb's orientation toward the Free Officers and the revolution was positive at the beginning. On the first page of *al-Risalah* and in the aftermath of the revolution, Sayyid Qutb wrote:

We the people recognize that today a new dawn appeared and that a new reign casts its shade on this valley. We recognize that the blessed move of the army made this dawn appear and it began this reign. This blessed move is not for the sake of an individual or a body or a party. Rather it is for the sake of us, the people. This new uprising alone tore up the political police, curtailed capitalism, gave freedom to workers' unions and prepared the ground for the establishment of trade unions on sound bases. . . . We know that the new move alone is the clean move, because its men are still living in hardship: they stay awake while people are asleep and live on coarse food.[8]

Sayyid Qutb was considered one of the intellectuals of the revolution and its mouthpiece among students, workers, and peasants. He was extremely loyal to Gamal 'Abd al-Nasser and had strong faith in his leadership.[9] Qutb wrote that he used to work for "more than twelve hours daily near the men of the Revolution, and with those surrounding them." Qutb adds that he was the object of their trust and that they nominated him for some important posts. "We also deliberated openly concerning the circumstances going on at that time, such as the matters of workers and the destructive communist movements among them, and the issue of transition, its duration and the constitution to be issued concerning it, etc."[10]

In an interview with Suleiman Fayyad, Sayyid Qutb mentioned that he used to hold meetings with members of the Free Officers at his home in Halwan while preparing for the revolution, and he showed Fayyad photographs of himself taken with the Free Officers at his house.[11] Mahmoud al-A'zab, an Egyptian officer belonging to the Muslim Brothers, is quoted as saying, "The army cannot forget that Sayyid Qutb is the father of the Revolution and the father of the revolutionaries. His modesty increases our attachment and veneration for him." al-A'zab adds that he visited Sayyid Qutb at his home on July 19, 1952. Some of the leaders of the July 1952 Revolution, including Colonel Gamal 'Abd al-Nasser, were there at the same time.[12]

Concerning the relationship of Sayyid Qutb with the Revolutionary Command Council (RCC), 'Adel Hammuda stated, "Those who were contemporaneous to the details of the first days and the first years of the Revolution emphasize that Sayyid Qutb had an office in the building of the leadership council of the Revolution (RCC), and that he used to reside semi-permanently there. . . . He and Sa'id al-'Aryan were entrusted with the task of changing the educational curricula. . . . At that time his writings and books were being distributed in the schools of the Ministry. . . . Also, the national hymns were taught to the students in the reading classes." 'Adel Hammuda added that when Sayyid Qutb held a conference on freedom of thought in Islam, Gamal 'Abd al-Nasser and Muhammad Naguib were among the first who blessed this step of his.[13] In August 1952, Sayyid Qutb delivered a lecture in the Officers' Club in al-Zamalek on intellectual and spiritual liberation in Islam. Partisan sources say that the lecture in which 'Abd al-Nasser, Anwar el-Sadat and a large gathering of the leaders of Egyptian society and from other Arab countries participated was transformed into a festival honoring Sayyid Qutb, his virtues, and his role in preparing for the July 1952 Revolution.[14]

The prominence of the independent Islamic propagandist who was close to the leaders of the Muslim Brothers and to the Free Officers in the aftermath of July 1952 Revolution was considered effective in supporting the search of the Brothers for greater cooperation with nationalist forces, that is, the Wafdists and the communists. As a sign of good intention toward other political forces, Qutb, in a press conference in August 1952, demanded the release of all prisoners including the communists who had fought against tyranny. Qutb described the communists as being "noble." In Qutb's opinion, they should be resisted not by iron and fire but by logic. This happened at a time when the Muslim Brothers were adopting a progressive program focusing on social justice and promoting equality in land ownership and distribution.[15]

On the other hand, some sources indicate that this positive position of Qutb toward the communists changed drastically after a few days in the aftermath of the labor disturbances at the Misr Fine Spinning and Weaving Company in Kafr al-Dawwar on August 12, 1952. Sayyid Qutb accused the communists of supporting the labor disturbances in the spinning and weaving complex. Qutb demanded that the RCC take a firm position against those who were behind the events. Sana' al-Misri says that Sayyid Qutb was an advisor of the RCC member and martial court chair, 'Abd al-Muni'im Ibrahim, who issued rulings that included the execution of two workers who participated in the events of Kafr al-Dawwar.[16] Qutb believed that in order to protect the July 1952 revolution at this early stage of its life, the RCC must strike with iron fist against all those trying to abort the revolution. He also called for the RCC to assume dictatorial power to insure the success of the revolution.

On the other hand, Sayyid Qutb sent an open letter to Egypt's president, General Muhammad Naguib, in the Cairene daily *al-Akhbar* on August 8, 1952, in which he demanded the establishment of a clean, "just dictatorship for six months for a comprehensive purgation which deprives corrupted ones of every constitutional activity, and which does not permit political freedom except to honest persons."[17] Anyone who traces the position of Sayyid Qutb vis-à-vis partisan pluralism in the pre–July 1952 regime will not be shocked by it. 'Adel Hammuda says: "He—as a man of letters—liked the expression (just dictatorship) without having—as a politician—sufficient experience to delineate the dimensions of that dictatorship, its danger, and even what is meant by it. . . . He did not define the specifications of the just dictator . . . and he did not tell us when the just dictator turns into an unjust dictator."[18]

With the cancellation of the elections, the dissolution of Egyptian parties in January 1953, arrests in the ranks of the army, and the emergence of the dictatorial regime (the Revolution Command Council), the international press called Egyptian President Muhammad Naguib "the just dictator" or "the refined dictator." President Naguib commented in his memoirs: "Because I was a just dictator, I was exposed to severe criticism from those who wanted a real dictator. . . . Those were dreaming of an Egyptian dictator. . . . However, I disappointed them . . . so they directed their thinking to Gamal 'Abd al-Nasser to undertake this role and I don't believe that he disappointed them."[19]

Sayyid Qutb believed that Egypt would never be relieved from its chronic suffering and pervasive problems unless free rein were given to the revolutionaries to restore the depleted country. The aims of the nation that were agreed upon did not allow for democracy because these aims became entrenched in the conscience of the nation and its collective mind. Therefore these aims did not require democracy in order to be realized. The evacuation of the British and liberation from feudalism and capitalism, however, were the conditions required, in Qutb's view, for democracy.[20]

It was reported that Sayyid Qutb served as an assistant to Gamal 'Abd al-Nasser, the secretary general of the Liberation Rally, upon its establishment on January 23, 1953. Qutb resigned from his post, however, less than one month later. Sayyid Qutb wrote that he worked with the men of the July 1952 Revolution until February 1953, "when my thinking and their thinking differed on the Liberation Rally, the method of its formation and other issues going on at that time which there is no need to detail. At the same time my relationship with the Brothers' Society became closer. From my viewpoint I considered it a valid field of work for Islam. In my viewpoint, it is the movement with no equivalent alternative for confronting Zionist and imperialistic Crusader schemes about which I knew a lot especially in the period of my stay in America. The result of these circumstances together was that I actually joined the Muslim Brothers Society in 1953."[21]

Some say that Sayyid Qutb resigned from the Liberation Rally because Gamal 'Abd al-Nasser withdrew Qutb's appointment as minister of education in the first cabinet formed by the Free Officers headed by Mohammad Naguib. As a result of this action, according to al-Damardash al-'Iqali, "Sayyid Qutb was extremely angry and he considered 'Abd al-Nasser responsible for the loss of his dream in the Ministry of Education which he expected to be appointed in as a reward for supporting the Revolution and promoting it."[22]

Others believe that Sayyid Qutb's dissatisfaction with the unIslamic policies of the RCC led him to submit his resignation from his position as assistant monitor in the technical research and projects division in the Ministry of Education on October 18, 1952, having worked for the ministry in different capacities since 1934. Sayyid Qutb's superior, Isma'il al-Qabbani, tried to convince Qutb to rethink his decision on several occasions, but to no avail. Finally, on December 30, 1953, the letter of resignation was submitted to the Council of Ministers of the RCC for approval. Qabbani tried to add two years to Qutb's total service for retirement purposes, but the RCC decided against that and accepted Qutb's resignation as of his letter dated October 18, 1952.[23]

Sayyid Qutb wrote about joining the Brothers: "Despite their hospitality as I joined their society, the sphere of work for me in their view was in cultural matters in the propagation division, the Tuesday lesson, the newspaper *al-Ikhwan al-Muslimum* (The Muslim Brothers) whose editor-in-chief, I became, and writing some monthly letters for Islamic cultural purposes. As for executive / organizational work, I remained remote from it."[24]

The Muslim Brothers and the Free Officers, 1953–1954

It is generally believed that some members of the ruling junta helped fuel the internal strife within the Muslim Brothers' ranks, which had been in existence since al-Hudaybi's assumption of the top leadership post in the society in 1951. It was hoped that by fueling the internal schism the organization would be brought under control. This schism reached a high point in October 1953 when top leaders of the executive committee, the Guidance Council, who opposed the leadership of al-Hudaybi were voted out of office. In November, this group, which was led by Salih 'Ashmawi, staged a brief rebellion within the organization to force the resignation of the General Guide, but to no avail. In December, the rebellion leaders were expelled from the society.[25] Al-Hudaybi's victory, according to Mitchell, was a severe blow to the Egyptian government, which "prompted its decision to dissolve the organization shortly afterwards."[26]

The protracted struggle between the Muslim Brothers and the RCC came to a breaking point on January 12, 1954, at the University of Cairo when Muslim Brothers speakers attacked government negotiations with Britain over the Sudan and the Canal Zone, describing the negotiations as a betrayal of national aspirations and calling for jihad against the British. At this student rally, the crowd was also addressed by the leader of the Iranian Islamic underground movement Fidaiyan-i Islam, Navab Safavi. During this rally, violent clashes erupted between the Muslim Brothers and pro-government students.[27] "Many eyewitness versions of the incident," Mitchell points out, "support the notion that it was government-provoked."[28]

The disturbances at the university gave the RCC the pretext to seek the long-awaited liquidation of the organization when the society was declared a political party and thus subject to the January 1953 law that abolished such entities. Muslim Brothers, including Sayyid Qutb and the rest of the top leadership, were promptly arrested, while Navab Safavi was expelled from Egypt.[29] Meanwhile, the power struggle between General Muhammad Naguib and Colonel Gamal 'Abd al-Nasser intensified. Nasser and his supporters in the RCC wanted the armed forces to lead the country exclusively, while Naguib, with the support of a united front of Wafdists, communists, and Muslim Brothers, wanted a return to constitutional government.

For a brief period in February and March 1954, Naguib appeared to have gained the upper hand in running the country. In March, he announced the imminent return of parliamentary rule by July 1954. The Muslim Brothers were released about the same time. However, a counter-offensive to abort Naguib's plans was carried out by the supporters of Nasser. Thus, between March 25 and March 27, union members and Liberation Rally partisans held massive demonstrations and general strikes to protest Naguib's plans for Egypt, which led to Naguib's ouster from key posts and his retention as only a figurehead president. The restoration of the parliamentary government, as a result, was cancelled.[30]

The final showdown between Nasser and the Muslim Brothers began to gather momentum following the RCC's acceptance of "heads of agreement" with Britain in late July 1954 for the complete British evacuation of the Canal Zone. This agreement was to signal the escalation of the Brothers' criticism of the regime through their weekly newpaper *al-Ikhwan al-Muslimun* and through secret pamphlets. The government countered with the same, accusing al-Hudaybi of negotiating a secret treaty with the British and reminding the people of al-Hudaybi's relations with the deposed Egyptian king and the discredited ruling classes.[31]

In September, six Muslim Brothers were stripped of their nationality because of their anti-RCC activities in Syria.[32] The opportune time for Nasser to eradicate the only power that stood in his way and his plans for the country came on October 26, 1954, when an alleged assassination attempt against Nasser by the secret apparatus of the society (through Mahmud 'Abd al-Latif) took place in al-Manshiyah Square in Alexandria while Nasser was addressing a Liberation Rally crowd. That evening, while Prime Minister Nasser was delivering his speech to a large gathering of citizens about Egypt's struggle and his nationalistic declaration of completion by the Evacuation Agreement, eight bullets were shot at him. In a long, dramatic pause, the prime minister stopped talking while the bullets whizzed by. Then he resumed his speech and demanded with gestures from his hand that the throng be quiet.[33]

In a few hours, these were the words of Gamal 'Abd al-Nasser broadcast from Radio Cairo to all parts of the Arab world: "Oh ye people . . . I am, Gamal 'Abd al-Nasser, from you. I redeem you with my blood. I shall live for you and die working for you. I shall struggle for your freedom and your honor, O free men. . . . O men . . . even if they kill me, I have placed in you self-respect. So let them kill me now. I have planted in this nation freedom, dignity and self-respect. For the sake of Egypt and for the sake of the freedom of Egypt I shall live; and I shall die for the sake of Egypt." Nasser and the RCC moved swiftly to crush the Muslim Brothers' effective political organization. A special People's Court implicated President Naguib in the alleged Muslim Brothers conspiracy, and he was quietly removed from his office and placed under house arrest in No-vember. Al-Hudaybi was sentenced to life imprisonment, while six others including leaders of the society and the secret apparatus such as Attorney 'Abd al-Qadir 'Awdah, Shaykh Muammad Farghali, Mahmoud 'Abd al-Latif, Hindawi Duweir, Ibrahim al-Tayyib, and Yusuf Tal'at were put to death by hanging on December 9, 1954.[34] With the elimination of General Naguib, the destruction of the So-ciety of Muslim Brothers and the suppression of all organized po-litical groupings, Nasser emerged by the end of 1954 as the undisputed ruler of Egypt.

QUTB'S EMERGENCE AS A MUSLIM BROTHER IDEOLOGUE, 1953–1954

Qutb's stature as a highly respected independent and progressive Muslim intellectual undoubtedly contributed greatly to his recruit-ment by General Guide Hudaybi to head one of the most powerful sections of the organization, namely, Qism Nashr al-Da'wah (The Propagation of the Message Section) early in 1953. Qutb was re-cruited to this prestigious position at a time when al-Hudaybi, leader of the society since October 1951, was reshuffling the top leader-ship of the society by replacing old members with his own partisans who were "relative neophytes in the Society," a move which was deeply resented by longtime members.[35] The Propagation of Islam Section was much sought after because of its "all important control over the instruments of communication." Furthermore, the control of the section by the partisans of al-Hudaybi became a continuing source of friction between those supporting the General Guide and his opponents led by Salih 'Ashmawi.[36]

In his capacity as the leader of this prestigious section, Qutb was in charge of organizing the society's call, including the supply of callers (du'at), for speeches and lectures inside and outside the soci-ety, journalism and the publication of Islamic-oriented literature, the spiritual, mental, and physical guidance of each Brother, and the sup-ply of missionary schools, which the society maintained, with a uni-fied curriculum.[37] Qutb was thus in charge of a section that was the "ultimate arbiter of the materials which were the stuff of the move-ment's ideology."[38]

Under the leadership of al-Hudaybi (and Qutb), there was a "change in tone and emphasis," and "substance, not slogans, became a priority" in the propagation of the Islamic call.[39] In Mitchell's words, "this meant a more consciously scientific approach to the problem of Islam. The section . . . began to make use of talents available to it among its professional members in the fields of law, economics, society, education, chemistry, engineering, and zoology; and in the training of the missionaries, the section began to introduce, into what had been almost a purely theological operation, more 'secular' currents of learning."[40]

Qutb's Writings in *al-Da'wah, al-Muslimun* and *al-Risalah*, 1952–1954

Qutb continued his prolific writing career, including publishing parts of his Qur'anic commentary that he began writing before the July 1952 Revolution. In these articles, Qutb tackled many issues facing Islam, the Muslim world, and society. On the local and national levels, he called for the revision of history books in order to correct the distortions that gave prominent place to Muhammad 'Ali and his dynasty, and that failed to give a worthier place for the Islamic revival in the eighteenth and nineteenth centuries as represented by the Wahhabiyyah and the Mahdiyyah movements in Arabia and the Sudan, respectively.[41]

Qutb attacked the Egyptian broadcasting services and called for restructuring them in order to protect the conscience and ethics of the people from the onslaught of the entertainment sector. He was highly critical of contemporary singers and songs and demanded that the revolution silence these voices forever, even if this resulted in violations of individual freedom.[42]

On the international level, Qutb accused the white man (al-rajul al-abyad), European or American, of being the number-one enemy of Egyptians and all other Arabs, and attacked vehemently the white man's stooges and legacy in various sectors of Egyptian society, such as in education and the press.[43]

He attacked French imperialism in North Africa and America's acquiescence in this oppression, and charged that UNESCO was a white man's front.[44] Western conscience, according to Qutb, was the same conscience that he saw with his own eyes in America when white people ganged up against a young black man and trampled him with their shoes.[45]

Reacting to the trials of the assassins of Hassan al-Banna, Qutb wrote that secular justice cannot avenge al-Banna's death; only Islamic justice can do so.[46] Qutb declared that the call to resume Islamic life is a call for a better world. Accordingly, in Qutb's view, the Islamic social system is the only regime that is based on "internationalism" in its truest form. Qutb charged that the Islamic system was attacked because if it resumed its way of life it would expel both imperialism and communism from Egypt and the whole Muslim world.[47]

Many of the articles that Qutb wrote in 1952 and 1953, and lectures that he delivered during the same period, were collected later in 1953 in a book titled *Dirasat Islamiyyah* (Islamic Studies).[48] Qutb's series of articles titled "Nahwa mujtama' Islami" (Toward an Islamic Society), which appeared in *al-Muslimun* between 1952 and 1953, were collected after Qutb's death and were published in 1969 under the same title, *Nahwa mujtama' Islami*.[49]

Qutb and the Weekly *al-Ikhwan al-Muslimun* (The Muslim Brothers), 1954

In December 1953, the society's Maktab al-Irshad (Guidance Council) decided to establish a weekly journal, *al-Ikhwan al-Muslimun*, under the chief editorship of Sayyid Qutb. All preparations had been made for the appearance of the weekly in January 1954 when unforeseen events aborted the target date: the society was dissolved on January 13 and its leaders, including Sayyid Qutb, were imprisoned for two and a half months until their release in early April.[50]

The much-awaited first issue of the weekly finally appeared on May 20, 1954. Only twelve issues of this publication were published; it ceased publication in August of the same year.[51] The diversified content of a typical issue of the fifteen-page illustrated weekly included editorials, news and political features on Egypt and the Muslim world, religious, and theological discussions, economics, social and literary features, and advertisements.

On the pages of the weekly, Qutb reiterated many of his views pertaining to the pressing issues facing Islam, the Muslim world, and society in general. Qutb wrote that the term *al-'Alam al-Islami* (The Muslim World) is not an emotional expression but rather a reflection of a reality in present world politics.[52] On another occasion, Qutb wrote that the Muslim world's deeply held system of belief was the main reason that this system of belief did not die in spite of attempts to destroy it by spiritual, intellectual, social, and political forces of colonialism. The strength of this system of belief, according to Qutb, emanates from Allah, and like Him it does not die.[53]

On literature and the arts, Qutb wrote that Islam is not opposed to the arts per se but only to the non-Islamic conceptions and values that are expressed in them. Art or literature derived from the Islamic conception, according to the chief editor, expresses in a sincere manner the subtle yet obvious abilities of the human being, depicting life purposes suitable for entities higher than "wolves."[54] On the same subject, Qutb wrote that art and life in Islam are movement oriented and are comprehensive and creative. The human soul's adoption of the Islamic conception of life inspires it to conceive arts differently from those inspired by materialistic conception. Islamic literature is thus an expression of the soul being overwhelmed by Islamic feelings.[55]

In another article, which can be interpreted as a warning to the RCC in view of the increasingly uneasy relationship between them and the Muslim Brothers, Qutb warned those taking the Egyptian people for granted that they do not understand the nature of the people. The signing of the 1936 treaty with Britain, according to Qutb, signaled the beginning of the end of the strongest party that was created by the 1919 revolution (i.e., the Wafd Party). Likewise, the assassination of Hassan al-Banna signaled the beginning of the end of the oldest throne in history.[56]

The publication of *al-Ikwan al-Muslimun* finally came to a halt in August 1954 as a result of a combination of factors, including chiefly the growing crisis between the RCC and the Muslim Brothers and the imposition of press censorship, which made it impossible for Qutb to publish a viable publication.[57]

Qutb's Other Activities with the Muslim Brothers and His Arrest, 1953–1954

Sayyid Qutb was also involved in various affairs of the Muslim Brothers and served the movement in various capacities, including serving as the representative of the society in Islamic conferences in Damascus and Jerusalem in March and December 1953. At the Damascus conference on social studies, Qutb delivered a lecture titled "al-Tarbiyah al-khuluqiyah ka-wasilah li-tahqiq al-takaful al-ijtima'i" (Ethical Education as a Means to Fulfill Mutual Responsibility).[58] Another lecture on the same topic was published in a twenty-page booklet in 1953 by the Mosque Committee of the Syrian University under the title *Nizam al-takaful al-ijtima'i fi al-Islam* (System of Mutual Responsibility in Islam).[59] In his booklet, Qutb described this as a system going beyond the domain of finance and charity into a more comprehensive way of life in which individual, family, society, and government, acting in a concerted Islamic fashion, shape the financial and economic well-being of society.

Little is known of Qutb's personal role in intrasociety friction, that is, between al-Hudaybi's partisans and those led by Salih al-'Ashmawi. Both were very close friends of Qutb. However, Qutb's loyalty and devotion to his leader al-Hudaybi were well known. Qutb's section on the propagation of Islam, in addition, was utilized to defend the actions of the General Guide against the dissidents Salih al-'Ashmawi, Muhammad al-Ghazali, and Ahmad Jalal, who were finally expelled from the society in December 1953.[60]

Sayyid Qutb's opposition to the secular policies of Nasser and the RCC and the July 1954 signing of the "heads of agreement" with Britain for the complete evacuation of the Canal Zone continued to manifest itself in his writings and public pronouncements. Following the demise of the weekly newspaper *al-Ikhwan al-Muslimun*, and in response to the rigid censorship and the anti-Hudaybi press campaign of the government, Qutb resorted to the only channels available to him, that is, underground activities including secret pamphlets to convey his message as well as that of the Brothers.[61]

Qutb is also credited with the secret bulletin *al-Ikhwan fi al-ma'rakah* (The Brothers in the Battle), which appeared in the summer of 1954, and with other secret pamphlets, chiefly *Hadhihi al-mu'ahadah lann tammur* (This Treaty Will Not Pass) and *Limadha nukafih?* (Why Do We Struggle?). The government accused Qutb of coordinating the anti-government incitements from the mosques' pulpits, and as such played an indirect role in the incitements that led to anti-government disturbances in the Rawdah mosque in late August 1954. Furthermore, Qutb was alleged to have coordinated the disappearance of the Muslim Brothers following the abortive attempt against Nasser's life on October 26, 1954.[62]

Following the crackdown on the society and the mass arrests of Muslim Brothers, a few, including Qutb, remained at large. After evading the police for several weeks, Qutb was arrested at his house in Hulwan on November 18, 1954.[63]

On November 22, 1954, Qutb was put on the witness stand in the trial of al-Hudaybi and repeated some alleged confessions he made during questioning about al-Hudaybi's plans to overthrow the government with the aid of Muhammad Naguib. He testified that al-Hudaybi provided him with the necessary money to buy a mimeograph machine to print the pamphlets.[64]

Qutb was not tried with the top leadership of the society in November and December of 1954, nor was he implicated in any activities of the secret apparatus of the society and the alleged attempt against Nasser's life. Instead, he was tried for his anti-government agitation and was sentenced to fifteen years of hard labor in July 1955, having been in the military hospital since May due to serious ailments.[65]

Concerning the attempt to assassinate Gamal 'Abd al-Nasser at al-Manshiyah Square, Sayyid Qutb insisted that a "foreign source was involved in it . . . and that the policy designed by Zionism and imperialist crusaders to destroy the Muslim Brothers movement in the area was planned in order to insure that the interests and schemes of these parties have been successfully realized."[66]

Hassan Hanafi, a leading academician and an Islamic left thinker in Egypt and the Arab world, comments on transformations in the life of Sayyid Qutb in light of the deterioration of relationships between the Muslim Brothers and the Free Officers and Qutb's arrest. He says that Qutb "developed naturally from literature to patriotism to socialism to discovering Islam as containing all these currents. Had his development continued in a natural way, he would have reached scientific socialism as synonymous to Islam, and he would have become one of the pillars of the Islamic left in Egypt and one of its first supports in the Muslim world."[67]

The hypothesis of Hassan Hanafi concerning scientific socialism as synonymous to Islam needs scrutiny. The materialistic bases of scientific socialism completely contradict the spiritual idealistic bases of the religious idea. The materialistic idea in its capitalistic and communist dimensions was totally rejected by Sayyid Qutb before and after his imprisonment, as his writings testify.

THE RADICALIZATION OF SAYYID QUTB AND THE INFLUENCE OF PAKISTANI ISLAMIST AL-MAWDUDI, 1954–1964

Sayyid Qutb remained imprisoned from November 1954 until May 1964, when he was freed for health reasons. Confinement was painful and severe, but as his health deteriorated with lung and heart complications he was transferred to hospitals, including the prison hospital of Liman Tura and the Munil University Hospital. His relatives were allowed to see him, and authorities provided him with the facility to pursue his writing career. The radicalization of Sayyid Qutb in prison and the emergence of his uncompromising revolutionary writings were influenced as well by the bloody events in Liman Tura prison on June 1, 1957. On that day, twenty-one jailed Muslim Brothers were killed for refusing to report to their daily hard labor of rock breaking. Qutb, a resident of the prison's infirmary, was "horrified by the barbarism" of the prison guards and "lost his last remaining illusions as to the Muslim character of the Nasser regime."[68]

As noted earlier, Qutb was permitted to work on his commentary *Fi Zilal al-Qur'an* as well his contract obligation for Dar Ihya' al-Kutub al-'Arabiyyah after the latter successfully challenged the government in the courts following the losses the publisher had suffered as a result of the author's imprisonment, but the government formed a censorship committee to screen Qutb's writings.[69] Despite censorship, Qutb managed to write many works that would eventually make him the leading ideologue of radical and jihadist Islamists. Indeed, Qutb's prison writings in 1954–1965 would become an integral part of Islamic resurgence in the next forty years. This resurgence would draw its strength from the unmitigated failures of the Arab regimes to build viable societies and from the repeated humiliation of the Arabs in their confrontation with Israel.

Qutb's radical terminologies such as al-Jahiliyyah (paganism) and al-Hakimiyyah (God's rule on earth) and the resulting takfir (excommunication) that characterize his controversial prison writings were influenced in part by Indian and later Pakistani radical Islamist Abu al-A'la al-Mawdudi. According to Muhammad 'Amarah, al-Mawdudi's concepts became the "common denominator among extremist factions in the Islamic awakening movements." The supporters of al-Mawdudi criticized Sayyid Qutb, however, for divesting al-Mawdudi's concepts of their specifically Indian circumstances and employing those concepts in a different Islamic Arab climate. Al-Mawdudi's supporters added that Qutb exaggerated some of these concepts in an extremist manner. The political environment in which al-Mawdudi's concepts had been born was the British imperialistic hegemony and the fear of the subjugation of Muslims by the Hindu majority, including the fear that the Islamic identity and character would disappear into Hindu India.[70]

Nevertheless, 'Adel Hammuda comments that the concepts of Abu al-'Ala al-Mawdudi infiltrated through the Brothers' cells after their first ordeal in 1948 and fascinated the minds of some of their young men. Although that ordeal was accompanied by circumstances similar to the 1954 ordeal (imprisonment, arrest, torture, and fabricated issues), the intellectual leadership of the Muslim Brothers believed that "generalization is a futility that should be stopped. The thinkers of the Brothers succeeded easily in stopping the stream before it pours down and sweeps away everything in its way. . . . However, the matter this time was more difficult. The ideas are not being called for by young men, rather Sayyid Qutb calls for them."[71]

Sayyid Qutb was exposed to al-Mawdudi's thought through *al-Muslimun* and through Arabic translations of al-Mawdudi's works, such as *Minhaj al-inqilab al-Islami* (The Method of Islamic Coup) and *al-Mustalahat al-Arba'a fi al-Qur'an* (The Four Terms in the Qur'an) that were issued by Al-'Urubah House for Islamic Call in Rawilpindy, Pakistan. Thus in the issues of the first year, 1951–1952, of *al-Muslimun* we find articles by al-Mawdudi entitled "The Spirit of Islam," "Proposals for the Islamic Constitution," "The Economic System in Islam," "The Basic Difference between Islam, Capitalism and Communism," and "Factor and Historical Influences behind the Capitalist System." The writings of al-Mawdudi thus became familiar in Egypt among Islamists in this period.

Sayyid Qutb had friends among prominent Muslim Indians, as we see in his firmly established relationship with Abu al-Hassan Ali al-Nadvi. This relationship is reflected in al-Nadvi's two books, *Madha khasira al-'alam bi-inhitat al Muslimin* (What Did the World Lose by the Degeneration of the Muslims?), for which Qutb wrote the introduction and commented on the author's concept of al-jahiliyyah (Paganism),[72] and *Mudhakirrat sa'ih fi-al-Mashriq al-'Arabi* (Memoirs of a Tourist in the Arab Orient), in which the al-Nadvi recounts his contacts with Qutb.

Besides the thirty-part commentary, which he completed in 1959 and the revision of its first thirteen parts, which was published in 1961, Qutb wrote major Islamic works considered by partisans to reflect the full maturity and purity of his movement-oriented Islamic conception. These works include *Hadha al-din* (This Religion of Islam), in 1962; *al-Mustaqbal li-hadha al-din* (Islam the Religion of the Future), in 1965; *Khasa'is al-tasawwur al-Islami* (Characteristics of the Islamic Conception), in 1962; *al-Islam wa-mushkilat al-hadarah* (Islam and the Problems of Civilization), in 1962; and his most controversial work by far and probably the one that was instrumental in sending him to the gallows, *Ma'alim fi al-tariq* (Milestones on the Road), in 1964. In addition, Qutb revised his seminal work, *Social Justice in Islam* during this time. Another major work, which is credited to this period and to the last days before his execution in August 1966, but appeared twenty years later, circa 1986, is *Muqawwimat al-tasawwur al-Islami* (Components of Islamic Conception).

AN OVERVIEW OF QUTB'S CONTROVERSIAL PRISON WRITINGS

Qutb's controversial prison writings, considered the revolutionary phase of his writing career, revolve around the idea that all societies on earth including the so-called Muslim societies are pagan societies (mujtama'at jahiliyyah), based on ignorance of the Divine guidance. Qutb writes that "our whole environment, people's beliefs and ideas, habits and art, rules and laws, is Jahiliyya even to the extent that what we consider to be Islamic culture, Islamic sources, Islamic philosophy and Islamic thought are also constructs of Jahiliyya.... We may say that any society is a Jahili society that does not dedicate itself to submission to God alone, in its beliefs and ideas, in its observance of worship, and in its legal regulations.... Our foremost objective is to change ... the Jahili system at its very roots."[73] This line of Qutb's thought led eventually to the excommunication (takfir) of all these pagan societies, and to radical Islamist jihadist interpretations of Qutb's ideas. There is no doubt that the prison environment and its repression were the nursery that hatched these takfir jihadist ideas. The first pagan "Kafir" (infidel) in Qutb's mind during his imprisonment was President Nasser and his regime.

Fi Zilal al-Qur'an (In the Shades of the Qur'an)

Fi Zilal al-Qur'an is the masterpiece work of Sayyid Qutb. It is written in a lucid and plain language. Paul Berman points out that "the total effect is almost sensual in its measured pace. The very title of *In the Shade of the Qur'an* conveys a vivid desert image, as if the Qur'an were a leafy palm tree, and we have only to open Qutb's pages to escape from the hot sun and refresh ourselves in the shade." Berman describes Qutb's work as a work large and solid enough to create its own shade, where its readers could repose and turn its pages, as he advised the students of the Koran (Qur'an) to do, in the earnest spirit of loyal soldiers reading their daily bulletin."[74]

Fi Zilal al-Qur'an is not a commentary in the traditional sense. Qutb avoids the grammatical, dialectical, and legal discourse that characterizes traditional commentaries, which according to Qutb, "conceals the Qur'an from my soul and my soul from Qur'an."[75] Instead, *Fi Zilal al-Qur'an* is a free expression of the author's feeling while reading Qur'anic verses. It is a "commentary of the heart" very similar in approach to Qutb's subjective poetry of the heart. The author's reflections and impressions while reading and living "in the shade of the Qur'an" fill him with spiritual, social, and humanistic inspirations, leading him, in addition, to freely express his feelings about the Qur'an's "wondrous" artistic beauty and its coordination of expression and portrayal.[76]

Sayyid Qutb's younger brother Muhammad, professor of Islamic Studies at King Abdul Aziz University in Mecca, describes *Fi Zilal al-Qur'an* as a commentary with a definite aim, which is "to disseminate the Islamic call and to delineate its system of education and discipline that is as essential for its continuity and progress today as it was for its prosperity throughout its unique history."[77]

Fi Zilal al-Qur'an has appeared in many editions and in many languages since the execution of Qutb on August 29, 1966. In addition to Cairo's Dar Ihy'a al-Kutub al-'Arabiyah's first and second edition of twenty volumes in 1952–1959, *Fi Zilal* was published in twenty volumes by Beirut's Dar al-Ma'arifah and Dar Ihya' al-Turath al-'Arabi in 1971, and most recently and (legally) a six-volume edition was published by Beirut's Dar al-Shuruq in 1973–1974. Many illegal reprints also have been and are still being circulated throughout the Arab and Muslim worlds.

Ma'alim fi al-Tariq (Milestones, 1964)

Qutb's revolutionary zeal is quite apparent in his most controversial work, *Milestones*, published in 1964, where he calls for the inevitable establishment of a true and just Islamic society and the overthrow through jihad of the existing Jahili (pagan) society, which is based on rebellion against God's sovereignty on earth and in the universe (al-Hakimiyyah). Qutb considered Egyptian and other Arab and Muslim societies as Jahili because God's sovereignty on earth in these societies is nonexistent.

The revival of Islam, according to Qutb in *Milestones*, is to be carried out and led by an Islamic "tali'ah" (vanguard) that will know the "milestones" of the road toward establishing the Islamic society with their basic reference being at all times the Holy Qur'an. Four chapters of *Milestones* were taken from Qutb's commentary *Fi Zilal al-Qur'an*. They were Chapter 2, "The Nature of the Qur'anic Method;" Chapter 8, "The Islamic Concept and Culture;" Chapter 4, "Jihad in the Cause of God;" and Chapter 3, "The Characteristics of the Islamic Society and the Correct Method of Its Formation."[78]

Following the uncovering of Qutb's 1965 underground vanguard apparatus and during the arrest, investigation and trial of Sayyid Qutb in 1965–1966, *Milestones* became prominent in Cairo's leading papers such as *al-Ahram*, *Ruz al-Yusuf* and *Al-Musawwar*, as well as the journal of the armed forces *al-Quwwat al-Musallaha*. Excerpts from the book were the focus of Qutb's questioning in December 1965 and his trial in April 1966 and were instrumental in sending him to the gallows on August 29, 1966.[79]

According to Radwan al-Sayyid, *Milestones* is "the founding text for the jihadist Islam. From between the lines of that booklet, all groups in jihadist Islam, in the Arab domain at least, came out. The text of Sayyid Qutb includes the two prevailing main theoretical ideas from which the jihadist groups set out and depend on: The idea of al-Jahiliyyah and the idea of al-Hakimiyyah."[80]

Sharif Yunis, like Radwan al-Sayyid, sees Qutb's 1965 underground vanguard apparatus that was guided by *Milestones* as "the moment of the ideological foundation of radical political Islam." Thus, the 1965 underground apparatus was not a simple extension of the Society of Muslim Brothers as mentioned in the government's accusations against Qutb, the apparatus, and the Muslim Brothers. Rather, "it was the first organizational expression for a new direction in the thought of political Islam which stands on the brink of secession from the political direction of the Muslim Brothers."[81]

The enemies of Sayyid Qutb claim that the purpose of *Milestones* is "to incite against what is not in Islam, poisoning the minds of Muslims and spreading corruption among them." In their view, *Milestones* is thus a word of truth by which falsity was intended, and in which Qutb established himself as a judge and ruler.[82]

A more sympathetic researcher, Ja'far Sheikh Idris, describes *Milestones* as representing "a new stage of the contemporary Islamic call in which propagation jumped from the stage of courtesy, hesitation, and apology to the stage of openness, challenge, and pride."[83]

Drafts of *Milestones* were distributed for study in Nasser's prisons during Qutb's imprisonment. Upon Qutb's release, the book was published by Wahbah Publishers in Cairo in 1964. Since that time, *Milestones* was reprinted many times, including the last legal printing by Beirut's Dar al-Shuruq, and was translated into many languages. *Milestones* has become, moreover, a basic reference for radical vanguard jihadist Islamic groups in the Arab and Muslim worlds in the last forty years.

Khasa'is al-tasawwur al-Islami was-muqawwimatih (The Characteristics and Components of Islamic Conception), Part 1 (1962)

This is the same work that Qutb promised to publish earlier titled *Islamic Thought Concerning God, Universe, Life and Man*.[84] The book revolves around the idea that it is necessary for the Muslim to have a comprehensive understanding of existence, humanity's place in this universal existence, the purpose of human existence, and consequently the method of human life, and the kind of regime that will realize this method, taking into consideration that the religion of Islam was revealed to lead humanity to realize the method of God on this earth, and to save humanity from leadership, method, and concepts that have deviated and gone astray.[85]

Qutb stresses in this work that his basic inspiration and first reference in the making this book is the Qur'an, having lived for a long period in the shades of the Qur'an.[86]

After concentrating on the confusions of distorted religious conceptions such as in Judaism and in Christianity, the book then focuses on the characteristics of Islamic conception.

The first, and the cornerstone, of all characteristics of Islamic conception is *al-Rabaniyyah* (Divinity). Islamic conceptions are the only Divinity-based conceptions.[87]

The second characteristic, which is derived from the first, is *al-thabat* (Stability) in the characteristics and components of Islamic conception. These characteristics and components are permanent, but the phenomena of practical life changes within the stable Islamic conception.[88]

The third characteristic is *al-shumul* (All-Encompassing), which revolves around the Divinity that rejects non-Islamic conceptions such as those of the so-called philosophers of Islam. This all-encompassing characteristic gives humans a deep understanding of life and the universe.[89]

The fourth characteristic is *al-tawazun* (Balance). In Islamic conceptions there are no excesses or exaggerations; therefore, this balance gives humans a leading role in running the affairs of this earth while keeping in mind the central role of Divinity and man's servitude ('Ubudiyyah) to God.[90]

The fifth characteristic is *al-Ijabiyyah* (Positiveness), which is the active positive relation between God and the universe on the one hand, and life and humanity on the other.[91]

The sixth characteristic is *al-Waqi'iyyah* (Realism), which is not based on abstract thought and ideals that do not exist in reality, but on an existing God who guides His creation to His existence.[92]

The seventh characteristic is *al-Tawheed* (Monotheism), which is also the first component of the Islamic conception based on Divinity and servitude to God. Islamic conception remains the only conception that is based on a pure monotheistic basis.[93]

Khasa'is al-Tasawwur al-Islami wa-muqawwimatih was written while Qutb was imprisoned in 1962. It was published by the same publishing firm that published the first and second editions of *Fi-Zilal al-Qur'an*, Dar Ihya' al-Kutub al-'Arabiyyah of Cairo. The most recent legal editions are being published by Beirut's Dar al-Shuruq.

Sayyid Qutb was working on Part 2 of this book, *The Components of Islamic Conception*, when he was executed on August 29, 1966.

Al-Islam wa-mushkilat al-hadarah (Islam and the Problems of Civilization, 1962)

The content of this work clearly indicates the impact of Qutb's stay in the United States in 1948–1950 on his thought. It is a rebuttal of Western materialistic civilization, which is leading humanity into the abyss and to destruction. To support his thesis, Qutb quotes extensively from a French eugenicist and a Nobel Prize winner (1912), Alexis Carrel, the author of *L'homme Cet Enconnu* (Man the Unknown, 1935) who lived and worked in the United States. Carrel posits that our knowledge of "al-insan" (The Human) is shrouded with "jahl mutbaq" (total ignorance).[94] This total ignorance, according to Qutb, is further exacerbated by setting up methods of human lives that are isolated from "Huda Alla" (God's guidance) and that persist in avoiding God's guidance.[95]

Qutb notes the contribution of Islamic civilization to the West in many areas of endeavors, and he traces the total ignorance to the separation of life and science from religion in European societies that led eventually to "al-fisam al-nakid" (the Hideous Schizophrenia).[96]

Darwinism or Darwinian theory, according to Carrel, was a setback to our understanding of humans, who became just another "animal" within the context of "the struggle of existence" and the natural selection process.[97] For Qutb, the human being is a very complicated being in organic, intellectual, and spiritual structures, and this complexity is clearly seen in every living person in each person's countless cellular structure. Our total ignorance is seen as well in the knowledge of our psychological and physiological complexes and the relations between feelings and the brain.[98]

Qutb devotes many pages to the negative development of Christianity from the time of the apostle Paul and Christianity's seizure of power at the time of Emperor Constantine (305 A.D.). Qutb asserts that Christianity became intertwined with paganism, unlike Islam, which was able to eradicate paganism totally. Qutb presents negatively the development of the phenomenon of monastic life in Christianity. It only added to the corruption of life in Europe, either extreme monasticism or extreme debauchery.[99]

When discussing the issue of "woman and relations between the two sexes," as exemplified in Islam, Qutb refers to his experiences in the United States in 1948–1950. Human sexual relations, according to an American young lady in her conversation with Qutb, are considered purely biological in nature just as the mating of any other animal. In another instance Qutb relates, a teacher told her students that premarital sexual relations between a 14-year-old girl and a 15-year-old boy are normal, for life is too short to delay. Qutb also gives several examples of how sexual permissiveness is encouraged in church gatherings and socials in the United States.[100]

Qutb dwells briefly on socioeconomic systems and traces the development of feudalism, capitalism, and Marxism in Europe and the West, each of which led in one way or another to enslaved humanity. Feudal crusaders were exposed to a more civilized Muslim world. Capitalism brought advancement to the individual and society, but at the same time it brought exploitation and the breakdown of morality and ethics as a result of absolute individual freedom. Marxism and its materialistic and dialectical systems, on the other hand, totally ignore the presence of the God who created the universe.[101]

Qutb quotes extensively from Alexis Carrel to show that contemporary civilization does not suit humanity. The modern factory's impact on the physiological and mental state of the laboror has been ignored in the organization of industrial life. The goal of maximum production with the least cost ignored the nature of the people who operate the machines, and as a result it alienated them. Thus, the assembly line robs the worker of the mental capacities and turns the worker into a machine performing the same partial task thousands of times daily. Carrel calls for the remaking of the human being by stressing each person's uniqueness, and in order to do that, we must destroy the structures of school, factory, and office and reject the principles of the technological civilization itself.[102]

Qutb cites many examples concerning the disintegration of European society as exemplified by one of the most advanced countries, Sweden, which has the most extensive welfare system in Europe and the West. Qutb quotes an Egyptian reporter of *al-Akhbar* daily of Cairo in Sweden, Mousa Sabri, who cites many statistics as to divorce rates, unmarried mothers, childless marriages, alcohol addiction, emotional disturbances, and other social ills. Qutb attributes this breakdown of society to the lack of faith in God.[103]

According to Qutb, the only assured way to overcome all the problems of civilization is to adopt the Islamic method of life. Islam does not reject industrial civilization, the roots of which are found in Islamic experimental science, but Islam does reject materialistic philosophies.[104]

Al-Islam wa-mushkilat al-hadarah was written during Qutb's imprisonment and was published in 1962 by the same company that published the first and second editions of *Fi Zilal al-Qur'an* and the first edition of *Khasa'is al-tasawwur al-Islami*, Dar Ihya' al-Kutub al-'Arabiyyah of Cairo.

Hadha al-Din (The Religion of Islam) and *al-Mustaqbal li-hadha al-Din* (Islam, the Religion of the Future)

Following the completion of his *Fi Zilal al-Qur'an* circa 1961, Sayyid Qutb targeted his writings to the imprisoned Muslim Brothers to boost their spirits amid their sufferings and torture, calling upon them to be steadfast and to persist in raising the banner of the Islamic way.[105] As a result he produced two books.

In *Hadha al-Din* (the Religion of Islam), Qutb says that Islam's realization in the life of humans "depends on the exertions of men themselves, within the limits of their human capacities."[106] More important "in determining victory or defeat in however the degree to which they truly, in themselves, represent this path (of Islam), and are able to give it practical expression in their personal conduct and behavior. . . . The truth of the faith is not fully established until a struggle (mujahadah) is undertaken on its behalf among people. . . . A struggle by word of mouth, by propagation, by exposition, by refuting the false and the baseless. . . . In this struggle misfortune and suffering will be encountered. . . . In times of victory, too, patience is needed."[107]

Qutb warns his readers of "idleness and negativism [which] contradict the purpose of human existence, as conceived by Islam, namely the vice-regency of God on earth, and the use of all that God has subordinated to man for the purposes of constructive activity."[108]

Qutb reminds the readers of the humble beginning of the first "brilliant generation of Muslims" [that is the Prophet, companions and followers] and assures them that "humanity, today and tomorrow, is not incapable, either by virtue of its inner nature or by virtue of its potentialities, of succeeding once again in its exertions provided that it takes the divinity ordained path as its guide."[109]

Qutb devotes considerable space to the rise of Islam and the negative environment surrounding the rise (age of ignorance) in the Arab world and the world surrounding it. Islam's rise and victory are attributed to the "potential of human nature to an exceptional generation of men, decreed and willed by God." Qutb calls the rise of Islam and the "brilliant" first generation "that unique leap forward in the history of mankind."[110]

The "first high tide of Islam" left much influence and many legacies in the formative stages of contemporary civilization. Once again Qutb dwells on the concept of Jahili society and Islamic society. He writes that there are two parties all over the world: "that of God and that of Satan. The party of God stands beneath the banner of God and bears His insignia. The party of the Devil embraces every community, group, people, race, and individual who do not stand under the banner of God. The *umma* (community) is the group of people bound together by belief, which constitutes their nationality. Land, race, language, lineage, common material interests are not enough, either singly or in combination, to form *umma*."[111]

Qutb concludes that "what is required is that a believing group ('usbah/tali'ah) place their hands in the hands of God and then march forth, the promise of God to them being the overriding reality for them, and the pleasure of God being their first and last aim."[112]

Hadha al-din (The Religion of Islam) was first published during Qutb's imprisonment in 1962 by Cairo's Dar al-Qalam. Since then it has been printed and reprinted, having been published legally by Beirut's Dar al-Shuruq in recent years. Likewise, it has been translated into many languages.

Al-Mustaqbal li-hadha al-Din (Islam, the Religion of the Future, 1965)

Qutb warns that "humanity is heading for the deep, awful precipice of destruction. The sages are ringing the bell . . . calling for help and rescue (and) searching for a 'saviour' with certain imagined features and properties. But these features and properties belong to this religion of Islam and to nothing else."[113]

Qutb classifies the non-Islamic system as "Jahiliyyah" because "these ignorant systems are built on the very same unsound basis from which Islam came to liberate people . . . and to demolish those ideologies which require the worship of man by man. God alone should be worshipped."[114]

Qutb focuses on the phenomenon prevalent in the West and in non-Islamic systems, which he terms "the hideous schizophrenia," the segregation or separation of religion from life. "Once people deviated from God's system, they had to continue following the fatuous ideologies of their own invention, leading predictably to their present miserable state wherein individuals suffer the terrible consequences of their ideological shortcoming, moaning from the pain inflicted upon them by their fellow men."[115]

Qutb devotes many pages to the development of Christianity from its earliest stages and traces the roots in Christianity that led to separation of religion from life, such as "the strictness of the Church regarding asceticism and abstinence and the moral laxity of the clergymen and the perfidiousness of their private lives." He adds, "The church, taking advantage of its disputes with emperors and kings over political power, exploited the people in the worst ways by imposing exorbitant taxes which it collected directly."[116]

Qutb envisions that the end of the white man is coming, as attested by English philosopher Bertrand Russell. According to Qutb, "the civilization of the white man has already exhausted its restricted

usefulness . . . because [it] did not issue from that Divine source and
origin [but] was established on bases repugnant to the nature of life
and human beings. . . . It is the problem of the hideous schizophrenia, which is the common denominator between all the systems prevailing in the white man's world where the Russians, the American,
the English, the French, the Swiss, the Swedes and all those who follow in the steps, whether in the east or west . . . all these stand on
the same precarious footing. . . . At present, one hears voices of
alarm coming from everywhere warning mankind of its catastrophic
end under the white man's faithless civilization."[117]

Once again and as he did earlier in his *Islam and the Problems of
Civilization*, Qutb quotes extensively from Dr. Alexis Carrel's *Man
the Unknown* to show clearly the many negative aspects of current
materialistic civilization. Likewise, Qutb quotes from former American Secretary of State John Foster Dulles's book *War and Peace* on
the encroachments of materialistic industrial civilization. Qutb criticizes both Carrel and Dulles because the "saviour" they are searching for emanates from the "science of man" according to Carrel and
"the church and its fathers" according to Dulles.[118]

According to Qutb, Islam alone "is recognized as the sole saviour
from the disastrous dangers toward which humanity is heading, at-
tracted by the glittering illusions of material civilization."[119]

Al-Mustaqbal li-hadha al-din (Islam the Religion of the Future)
was first published, after the release of Qutb from prison in 1965,
by the same publishing firm that published *Milestones* in 1964,
Wahbah Publishers in Cairo. Like Qutb's other books and tracts,
this work was printed, reprinted, and translated into many languages.

Qutb's Prison Poems

Qutb composed poems that were smuggled out of prison and eventually were published by Islamists in Jordan. These poems are found in the
periodical *al-Kifah al-Islami* (The Islamic Struggle), no. 29, July 26, 1957,
and in an anthology, which appeared also in Amman, Jordan, titled *Lahn
al-Kifah* (The Melody of Struggle). These poems were clearly written in
opposition to President Nasser and his regime. In "Hubalon . . . Hubal,"
Nasser is compared to the pre-Islamic pagan idol Hubal, a chief deity of
Mecca and al-Ka'bah. Nasser is being worshipped by the sheep of the
flock, that is, the masses. The few free men are in prison. In the second
but much larger poem, "My Brother" (Akhi), Qutb once again targeted

his words against President Nasser, and in the process he calls on his fellow Islamist brothers who are in prison to be steadfast in their struggle and not to turn back.[120] A sample from each poem follows:

Hubalon . . . Hubal

Hubalon . . . Hubal
It is the symbol of stupidity, ignorance and deception,
Don't ask, O! my friend, those throngs
To whom belong worship, reward and submission,
Leave them, they are only the sheep of the flock,
Her worshipped one is an idol which
Uncle Sam sees,
The dollar guaranteed to bestow on it respect
And the flock moved around in dumbness . . . O! hero

Hubalon . . . Hubal
It is the symbol of treason, treachery and deception,
Fake glories were formulated for him,
And the dumb one believed them to be true,
The free and proud one denounced the
Explicit lie and refuted it;
But free men in this time are few in number,
So let them enter the terrible prison
And have good patience,
And let them see the most cruel novel
For every tyrant has an end,
And for every creature there is death,
Hubalon . . . Hubal
Hubalon . . . Hubal

My Brother

My brother, you are free behind the dams;
My brother, you are free with those fetters;
If you seek protection in God,
The slyness of slaves will not harm you

My brother, the armies of darkness will be annihilated,
And a new dawn will rise in the universe;
So set the radiance of your soul free
You will see the dawn gazing at us from afar.

My brother, today I am headstrong;
I demolish the rocks of the unshakable mountains;
Tomorrow I will crush the heads of the serpents
With the pickaxe of salvation until they are annihilated.

My brother, if we die we shall meet our beloved ones,
For the gardens of our God were prepared for us,
And their birds fluttered around us;
So blessed are we in the abodes of immortality.

My brother, proceed and do not turn back,
Your road has been tinged by blood,
And do not turn around here or there,
And do not look at anything except heaven.

QUTB'S RELEASE FROM PRISON, 1964

During his ten-year imprisonment, Qutb worked very closely with
fellow inmate Muhammad Yusuf Hawwash in studying the Qur'an.
Muhammad Hawwash, according to his wife, "would benefit from
and learn the thought, culture, knowledge, and depth of the martyr
Sayyid, while Sayyid would learn about the history of the Muslim
Brothers, their organization, methodology, and anything related to
the 'Society' from the martyr Muhammad, because he had joined it
before him." Hawwash told his wife, "Every chapter and every
phrase in the books of Ustaadh (Teacher) Sayyid, I know when it
was written, what the occasion was, and the debate over it when it
appeared as it did." Hawwash became an avid reader and critic of
Qutb's writings. Qutb and Hawwash concluded that the Islamic
movement had reached a stage that was very similar to the stage experienced by the early Muslims as a minority of believers in Mecca,
that is, the stage of weakness. Therefore Muslims would have to prepare themselves by concentrating on translating the creed and the
ideas into a perceptible Islamic way of life led by a vanguard.[121]
    This explains why Qutb handpicked Hawwash to be his desig-
nated successor as the spiritual leader of the underground vanguard
apparatus following Qutb's arrest in August 1965. Subsequently
Qutb and Hawwash were executed by the Nasser regime in 1966.
    Between 1962 and 1964, vanguard families were organized in the
prisons such as al-Qanater Prison. The aim of these families was to

study together and to be guided by directed books including the preliminary chapters of the books *Ma'alim* and *Fi Zilal al-Qur'an* as well as the explication of Ibn Katheir and other books by Ibn Hazm, al-Shafi'i, Ibn Taymiyyah, Ibn 'Abd al-Wahhab, Muhammad Qutb, and Abu al-'Ala al-Mawdudi. Some Islamist prisoners refused to join these families because the program did not develop from the legitimate frameworks of the Muslim Brothers such as the Guidance Council. Sayyid Qutb admits that he had no "executive administrative duty in the Society which gives him the legitimate right in putting a movement plan. . . . The Guidance Council alone has this right and it is the one which is authorized. I am neither a member of the Council nor authorized by it in any thing."[122]

Qutb was released from prison in May 1964 as a result of the personal intervention of the late Iraqi President 'Abd al-Salam 'Aref. Sayyid Qutb wrote, "After my release, his excellency the ambassador of Iraq in the United Arab Republic visited me and conveyed to me the greetings of his excellency President 'Abd al-Salam 'Aref. The ambassador also told me that the president is happy for the success of his mediation with his excellency President Gamal 'Abd al-Nasser. He inquired about my health and whether I had any requests he could fulfill."[123] According to 'Umar al-Talmasani, the third General Guide of the Muslim Brothers (that is, after Hassan al-Bana and Hassan al-Hudaybi), Sayyid Qutb told al-Talmasani upon Qutb's release from prison in 1964, when al-Talmasani was in prison, that the Iraqi republic wanted Qutb to work in Iraq in the field of education and that Qutb wanted al-Talmasani's opinion in the matter. Al-Talmasani told Qutb that he should accept that offer, out of fear for Qutb from the regime. Ultimately, Qutb decided to stay in Egypt "to defend his convictions."[124]

CHAPTER 8

MARTYRDOM, POSTHUMOUS IMPACT, AND GLOBAL JIHAD, 1965–PRESENT

The violence with which the Brothers were treated in 1954 based on an incident contrived for them and not devised by them which is al-Manshiyah . . . established the idea of retaliation by force against aggression if it is repeated. If we had known that arrest is merely an arrest, which ends up with a fair trial and legal penalties—even on the basis of positive laws, which are in effect, nobody would have thought of retaliation by force against aggression. I know that there is no practical value now in deciding upon this truth. However, it is a truth which I must record in my last words. *(Sayyid Qutb on the eve of his execution in 1966)*

Sayyid Qutb's call for loyalty to God's oneness and to acknowledge God's sole authority and sovereignty was the spark that ignited the Islamic revolution against the enemies of Islam at home and abroad. The bloody chapters of this revolution continue to unfold day after day. *(Ayman al-Zawahiri of al-Qaʿeda, 2001)*

QUTB'S 1965 UNDERGROUND VANGUARD APPARATUS

The beginning of this group goes back to 1962 when Egyptian Islamists Zaynab al-Ghazali and 'Abd al-Fattah Isma'il, with the
knowledge of the General Guide of the Brothers, Hassan al-
Hudaybi, established a study group. They contacted the imprisoned
Qutb through his sister Hamidah and asked for his guidance through
a course of readings, including his writings *Fi-Zilal al-Qur'an*, the
rough drafts of his controversial work *Ma'alim* (Milestones), and his
instructions. The group decided with Qutb's instructions and the approval of al-Hudaybi, to undergo thirteen-year educational program
cycles until 75 percent of the citizens of Egypt who would be sur-
veyed were firmly convinced of the need for Islamic rule and that
Islam is both a religion and a state. Then the group would call for
an Islamic state. If the survey found only 25 percent who were convinced of the need for an Islamic state, then the group would revert
back to the thirteen-year educational program cycles. (The thirteen
years are equivalent to the Prophet's years of Islamic propagation in
Mecca).[1]

Following his release from prison in May 1964, Qutb was contacted by 'Abd al-Fattah Isma'il, a Muslim Brother who was imprisoned in 1954 but released in 1956. Isma'il asked Qutb to become
a spiritual advisor to the group of Brothers that had been in touch
with him since 1962.

According to Qutb, he agreed to serve as an advisor to the group
only to discover its underground nature by December 1964 or January 1965. However, Qutb decided to continue with his task, hoping that his spiritual leadership of this clandestine apparatus, which
had been in existence since 1959 under 'Abd al-Fattah Isma'il, 'Ali
'Ashmawi and others, would change its goal, which until then had
been vengeance for the Muslim Brothers' debacle of 1954. Instead,
Qutb wanted to abandon this and to develop in the process the vanguard of Islamic society, envisioned in *Ma'alim*, which requires long-
range Islamic education. Qutb chose his prison mate from 1954 to
1964 and the person who was most familiar with his thought,
Muhammad Yusuf Hawwash, to be his heir to the spiritual leadership of the apparatus.

Some leaders of the apparatus in their meetings with Qutb, however, began to raise questions concerning to the imminent possibility of the apparatus being uncovered and the inevitable reaction that
would undoubtedly entail the replay of the 1954 "inquisition." Fol-

lowing discussions in early May 1965, it was decided to prepare contingency plans "to repel aggression if it occurs" (radd al i'tida idha waqa'), which would involve seventy vanguard members of the secret apparatus. These would entail, among other things, the assassination of public figures in order to create enough confusion in the country to allow the apparatus and its members to disappear. Before his arrest, Qutb instructed the apparatus to cancel the plan, only to follow it with another message that instructed the members to execute the plan if the regime uncovered their activities. The plan was never carried out.[2]

Before his execution in August 1966, Sayyid Qutb wrote: "The violence with which the Brothers were treated in 1954 based on al-Manshiyah (Alexandria) incident contrived for them and not devised by them is what established the idea of retaliation by force against aggression if it is repeated. . . . If we had known that arrest is merely an arrest which ends up with a fair trial and legal penalties—even on the basis of positive laws which are in effect—nobody would have thought of retaliation by force against aggression. I know there is no practical value now in deciding upon this truth. However, it is a truth which I must record in my last words."[3]

QUTB'S REARREST AND EXECUTION, 1965–1966

On July 30, 1965, Sayyid Qutb's brother Muhammad was arrested without charge. Sayyid protested this arbitrary action by the government in writing and in person, only to be arrested himself a few days later on August 9. The Qutb brothers' arrest signaled the beginning of the government's massive arrest of Muslim Brothers under a total blackout of news lasting through August. This heavy-handed response by the government came in the aftermath of the alleged confessions of one of the leaders of the apparatus. The confessions of this leader, according to some sources, played a decisive role in implicating Qutb and others in the alleged conspiracy to overthrow the regime. It is said that in return for his damaging and incriminating confessions, this leader was treated with leniency, was released from prison early and was allowed to emigrate to the United States.[4] The first public disclosure of the alleged conspiracy was made in the semiofficial daily newspaper *al-Ahram* on September 7, 1965, in which it was alleged that the Muslim Brothers in the secret apparatus were planning to assassinate public figures, including Pres-

ident Nasser, and to destroy factories, public utilities, means of communications, and other structures and resources in order to create
enough confusion to possibly cause the downfall of the Nasser regime and its replacement by the apparatus.[5]

Much publicity was given to the alleged conspiracy in Egypt's
daily and periodical press. As noted earlier, Qutb and his work
Ma'alim fi al-tariq received a big share of this publicity, which could
be seen in the daily press and in the issues of such leading Cairene
periodicals as *Ruz al-Yusuf*, *al-Musawwar*, and the journal of the
armed forces, *al-Quwwat al-Musallahah*.

In addition, *Ma'alim fi al-tariq* (Milestones on the Road) received
the special attention of the state security prosecutor's office in building its case against Sayyid Qutb. Excerpts from the book were the
focus during Qutb's questioning on December 21, 1965, and during
his trial by a military court on April 12, 1966.[6] Hassan Hanafi commented on the rearrest of Sayyid Qutb by saying: "No sooner had
the wound of the first imprisonment healed then it was opened, and
widened until it festered in the second imprisonment. The Egyptian
Revolution is responsible for *Milestones on the Road* because had
Sayyid Qutb not been within the walls of prisons, the social stage
would have developed into a revolutionary struggle and he would
have become one of the great revolutionaries the like of Guevara,
Mao Tze Dong, Hoche Minh, al-Afaghani, Capucci and al-Khomeini.
The Egyptian Revolution is responsible for transforming the battle
of Islam and Capitalism into the battle of Islam and al-Jahiliyyah."[7]

A sample of Qutb's controversial thought from *Ma'alim*, which
was quoted by the prosecutor's office runs as follows:

It is necessary that there should be a *vanguard* which sets out with
this detemination and then keeps walking on the path, marching
through the vast ocean of "Jahiliyyah" which has encompassed
the entire world. During its course, it should keep itself somewhat
aloof from this all encompassing "Jahiliyyah" and should keep
some ties with it. It is necessary that this *vanguard* should know
the land marks and the milestones of the road toward this goal. I
have written "Milestones" for this *vanguard*, which I consider to
be a waiting reality about to be materialized.

Our foremost objective is to change the practices of this society.
Our aim is to change the "Jahili" system at its very roots, this system which is fundamentally at variance with Islam and which,

with the help of force and oppression, is keeping us from living the sort of life which is demanded by our Creator.

The homeland of the Muslim, in which he lives and which he defends, is not a piece of land; the nationality of the Muslim, by which he is identified, is not the nationality determined by a government; the family of the Muslim in which he finds solace and which he defends is not blood relationships; the flag of the Muslim, which he honours and under which he is martyred is not the flag of a country; and the victory of the Muslim, which he celebrates and for which he is thankful to God, is not a military victory.[8]

On August 21, 1966, Sayyid Qutb, his former colleague in prison and his successor in leading the secret apparatus Mohammad Yusuf Hawwash, and the person who was the first contact link between Qutb and the apparatus, 'Abd al-Fattah Isma'il, were sentenced to death by hanging by a military tribunal for their alleged attempt to overthrow by force the regime of President Nasser. Despite protests from all parts of the world, including protests from Amnesty International, the head of the lawyers' union in France, lawyers from Switzerland, Morocco, and Sudan, and requests for clemency from prominent Arab and Muslim personalities, the sentence of execution was carried out in the early hours of the morning of Monday, August 29, 1966.

There was no logical explanation or justification for the executions of 1966. The regime of the late President Nasser did not need these executions in order to firmly establish the pillars of rule, as he needed such executions at the end of 1954 when he liquidated the elements whom he saw as determined to destroy him at the formative stages of his regime. The Egyptian political system in 1966 was standing on solid ground popularly, politically, economically, and internationally. These executions and the preceding executions of 1954 will remain a black page in the history of the Arab liberation movement, which the late president symbolized.

It is true that President Nasser's regime was able to eliminate Sayyid Qutb physically. However, the same thing cannot be said of the regime's attempts to eliminate his revolutionary ideas contained in his prison writings. By eliminating Qutb, the regime, intentionally or unintentionally, created a new martyr for the Islamic resurgence of the past forty years, whose revolutionary writings have become a manifesto for Islamists and global jihadists everywhere.

While President Nasser's pan-Arab ideas were reaching their zenith by the time of Qutb's execution in 1966, forty years later these same ideas have been marginalized by the Arab regimes and have failed to win the hearts of the Arab masses. In addition, the unmitigated failures of the Arab regimes to build socioeconomic justice in their societies, and their failures in both war and peace with the Israelis, have only served as a fertile ground for the proliferation and growth of Qutb's ideas in both the Arab and Muslim worlds.

Qutb's books have been translated into most languages that Muslims read. For example, the translation of his books into Persian has been carried out by the "Rahbar of the Islamic Republic, Ayatullah Sayyid Ali Khamenei himself."[9] In the 1960s and 1970s many Afghan religious figures were influenced by the Muslim Brothers. Qutb's ideas were of interest in the faculty of religious law in Kabul, and "the scholar (later President) Burhanuddin Rabbani translated him into the Afghan language of Dari." Moreover, Qutb's writing has "exercised a formative influence on the Taliban."[10]

Qutb's influence has been felt on the Moro Islamic Liberation Front in the Philippines and on Islamists in Europe and the former Soviet republics. Qutb's thought has spread as well with al-Qa'eda's international network.[11]

As for the impact of Qutb's thought on Arab countries neighboring Egypt, one can detect it in the Islamic Salvation Front and the Armed Islamic Group (GIA) in Algeria as well as in HAMAS in Palestine.[12] The Islamic jihad in Palestine views itself as "the Islamic vanguard Sayyid Qutb talks about." Thus, Qutb's writing constitutes the guide for the ideas and practices of the movement.[13] Sa'id Hawwa, a leader of the Muslim Brothers in Syria, translates the concepts of Mawdudi and Qutb concerning al-Jahiliyyah and al-Hakimiyyah in an extreme excommunicating spirit, calling for the militarization of the Muslim Brothers and their transformation into "fighting families and phalanges."[14]

Had the regime not executed Sayyid Qutb, there would have been a fair possibility that Qutb would have clarified many of the controversial terms he had posited in his writings. Instead, with Qutb gone, his writings were left wide open for radical interpretations of all kinds, which led many circles in the West since September 11, 2001, to dub him "the godfather ideologue of Osama bin Laden, Ayman al-Zawahiri, and al-Qa'eda."

One only needs to search the web for Sayyid Qutb to realize the extent to which he has been demonized throughout the world, and the extent to which his ideas have been presented in the West by many anti-Arab and anti-Muslim sources as forming the ideological corner-stone of the so-called Islamic Terror.

Among the more prominent widely read articles appearing on the web since September 11, 2001, which focus totally on Sayyid Qutb, is Paul Berman's article titled "The Philosopher of Islamic Terror," which was published by the *New York Times Sunday Magazine*, on March 23, 2003, but which has been disseminated widely since then via web sites.

Likewise, Sayyid Qutb's writings have been harshly treated by some Muslim clerics in the Arab world. His Qur'anic commentary *In the Shades of the Qur'an* and his controversial *Milestones* have been declared as innovations and deviations from the Islamic dogma and teachings. According to these clerics, a beginning student of knowledge "who is incapable of distinguishing between the fat and the thin" should not read the writings of Qutb because they would misguide the student and lead the student to deviation. That is what has happened in the case of the al-Takfir wa-al-Hijrah (Penance and Retreat) group in Egypt who were misled by Qutb's writings and who as a result deviated from the Islamic dogma.[15]

Likewise, Qutb's notion put forth in *Milestones* that claims, "(the Islamic Ummah / Nation)" has ceased to exist, and most recently re-iterated by his follower, Shaykh Salman al-'Awda, in his *al-Ummah al-Gha'ibah* (The Absent Ummah / Nation), to excommunicate the whole nation on the grounds of Jahiliyyah (Paganism), are rejected totally as innovations and deviations, for the Islamic Ummah is for-ever present as a reality and will always include among its members truthful believers, hypocrites, and disbelievers.[16] These deviations and innovations, such as those of Sayyid Qutb and others, lead to "evil mistakes in the Islamic dogma," say those refuting Qutb's writ-ings. Accordingly, it is "obligatory upon the people of knowledge to clarify the truth . . . (and) whoever refutes them, then he is regarded as a *mujaahid* in the Path of Allah."[17]

Qutb's Last Recorded Ideas before His Execution: *Muqawwimat al-Tasawwur al-Islami* (Components of the Islamic Conception, circa 1986)

The last words and ideas of Sayyid Qutb are exemplified in his book *Muqawwimat al-Tasawwur al-Islami* (Components of the Is-lamic Conception), which he finished writing prior to his execution on August 29, 1966. The book was not published, however, until twenty years later (circa 1986), with the last two chapters "Haqiqat al-haya" (The Truth of Life) and "Haqiqat al-insan" (The Truth of Man) missing even though an outline of each chapter is presented in the book. The following chapters are included:

1. "Wijhat al-bahth" (Direction of Research)
2. "Muqawwimat al-tasawwur al-Islami" (Components of the Islamic Conception)
3. "Uluhiyyah wa-'Ubudiyyah" (Divinity and Servitude to God)
4. "Haqiqat al-'Uluhiyyah" (The Truth of Divinity)
5. "Haqiqat al-Kawn" (The Truth of the Universe)

In his introduction to the book, Muhammad Qutb writes that his brother Sayyid put in this book in particular the essence of his belief experience. Sayyid Qutb also reached the pinnacle of his expression in it, which expresses extremely profound issues in gushing flowing terms as if it is a hymn that is sung and not an idea that is "formulated."[18]

Again, and following the example of *Milestones*, Sayyid Qutb posits controversial ideas based on an essential idea that there are two rules for conceptualizing life throughout times: Islam and Jahiliyyah. From a religious law perspective, Jahiliyyah is basically not valid from the beginning. It has no right to exist. Subsequently, there is no meeting between Islam and al-Jahiliyyah at any stage of the road. The crucial separation is at the crossroad. There is neither jesting nor equivocation in the crucial separation. For such an instance Almighty God says in Qur'an 5:44: "*Do not be afraid of men but fear me. And do not buy with my verses a little price. Those who do not rule by what God sent, they are infidels.*"[19]

Qutb again repeats the idea of the believing vanguard who will carry the message and transform it into a perceptible reality and who recognize the nature of Islam and know its means. The vanguard recognizes human real needs in a growing renewing life, a life in which dynamism is one of its qualities and is derived from the Islamic conception itself. The vanguard is proud of this conception and its requirements in order to confront al-Jahiliyyah, its conceptions, values and situations. It disapproves from the beginning, in the whole and in details, the legitimacy of the existence of this earthly international Jahiliyyah.[20]

Sayyid Qutb defines the Components of the Islamic Conception as being "a collection of basic creed truths which establishes in the mind and heart of the Muslim that special conception of existence and the creative ability and providential will behind it, as well as the ties and connections which exist between this existence and this will."[21] These (components) are not made by humans or the human mind; "rather the latter receives them from their divine source . . . and it has to abide by what it receives from that authentic source in the linguistic or idiomatic indication of the text in which these components are mentioned without interpretation—as long as the text is precise as seen in Qur'an 59:7: *What the Apostle brought forth to you, abide by it, and abstain from what He prohibited you.*"[22]

Sayyid Qutb also rejects the idea that there is any relationship between the Islamic concepts and that grim depressing picture, which is called " 'Islamic philosophy' or 'scholastic theology' or 'theology' . . . which is remote from the nature of Islamic concepts and the nature of Islamic methodology."[23]

Starting from Islamic constants, which include the belief that Almighty God "created everything in this existence," Qutb writes that the Islamic concepts reveal that persistent motion and continuous transformation are the constant and steady law of this novel and ephemeral existence. This persistent motion and this continuous transformation are particularly the law of life and its rule. However, Qutb ascribes this persistent motion and this continuous transformation to God's will and His preordaining.[24]

Sayyid Qutb deals with the position of Islam vis-à-vis "distorted Judaism" and "distorted Christianity" and their false and devious beliefs that conflict with the essence of Islam which is "monotheism." Although they do not deny God, "they were as such false beliefs because they deviated from the heavenly origin." Starting from the Islamic principle of no compulsion in religion, Sayyid Qutb writes that Islam gave Jews and Christians (People of the Book) freedom of choice: either embracing Islam or paying al-Jizyah (poll-tax). Islam guaranteed protection and care for them and safeguarded their souls, honor, and property. Islam treated them amicably by permitting Muslims to marry from them. Islam also allowed Muslims to eat from their food. The Apostle of God and his successors entrusted them to the Muslims' charge. According to Qutb, the People of the Book always conspired against the Muslims and Islam. The Crusades, the brutal massacres of Muslims in al-Andalus (Muslim Spain), and modern imperialism were examples of the total war that the People of the Book declared against Islam and Muslims. In addition, the catastrophe caused by the Tartars in their destruction of Baghdad and the caliphate was a result of the slyness of Jews and Christians.[25]

There are some who severely criticize Qutb's position vis-à-vis Jews and Christians and accuse him of interpreting Qur'anic verses, which are called "the verses of the sword," especially the Jizyah (poll-tax) verse, which calls for fighting the People of the Book until they pay the poll-tax out of humiliation. The Jizyah (poll-tax) in this context is "the land tax imposed on infidels out of humiliation and servility." According to 'Abd al-Ghani 'Imad, this prevailing attitude in political Islam "does not take into consideration the preponderant opinion among jurisprudents which considers al-Jizyah (poll-tax) as a cash alternative for performing the duty of defending the homeland and the soul."[26]

QUTB'S CONTROVERSIAL APPROACHES

Individual Interpretation of the Qur'an

Qutb's writings, like those of other Muslim revolutionary writers, are grounded in and justified by quotations from the Qur'an. Yvonne Yazbeck Haddad points out the following:

> They quote them [Qur'anic verses] repeatedly in an effort to instill Islamic consciousness, calling on fellow Muslims to renounce defeatism and the feelings of subservience, irrelevance and inferiority which appear to be the by-products of European colonialism and repeated Israeli victories. . . . As citizens of the best nation, Muslims are assured of the leadership role. Their ideology supersedes that of the two contending systems in the world, capitalism and Marxism. Muslims need not choose between one or the other. They have their own superior order which has divine validation.[27]

It is clearly apparent that Qutb's long and serious study of the Qur'an, which he began in 1939, is clearly manifested in all the controversial works that Qutb wrote in prison, including his last work that he was still writing in prison on the eve of his execution on August 29, 1966; *Muqawwimat al-tasawwur al-Islami*.

Concerning the Qur'anic quotations, Sayyid Qutb held that the

Qur'an is the first source from which the Muslim derives the components of Islamic conception. Qutb adds that "this is a conviction we derive from long companionship with this Qur'an and long personal practice of writing for a long period of my lifetime."[28] Qutb describes the method he uses when quoting the Qur'an as follows:

> I followed a methodology which might somehow be strange to the modern reader who grew accustomed—even in pure Islamic research—to see Qur'anic verses being brought in for mere quotation. The methodology which we followed here is to the contrary of this. Our methodology attempts to make the Qur'anic text the original which undertakes deciding upon the facts which the research consists of, and to make our human expression a mere helping factor which makes the Qur'anic text understandable—as far as possible—for the reader. We want to establish familiarity between the reader of this research and the Qur'an itself. Ultimately, we want this reader to grow accustomed to dealing directly with the Qur'an itself whenever he needs the truth in one of the affairs of life and he wants to arrive at the truth in these affairs.[29]

Sayyid Qutb's Qur'anic approach is similar to that of the Reformation's biblical approach. Michael J. Thompson makes a comparison as follows:

> All forms of fundamentalism are an attempt to reach back to the past to regenerate the present. . . . It had its greatest moment within Christianity itself during the Reformation with Luther's entire project of reinventing Christianity through the return to the purity of Christian texts (with the doctrine of *sola scriptura*) and by turning away from the institutions of the church . . . toward the content of the individual's soul.[30]

'Imad criticizes Qutb's approach and sees a danger in setting free the concept of individual freedom in understanding the Qur'an, which leads to the destruction of a tremendous heritage of rules and methodologies that regulates the principles of interpretation and rules of interpretation (tafsir) of the Qur'an. 'Imad adds that free individual interpretation will only open the door wide for contradictory interpretations depending on the number of groups and readers. "Leaving the interpretation for the individual to understand the Qur'an according to one's ability is an extremely serious matter since most people find it difficult to read the Qur'an; so can these understand and interpret it?" 'Imad concludes.[31]

Sayyid Qutb's approach, which was expressed earlier in *Khasa'is al-tasawwur al-Islami* and led to radical interpretations was criticized earlier by the General Guide of the Muslim Brothers, Hassan Isma'il al-Hudaybi, during the debacles of 1954 and 1966. Al-Hudaybi was in prison during this whole period. Al-Hudaybi wrote his now famous tract, *Du'at la qudat* (Preachers and not Judges), to rebut Sayyid Qutb's controversial prison thought and the resulting radical interpretations.

Al-Hudaybi writes that an individual interpretation of the Qur'an, which shies away from the "Hadith" (Prophet's sayings), "violates the decisive and explicit texts of the Noble Qur'an and undoubtedly goes astray in knowing the truth of God's judgment." Al-Hudaybi clarifies his stand as follows:

> It is incumbent upon anyone who embarks upon dealing with the Holy Qur'an and the noble prophetic sayings that he is qualified for this, by fulfilling the conditions put by God on the one who embarks upon this matter. It is imposed upon him to investigate according to his capacity the ruling of the Holy Qur'an, the sayings of the Prophet, the ranks of the transmitters, the qualities of the transmitters, and distinguishing between authentic attributed sayings from weak attributed sayings. It is also imposed upon him to learn how to establish the proofs by which he distinguishes between truth and falsity and how to deal with what is apparently conflicting.[32]

Criticism by Sheikh Yusuf al-Qaradawi

The noted Egyptian Islamist propagator and a leading Islamic thinker Sheikh Yusuf al-Qaradawi rebuts Qutb's selective approach when quoting the Qur'an. Al-Qaradawi says there are many Qur'anic verses that call for peace with non-Muslims who do not enter into conflicts or wars with Muslims, which Qutb totally ignores. These include, for example, Qur'an 8:61: "*And if they incline to peace, incline thou also to it, and trust in Allah. Lo! He is the Hearer, the Knower*"; Qur'an 60:8: "*Allah forbiddeth you not those who warred not against you on account of religion and drove you not out from your homes, that ye should show them kindness and deal justly with them. Lo! Allah loveth the just dealers*"; and Qur'an 4:90: "*So, if they hold aloof from you and wage not war against you and offer you peace, Allah alloweth you no way against them,"* among many other verses of the Qur'an.[33]

Al-Qaradawi criticizes Qutb for quoting "sword-oriented" uncompromising verses such as those in the Medinan Sura 9 (al-Tawbah/al-Bara'at), which Qutb believed had abrogated earlier Meccan verses (nasakhatha Ayat al-Sayf). In the process, Qutb called for continuous jihad against all pagan societies, including the so-called Muslim societies, until the Islamic society and Shari'ah (Islamic law) prevail.[34]

Christians and Jews (People of the Book), who had a special status as protected people who paid the Jizyah (poll-tax) for being exempted from military service, are not an exception to the rule in Qutb's uncompromising stance toward all non-Islamic societies. Thus, Qutb quotes Qur'an 9:29: *"Fight against those among the People of the Book who do not believe in God and the Last Day, who do not forbid what God and His Messenger have forbidden, and who do not consider the true religion as their way of life, until they are subdued and pay Jizyah."*[35]

On this issue, Qutb also quotes Qur'an 9:30: *"The Jews say: Ezra is the Son of God, and the Christians say: The Messiah is the Son of God. These are mere sayings from their mouths, following those who preceded them and disbelieved. God will assail them: how they are perverted."*[36] In addition, Qutb often quotes Qur'an 9:31: *"They have taken as lords beside Allah their rabbis and their monks and the Messiah son of Mary, when they were forbidden to worship only one God. There is no God save Him. Be he glorified from all that they ascribe as partner (unto Him)!"*[37]

Jihad for the Cause of Allah and the Establishment of Islamic Society

The word *jihad*, which is derived from the trilateral Arabic root *jahad* (to strive, to endeavor, to exert oneself) and the verb *jaahada* (to fight for a cause, or to wage holy war against infidels) means exertion of one's power in Allah's path, that is, to spread the belief in Allah and to make his word supreme over this world.[38]

According to Majid Khadduri, Islamic jurists have delineated four types of jihad obligations: jihad by heart, jihad by tongue, jihad by hand, and jihad by sword. Jihad by heart is concerned with combating the devil and evil things and was regarded by the Prophet as the "greater jihad." Jihad by tongue and hand is associated with the

Qur'anic injunction "Enjoining the right and forbidding the wrong," while the fourth meaning, the jihad by sword, focuses on fighting unbelievers and enemies of the faith.[39] The fourth meaning of jihad is not considered among the five pillars of Islam, which are duties observed by individuals (Fard 'Ayn). On the other hand, jihad is regarded by all jurists as a collective duty (Fard Kifaya) by all Muslims when the Muslim community and the faith are subject to aggression.[40] Sayyid Qutb and jihadist Islamists disagree with these understandings. They insist that jihad is an individual obligation as well as a collective duty and one of the pillars of Islam. For example, jihad is the central theme in Muhammad 'Abd al-Salam Faraj's tract "The Forgotten Pillar" (al-Farida al-Gha'ibah), which served as a guide to the al-Jihad group in Egypt. The same group, led by Faraj, Khaled Islambouli and others, carried out the assassination of President Anwar el-Sadat of Egypt in October 1981.

Qutb's View of Jihad

Qutb's basic ideas about jihad are found in Chapter 4 in his controversial work *Ma'alim* (Milestones), published in 1964, a work which was instrumental in sending him to the gallows on August 29, 1966, and which has become a manifesto for jihadist Islamists.

Qutb quotes extensively in this chapter, which appeared originally in his Qur'anic commentary *Fi Zilal al-Qur'an*, from the book *Zad al-Ma'ad* of Ibn Qayyim al-Jawziyyah.[41] Al-Jawziyya was a leading disciple of the medieval Islamic thinker who was the forerunner of modern jihadist Islamists and a central figure often quoted by leading jihadist Islamists, Ibn Taymiyyah (1263–1328 A.D.).[42]

Jihad is a central theme in Qutb's work. The aim of jihad is to uproot the Jahili way of life and replace it by Allah's sovereignty on earth (al-Hakimiyyah) through a vanguard whose basic task in the long journey is the realization of a Shari'ah-based Islamic society and "a way of life which on the one hand conserves the benefits of modern science, and technology, and on the other, fulfills the basic human needs on the same level of excellence as technology has fulfilled them in the sphere of material comfort."[43]

Qutb's basic premise concerning jihad revolves around the idea that God's rule on earth can only be achieved through the Islamic system, which is "ordained by God for all human beings, whether they be rulers or ruled, black or white, poor or rich, ignorant or learned. Its law is uniform for all and all human beings are equally responsible within it. . . . [Thus] Jihad in Islam is simply a name for striving to make this system of life dominant in the world."[44]

Qutb adds that there are "many practical obstacles in establishing God's rule on earth, such as power of the state, the social system and tradition and, in general, the whole human environment. Islam uses force only to remove these obstacles so that there may not remain any wall between Islam and individual human beings, and so that it may address their hearts and minds after releasing them from these material obstacles, and then leave them free to choose to accept or reject it."[45]

Qutb is highly critical of Muslim thinkers who say that Islam calls for "defensive war." He brands them as a "product of the sorry state of present Muslim generation [and] has nothing but the label of Islam and has laid down its spiritual and rational arms in defeat."[46]

The place of "Jihad through sword" is "to clear the way for striving through preaching," for Islam is not a "defensive movement" in the narrow sense, which today is technically called a "defensive war," a narrow meaning that has been adopted by defeatists. The true character of Islam is a "universal proclamation of the freedom of man from servitude to other men, the establishment of the sovereignty of God and His Lordship throughout the world, the end of man's arrogance and selfishness, and the implementation of the rule of the Divine Shari'ah in human affairs."[47]

To support his views of jihad, Qutb draws on Ibn Qayyim al-Jawziyyah's understandings of Qur'anic verses that are related to jihad in Islam, including the evolution of the concept from the Meccan period to the Medinan period. In the first thirteen years of his messengership, that is, during the Meccan period when Muslims were a minority surrounded by a hostile environment, the Prophet "called people to God through preaching, without fighting or Jizyah, and was commanded to restrain himself and to practice patience and forbearance."[48] Following the migration to Medina (622 A.D.) and the establishment of the Islamic state, the Prophet was given permission "to fight those who fought him, and to restrain from those who did not make war with him. Later he was commanded to fight polytheists until God's religion was fully established."[49] When the "sword verses" of the Qur'anic Sura of Tawbah (Repentance) were revealed, details of treatment of nonbelievers were posited, including treatment of hostile elements of the "People of the Book." According to Ibn Qayyim al-Jawziyyah, as quoted by Sayyid Qutb, "unbelievers were of three kinds: adversaries in war, people with treaties, and Dhimmies (non-Muslims residing in a Muslim state whose protection and rights, the Muslim government was responsible for. They are required to pay a Jizyah tax). People with treaties eventually became Muslims . . . while there were (Dhimmies) with whom peace was made and people with whom war was continuous."[50] Qutb reminds "defeatists" that both the Qur'an and traditions of the Prophet praise jihad, and with history of Islam full of jihad "the heart of every Muslim rejects the explanation of Jihad invented by those people whose minds have accepted defeat." Qutb asks the defeatists the following: "What kind of a man is he who, after listening to the commandment of God and Traditions of the Prophet—peace be on him—and after reading about the events which occurred during the Islamic Jihad, still thinks that it is a temporary injunction related to transient conditions and that it is concerned only with the defense of the borders?" Qutb continues by stressing that "in the verse giving permission to fight, God has informed the believers that the life of this world is such that checking one group of people by another is the law of God, so that the earth may be cleansed of corruption."[51]

THE IMPACT OF QUTB'S THOUGHT AND THE RISE OF RADICAL GROUPS IN EGYPT

The execution of Qutb on August 29, 1966, had an effect contrary to that first intended. Instead of eliminating the threat of Qutb's revolutionary thought, as exemplified in *Ma'alim*, the execution only added a new martyr and a new name to the list of noted Muslim revivalists of the past one hundred years such as Jamal al-Din al-Afghani, Muhammad 'Abduh, Hassan al-Banna, and Abu al-'Ala al-Mawdudi. The great importance of Qutb's thought is well attested by the republication and the translation of his works into many languages, the worldwide interest in his commentary, and the appearance of dozens of books, researchers, and articles that deal with his life and thought.

Qutb's thought assumes further importance in light of the development in the 1970s of Muslim groups in Egypt whose doctrine was formulated in Nasser's prisons under the guidance of Qutb's writings, especially the Qur'anic commentary and *Ma'alim*. Because of their uncompromising stance, some of these groups are referred to in the Egyptian press as "Qutbists" (Qutbiyun).[52] The suppression of the Muslim Brothers in the 1950s and 1960s, the execution of many of that society's prominent leaders in 1954 and 1966, and the abuses in Nasser's prisons led young members of the society to seek an escape from their plight through radical political solutions to their problems in accordance with their own interpretation of Qutb's writings.

Indeed, Qutb's writings on the Jahili society, especially his charge that all contemporary societies including that of Egypt are Jahili because they do not submit to God's rule (Hakimiyyah), as well his articulation of the notions of "al-'uzlah al-shu'uriyyah or al-mufasalah al-shu'uriyyah" (separation by feelings and conscious as opposed to physical separation) from such a society, had a far-reaching effect. Qutb's writings on Jahili society led to radical interpretations of his thought and to the development of the ideas of withdrawal from society, branding with unbelief (Kufr) those Muslims who chose not to withdraw.[53]

Salim al-Bahnasawi says that the takfir (excommunication) thought has two wings: the "complete separation" wing, which claims that it is the Community of the Muslims and whom the government calls "al-Takfir and al Hijra" (Penance and Retreat), and the "conscious/feelings separation" wing, which reveals the opposite of what it conceals; so this wing spreads the infidelity of the Muslim, then it pretends otherwise and claims that it belongs to the Muslim Brothers while seeking to destroy their group and their thought. This wing ascribes its innovation to Sayyid Qutb.[54]

Shabab Muhammad Group

The influence of the thinking of Sayyid Qutb became salient on the Shabab Muhammad group (known as the Military Technical Organization) under the leadership of Palestinian Doctor Saleh Siriyyah, an educational specialist who, with some of his students, led an armed attack in April 1974 against the Military Technical College as a first step to overthrow the regime of President Anwar el-Sadat and to lay the foundations of the Islamic state under the leadership of Hizb al-Tahrir al-Islami (the Islamic Liberation Party). Hizb al-Tahrir al-Islami was founded in Jerusalem in 1952 by a group of Palestinians led by religious court judge Taqiy al-Din al-Nabhani (1905–1977), a Palestinian refugee from the Haifa region. Al-Nabhani had completed his religious training in Cairo's al-Azhar University, where he met the colleagues with whom he founded Hizb al-Tahrir, Sheikh 'Abd al-Qadim Zallum from Hebron and Sheikh Ahmad al-Da'ur from Qalqilya. Al-Nabhani served as a religious court judge in Hebron during the British Mandate and in Amman during the Jordanian rule of the West Bank and Arab Jerusalem. From its inception, Hizb al-Tahrir focused on the dire need to restore the Islamic caliphate.[55]

Researcher 'Abd al-'Ati Muhammad Ahmad writes that Saleh Siriyyah was detained at the prison of appeals before his execution, while the remaining members of his faction, about eighty individuals, were detained at Leman Turah farm prison. At Leman Turah, friction and contact occurred between those individuals and a number of Muslim Brothers who had been imprisoned when Sayyid Qutb's secret vanguard apparatus was uncovered in 1965. This led to increasing the influence of Sayyid Qutb's ideas on the members of the group of the Military Technical Organization "many of whom sided with these ideas."[56] Siriyyah left an unpublished manuscript titled *Risalat al-iman* (The Epistle of Faith), which has many similarities with the thought of Sayyid Qutb, especially Qutb's declaration of all societies including Muslim societies as Jahili and all political systems in the Muslim world as infidel (hukm kafir).[57]

Shukri Mustafa

Shukri Mustafa, a native of the village of Abu Khurus, south of the city of Asyut, was arrested while attending an agricultural college in Asyut in 1965. In Abu Zu'bul prison, Mustafa became a member of Jama'at al-Muslimin (the Society of Muslims) founded by 'Ali 'Abdu Isma'il, which was known by its enemies as "al-Takfir wal-al-Hijra" (Penance and Retreat). The group's radical interpretation of Qutb's ideas concerning the vanguard, the nucleus of Islamic society, led the group to separate itself from others in prisons, as they considered the others to be infidels. According to Jama'at al-Muslimin, their nascent Islamic society was in the phase or weakness similar to that experienced by the Prophet Muhammad during his thirteen-year preaching phase in Mecca. Therefore, the group believed that it had to build its strength in isolation from Egyptian society, including the migration (hijra) away from the corrupting influence of Jahili society, before the group could wage an offensive stance toward this infidel society. In 1969, the group's founder and leader, 'Ali 'Abdu Isma'il, renounced the ideas of the group and returned to the ranks of the mainstream Society of Muslim Brothers, while Shukri Mustafa insisted on preserving the group and its ideas. In 1974, after President Sadat adopted a more conciliatory posture toward the Islamic groups, many Islamists in prison since 1965, including Shukri Mustafa, were released. Shukri Mustafa reestablished the Society of Muslims outside the prison soon after.[58]

Although in the beginning this group was considered a collection of maniacs "who wished to seclude themselves from contemporary society," it gradually drew the attention of the authorities after they waged "punitive campaigns against dissidents from the group." This led to intervention by the authorities and to confrontation with Sadat's regime. In 1977, the group became more prominent after kidnapping the former minister of Awqaf (Islamic Religious Endowments) Sheikh Muhammad Hussein al-Dhahabi and assassinating him after the government refused to give in to the kidnappers' demands, which included, among other things, pardon for the arrested members of the group, publishing Shukri's book *The Caliphate*, and payment of a ransom. Eventually, Mustafa was arrested, tried, and executed.[59]

Shukri Mustafa accepted the joining of new members to his group from another group who differs with it in thinking and mode of action. Mustafa thus accepted the membership of Hassan al-Hellawi, Muhammad al-Sayyid Jad al-Karim, Mustafa 'Abdul-Mun'im, and Talal al-Ansari, who were among the the most prominent leaders of the Shabab Muhammad group, or the Military Technical Organization, formed by Salih Siriyyah in 1974.[60]

Jama'at al-Muslimin (the Society of Muslims, or the Penance and Retreat group) disappeared after the trial of Shukri Mustafa and his execution in 1978. Kepel indicates that the achievements and mistakes of the group gave intellectual "food for thought" to others, especially the al-Jihad group that embraced the conspiracy that led to Sadat's assassination.[61] The al-Jihad group belonged to the same milieu, but it totally rejected the idea of withdrawal from society and chose instead to wage a holy war against the infidel ruler so that it could establish God's rule on earth (al-Hakimiyyah), even though both groups agreed that all political regimes in the Arab and Muslim worlds are pagan and infidel states and thus it is necessary to fight them and to replace them with truly Islamic regimes.[62]

Al-Jihad Group and al-Gama'ah al-Islamiyyah

This jihadist Islamic movement found its expression in *al-Farida al-gha'ibah* (The Forgotten Pillar) of Muhammad 'Abd al-Salam

Faraj, the ideologue of the al-Jihad group who calls in his tract for holy war against the regime that does not rule in accordance with Islamic law (Shari'ah). The practical aspects of the Islamic faith and dogma that are required from individual Muslims (Fard 'Ayn) are the following five pillars:

1. The recital of the Creed (There is no god but God / Allah and Muhammad is the Prophet of God)
2. The five stated periods of daily prayers
3. The payment of poor-tax / legal alms / al-Zakat
4. The thirty days of fast in the month of Ramadan
5. The pilgrimage to Mecca

The forgotten pillar, according to Faraj, is jihad. Jihad, in Faraj's view, should become an individual obligation, a position that the great majority of jurists disagree with. Jihad is regarded by jurists as a collective duty (Fard Kifaya) by all Muslims when the Muslim community and the faith are subject to aggression.[63]

Faraj accuses rulers of being apostates from Islam, "nourished at the table of colonialism, be it Crusader, Communists, or Zionist." The first target of jihad according to Faraj is the enemy at home, with external enemies coming later. Faraj based his arguments on quotations from jihadist jurist Ibn Taymiyyah and his *al-Fatawa al-kubra* (The Great Religious Rulings).[64] Faraj finished writing his tract, *al-Farida al-gha'ibah*, in 1981 prior to the assassination of President Sadat in October of that year. Faraj was very critical of the ideas posited earlier by Shukri Mustafa and his group concerning "migration and separation" during "the period of weakness." According to Faraj, there is no such a thing as a period of weakness. There is only the immediate obligation of jihad.[65] The Jihad group included in its ranks, among others, Lieutenant Khaled Islambuli, who led the military group that assassinated President Sadat on October 6, 1981.

Rif'at Sayyid Ahmad reports that as early as 1958 a student of Sayyid Qutb in prison, Nabil Bur'i, called for armed struggle against the regime. The same Nabil Bur'i organized an underground group that included Isma'il al-Tantawi, another student of Sayyid Qutb; physician Ayman al-Zawahiri, a future leader of al-Qa'eda; and Major 'Isam al-Qamari. Later, al-Zawahiri and his group established contacts with Muhammad 'Abd al-Salam Faraj, who in turn formed a group headed by Lieutenant Colonel 'Abboud al-Zumar, who would later lead with other army officers the planning and implementation of the assassination of President Sadat. Muhammad 'Abd al-Salam Faraj, in addition, managed to unite the two jihadist wings of the Islamic movement, that is, the Jihad group whose strength was in northern Egypt and "al-Gama'ah al-Islamiyyah" (the Islamic group) whose strength was in middle and southern Egypt (al-Sa'eed). These same groups would eventually lead armed struggle against the regime of President Hosni Mubarak in the 1980s and the 1990s.[66]

In the aftermath of the assassination of President Sadat, a disagreement took place in prison concerning the leadership of the united jihad organization in light of the execution of its leader, Muhammad 'Abd al-Salam Faraj. The leaders of the Islamic group insisted that the blind cleric and jihadist ideologue Sheikh 'Omar 'Abd al-Rahman should become the leader (the Amir, or Prince), while the Jihad group insisted that the leadership should go to the member with the most political and military awareness, that is, the imprisoned 'Abboud al-Zumar. As a result, the united organization split into two parts, the al-Jihad group and the Islamic group, in 1982–1983. Physician Ayman al-Zawahiri's name became prominent in 1993 and in 1997 in the aftermath of his attempt to reorganize the al-Jihad group.[67]

GLOBAL JIHAD: AYMAN AL-ZAWAHIRI, OSAMA BIN LADEN, DR. 'ABDALLAH 'AZZAM, SHEIKH 'OMAR 'ABD AL-RAHMAN, AND MULLAH FATEH KREKAR

Physician Ayman al-Zawahiri, al-Jihad, and al-Qa'eda

Two names, those of Egyptian physician Ayman al-Zawahiri and blind cleric Sheikh 'Omar 'Abd al-Rahman, would become prominent in the West in the 1990s and the early 2000s. Ayman al-Zawahiri would become in the late 1990s and early 2000s the second man in command, after Osama Bin Laden, of al-Qa'eda (the Base), an organization of global jihadist Islamists made up of Arab and other Muslim veterans of the Afghanistan war against the Soviet Union. Al-Qa'eda became prominent after September 11, 2001, when they crashed two jets into the World Trade Center towers in New York, another jet into the Pentagon, and another in a Pennsylvania field, resulting in the deaths of several thousand people. As a result, President George W. Bush declared "war against terrorism" and subsequently led a war against al-Qa'eda and the Taliban, the strict and conservative regime of Islamists who ruled Afghanistan and hosted al-Qa'eda in 1996–2001. Osama Bin Laden eluded capture and issued several videotaped and audiotaped messages on several occasions. In the videotapes one can always see the bespectacled Ayman al-Zawahiri appearing by the side of Bin Laden.[68]

Born on June 19, 1951, Ayman al-Zawahiri began his activism at the early age of fifteen, while attending secondary school in Cairo's suburb, Maadi, in 1966 in the aftermath of events surrounding the uncovering of Sayyid Qutb's underground vanguard apparatus in 1965. Sayyid Qutb's writings and the eventual execution of Qutb in August 1966 left deep impressions on al-Zawahiri. Al-Zawahiri became convinced then that young Muslims must organize themselves in order to defend Islam. In 1966–1967, Ayman and a group of high school students formed an underground apparatus, which was led by Nabil al-Bur'i, a jihadist student of Sayyid Qutb. The group's basic objective was to set up an Islamic government in Egypt through a military coup. This apparatus continued in the 1970s. Al-Zawahiri eventually became its leader and was joined by Nabil al-Bur'i, Isma'il al-Tantawi, 'Isam al-Qamari, and others who would play a role in the preparations that led to the assassination of President Sadat.[69]

Mohammad Salah of London's Arabic language daily, *al-Hayat*, commented on al-Zawahiri's early involvement in organized work that "people usually start in their 20's [but] for Zawahiri working so young with these groups allowed him to develop a very organizational brain, which was able to create sophisticated organizations."[70]

Al-Zawahiri graduated from medical school in 1978 and was posted as a surgeon in the Egyptian army for the next three years. Al-Zawahiri's studies of medicine at the University of Cairo (1974–1978) coincided with the flourishing of Islamists' activities on university campuses at the time when President Sadat was using the Islamic elements to counter the Nasserite and radical leftist forces who were deeply entrenched in society in the aftermath of President Nasser's death in 1970. At this time, student Islamist groups like the Gama'ah al-Islamiyyah (the Islamic Group) were in control of Egyptian campuses. President Sadat's visit to Israel in 1977 and the eventual signing of the Camp David Accords in 1979, however, ended the working relationship between Sadat and the Islamist groups. By 1980, all student groups were outlawed.[71]

In the meantime, radical Islamic groups were encouraged by the successes of the Iranian Islamic revolution led by Khomeini in 1979. In the same year, three of the jihadist underground groups merged to form the Jihad organization. In the summer of 1980 and again in March 1981, al-Zawahiri traveled to Peshawar, Pakistan, to tend to the medical needs of Afghan refugees who were fleeing their country in the wake of the Soviet invasion of Afghanistan. Al-Zawahiri was impressed by the "miracles" of the jihad against the Soviets and regarded Afghan jihad as "a training course of the utmost importance to prepare the Muslim *mujahideen* to wage their awaited battle against the superpower that now has sole dominance over the globe, namely, the United States."[72]

In the wake of the assassination of President Sadat on October 6, 1981, hundreds of Islamic radicals were rounded up, including al-Zawahiri, who did not agree with the timing of the assassination. Instead, al-Zawahiri had wanted the group to wait until the opportunity was ripe for a military coup. Al-Zawahiri spent three years in prison, obtaining his release in 1984. Soon after that, he left Egypt to go to Saudi Arabia to work in a Jeddah medical clinic. There he met Osama Bin Laden, a very wealthy young Saudi who had received his education in the schools of Jeddah and who studied management and economics at King 'Abd al-'Aziz University, where leading Islamists taught, including Sayyid Qutb's brother Muhammad Qutb and a global jihadist who led the mujahideen, the holy war warriors in Afghanistan in the 1980s, Dr. 'Abdallah 'Azzam. Like al-Zawahiri, Osama was radicalized by the Soviet invasion of Afghanistan. Soon both were in Pakistan to help the Afghan mujahideen.

In Egypt, in the meantime, al-Zawahiri's radical Islamic jihadist thought was proliferating among young Islamists through his underground pamphlets titled *al-Rasa'il al-safra'* (The Yellow Letters) and other writings.[73] In his biographical work *Knights under the Prophet's Banner*, which was serialized in London's *al-sharq al-Awsat* newspaper in 2001–2002, al-Zawahiri traces various stages in his life including his experiences in Afghanistan and confrontation with the United States. The book was smuggled from inside Afghanistan to Peshawar in Pakistan and finally to London at the time when U.S. air strikes were pounding the hideouts of al-Qa'eda bases in Afghanistan, causing the deaths of noted al-Qa'eda leaders such as Abu Hafs al-Masri, Nasr Fahmi Nasr, and Tariq Anwar.[74]

In his book, Ayman al-Zawahiri stresses the impact of Sayyid

Qutb's life and thought on the jihadists and the Islamic revolution. Qutb's affirmation of God's oneness and sovereignty, his call for battle against man-made laws that totally contradict God's Shari'ah, "helped the Islamic movement to know and define its enemies. It also helped it to realize that the internal enemy was not less dangerous than the external enemy and that the internal enemy was a tool used by the external enemy as a screen behind which it hid to launch its war on Islam." Concerning Qutb's 1965 underground vanguard apparatus and its plans for "retaliatory blows" against the Nasser regime in case the regime uncovered Qutb's group, al-Zawahiri writes that "the meaning of the plans was more important than their material strength. The meaning was that the Islamic movement had begun a war against the regime in its capacity as an enemy of Islam."

As a result of Qutb's execution by the Nasser regime, according to al-Zawahiri, Qutb's words became more influential than those of any other scholar. Qutb had refused to ask for a pardon from President Nasser for his death sentence to be commuted. Qutb had answered instead: "the index finger (which holds the prayer beads) that testifies to the oneness of God in every prayer refuses to request a pardon from a tyrant." Thus, "he became an example of sincerity and adherence to justice . . . and paid his life as a price for this." The Egyptian regime thought that it had dealt a deadly blow to Islamists with the execution of Sayyid Qutb. However, Qutb's ideas were "the beginning of the formation of a nucleus of the modern Islamic jihad movement in Egypt." Al-Zawahiri claims that the underground jihad, which al-Zawahiri had joined at an early age, was that nucleus of Islamic society.[75]

Osama Bin Laden, Dr. 'Abdallah 'Azzam, Ayman al-Zawahiri, and al-Qa'eda

In Pakistan, Bin Laden and al-Zawahiri worked together with the doyen of the Arab mujahideen against the Soviets, the Palestinian Dr. 'Abdallah 'Azzam, a member of the Society of Muslim Brothers. 'Azzam, a graduate of Damascus University and al-Azhar University in Cairo and a devout student of Sayyid Qutb's thought, acknowledges the profound influence of Sayyid Qutb's thought on him. Qutb had shaped his intellectual orientation.[76]

'Azzam, a native of the West Bank town of Silat al-Harithiyya in the Jenin district, is the first global jihadist par excellence and was considered, until his assassination in 1989, the doyen of jihadists and its main fund raiser. 'Azzam is often quoted by Islamists. According to one of his famous dicta: "Love of jihad has taken over my life, my soul, my sensation, my heart and my emotions. If preparing [for jihad] is terrorism, then we are terrorists. If defending our honor is extremism, then we are extremists. If jihad against our enemies is fundamentalism, then we are fundamentalists." 'Azzam's book *al-Difa' 'an aradi al-Muslimin ahamm furud al-a'yan* (The Defense of Muslim Lands, the Most Important Personal Duty), which appeared in 1987, became a manifesto for jihadists everywhere. The book's central theme is that Islamic land that was under Islamic rule must be returned only through jihad, and it is a personal duty of every Muslim to participate in the jihad in order to restore Muslim land to Islamic rule. 'Azzam has become a role model for many jihadist organizations, including the Palestinian HAMAS.[77]

In Peshawar, Pakistan, 'Azzam lectured at the College for Preaching and Jihad, from which many mujahideen who fought against the Soviets in Afghanistan graduated. Earlier he taught briefly at the University of Jordan, at King 'Abd al-'Aziz University in Jeddah, and at the International Islamic University in Islamabad, Pakistan. 'Azzam became the spiritual mentor of Bin Laden. They met at the College for Preaching and Jihad in Peshawar and began working jointly to set up the infrastructure for the service of the mujahideen volunteers who came to fight the Soviets, such as Maktab al-Khidamat (MAK) for recruiting, services, and training. 'Azzam named this project "al-Qa'eda al-Sulba" (The Firm Base).[78]

In 1986, 'Azzam and Bin Laden took part in the battle against the Soviets in Jalalabad. However, Bin Laden differed with 'Azzam as to the scope of jihad. 'Azzam believed that jihad cannot be waged against Muslims, while Bin Laden and al-Zawahiri espoused the idea that a holy war must be waged in Muslim lands as well, such as in Egypt and Saudi Arabia.[79]

'Abdallah 'Azzam's global jihadist career in Pakistan and Afghanistan came to an end on November 24, 1989, when 'Azzam and two of his children, Muhammad and Ibrahim, were assassinated in Peshawar by alleged Soviet agents.[80]

In 1989, Soviet invasion and occupation of Afghanistan came to an end. Many Afghan Arab mujahideen returned home early in the 1990s to Egypt or to Algeria to continue their jihad against the "infidel" regimes. Others volunteered their jihadist services in the three-year war in the Balkans or in the war of independence of Chechnya.

Others, such as Bin Laden and al-Zawahiri, met prior to leaving Afghanistan to discuss the future of jihad. This meeting resulted in the reemergence of al-Qa'eda (The Base), which comprised individual Afghan war veterans from the Muslim world and groups including the Jihad group of Egypt. The financial aspects of this newly founded organization were under the control of Bin Laden.[81]

Among the Egyptian jihadist members of al-Qa'eda and followers of al-Zawahiri who became prominent following September 11, 2001, were Mohammad 'Atef, also known as Abu Hafs al-Misri, who was in charge of the military wing of al-Qa'eda and whose name along with that of al-Zawahiri became associated with many deadly anti-American operations in Saudi Arabia, Africa, and Yemen in the 1990s; and Muhammad Makkawi, also known as Seif al-'Adl, who, according to one of Lawrence Wright's sources, as early as 1987 suggested that the "Jihad group hijack a passenger jet and crash it into the Egyptian People's Assembly." The source asserts that Seif al-'Adl thus "is the father of September 11th." Al-Zawahiri visited the United States on two occasions, in 1989 and 1993, to raise funds for jihadist activities in Afghanistan. Earlier, President Reagan "compared the *mujahideen* (in their struggle against the Soviets in Afghanistan) to America's founding fathers." In 1989, al-Zawahiri visited "the *mujahideen*'s Services Bureau branch office in Brooklyn." In the spring of 1993, al-Zawahiri came as a representative of the Red Crescent of Kuwait and stayed in California, where he visited Santa Clara and mosques in Sacramento and Stockton. Financially, al-Zawahiri's visit was a failure.[82]

Al-Zawahiri and his Jihad group froze all their activities in Egypt between 1981 and 1994. Fathi al-Shaqaqi, the founder and head of the al-Jihad group in Palestine until his assassination by the Israeli Mossad, suggested to al-Jihad groups in Egypt that they focus their jihadist activities against Israel. Al-Zawahiri was firm in his dictum that "the road to Jerusalem passes through Cairo." Later, when al-Zawahiri allied himself with Bin Laden, that dictum was adjusted to mean that "The road to Jerusalem passes through Washington."[83]

In May 1996, al-Zawahiri and Bin Laden were expelled from Sudan, leading Bin Laden to take refuge in Jalalabad in eastern Afghanistan, then under Taliban control. Al-Zawahiri and his companions traveled to Chechnya to set up "a new home base" for his group, but they were arrested in Dagestan for "entering the country illegally." The group was released later. Al-Zawahiri then joined

Bin Laden in Jalalabad in May 1997, where Islamists from all over the world were joining Bin Laden's training camps.[84]

In the February 23, 1998, issue of London's *al-Quds al-'Arabi* (The Arab Jerusalem) daily, al-Zawahiri was one of the signatories along with Bin Laden and an alliance of jihadist groups from Egypt and from throughout the Muslim world, Europe, Asia, and Africa announcing the formation of al-Jabha al-Islamiyyah al-'Alamiyyah li-Qital al-Yahud wa-al-Salibbiyyin (International Islamic Front for Jihad against the Jews and Christians) and issued a religious ruling (fatwa) authorizing an individual duty (Fard'Ayn) on every Muslim to kill Americans and their allies in any country "in which it is possible to do it."[85] Open warfare now erupted between the United States and al-Qa'eda. The U.S. Central Intelligence Agency (CIA) kidnapped many Jihad cell members in Azerbaijan and Albania. In response, jihadists carried out suicide bombings that destroyed the American embassies in Kenya and Tanzania in the summer of 1998. On August 20, 1998, Tomahawk cruise missiles were targeted at Bin Laden, al-Zawahiri, and other al-Qa'eda leaders, but they missed their targets. By June 2001, the Islamic Jihad group of al-Zawahiri and al-Qa'eda merged to form Qa'edat al-Jihad (The Base of al-Jihad). The leadership was for the most part Egyptian and Saudi. On September 11, 2001, al-Zawahiri, Bin Laden, and other jihadists fled to the mountains to listen to the radio's reports concerning the suicide attacks on the World Trade Center and the Pentagon. It is believed that al-Zawahiri was one of the masterminds behind the planning for September 11.[86] Hamid Mir, a Pakistani journalist and a biographer of Bin Laden, concluded that "the real brains of the outfit [al-Qa'eda] stand in Bin Laden's six-foot five-inch shadow, specifically Egyptian radical Ayman al-Zawahiri."[87] Attorney Muntasir al-Zayyat, a biographer of al-Zawahiri, claims that "Ayman is for Bin Laden like the brain to the body."[88]

It was reported that al-Zawahiri's wife and several children were killed during the heavy bombardment of the mountains in Afghanistan in November or December 2001.[89] Many videotapes and audiotapes of al-Zawahiri have appeared, however, on the Arabic satellite stations since 2001. A recent audiotape appeared on an Aljazeera satellite station on Friday, October 1, 2004, calling on Muslim opinion and experienced leaders to formulate a unified command for the Islamic resistance. In that audiotape, al-Zawahiri urged young Muslims to begin preemptive strikes and "not to wait any longer, otherwise we will be devoured, one country after the other." Al-Zawahiri reminded listeners that liberating Palestine is an individual duty (Fard 'Ayn) for every Muslim, that Muslims cannot give up Palestine even if the whole world does so. But al-Zawahiri warned that limiting the battle to fighting the Jews alone "will not restrain America and the Crusaders against us." He urged fighters to carry on even if al-Qa'eda leaders were killed or arrested.[90]

Concerning Sayyid Qutb and the events of September 11, 2001, John C. Zimmerman writes that Qutb was "relatively unknown in the West" prior to these attacks, even though he was credited with "formulating the extreme religious view of Egyptian Shaykh Umar 'Abd al-Rahman, who is currently in prison for his role in the 1993 attack on the World Trade Center."[91] Zimmerman points out that the September 11 attacks can be understood only if one understands the ideas of Sayyid Qutb, "the intellectual godfather of the various modern radical Islamic movements including al-Qa'eda." Qutb's writings comprise extreme hostility toward the West, insistence on establishing a Shari'ah-based society, the overthrow of governments not ruled by Shari'ah through jihad, hatred of Jews, and distrust of Christians.[92]

Blind Cleric Sheikh Omar 'Abd al-Rahman and al-Gama'ah al-Islamiyyah

Another prominent jihadist Islamist, a contemporary of al-Zawahiri whose name became prominent in the West in the 1990s, is the blind cleric Sheikh Omar 'Abd al-Rahman, who immigrated to the United States and established himself as a prominent jihadist cleric in his community mosque in Jersey City, New Jersey. Sheikh Omar was arrested in 1993 in connection with the World Trade Center bombing in New York in the same year. A jury returned a guilty verdict on five counts, including "seditious conspiracy against the U.S. government; solicitation to murder President Hosni Mubarak of Egypt; conspiracy to bomb; and solicitation to bomb a U.S. military installation." The verdict was criticized on the ground that it took only thirty-six hours of jury deliberations to reach such a verdict, which was highly unusual in a trial in which there were ten defendants, 200 witnesses, and 1,000 exhibits." Defense Attorney Abdeen Jabara said that "we expected convictions, but not to such an overwhelming extent."[93] Sheikh Omar is serving a life sentence in a federal prison in Springfield, Missouri. By August 2004, Sheikh

Omar's Egyptian attorney Muntasir al-Zayyat was planning to travel to the United States to seek Sheikh Omar's release on health grounds.[94]

Sheikh Omar's career began with his graduation from Cairo's al-Azhar University in 1965, majoring in religious studies. He cites in his book *Kalimat Haq* (A Word of Truth) the various sources that enriched his religious education in jurisprudence, Hadith (the sayings and deeds of the Prophet), Qur'anic commentaries and exegesis, Qur'anic sciences, and other references. He lists Sayyid Qutb's *Fi Zilal al-Qur'an* as one of these references.[95] Sheikh Omar became an anti-President Nasser activist, criticizing Nasser and the regime, which led to his arrest on several occasions between 1968 and 1970. Upon the death of President Nasser in September 1970, Sheikh Omar issued a religious ruling forbidding people to pray for the dead president, which led him to eight months of imprisonment.[96]

In the meantime, President Nasser's successor, Anwar el-Sadat, approached the Muslim Brothers for support and told them that he would "allow them to preach and to advocate, as long as they don't use violence." This way the religious elements would form a support group for Sadat to counter the influences of the deeply entrenched Marxists and Nasserites. "But what Sadat didn't know," writes Lawrence Wright, "is that the Islamists were split. Some of them have been inspired by Qutb. . . . Sadat emptied the prisons, without realizing the danger that the Islamists posed to his regime."[97]

Forbidden to be active politically, Islamists became active instead in professional and student unions. By 1973, young Islamic radicals calling themselves al-Gama'a al-Islamiyyah (The Islamic Group) appeared on university campuses to radicalize the student bodies. Growing beards and wearing the veil among students "became fashionable."[98]

Sheikh Omar 'Abd al-Rahman, now a teacher of Islamic religion at al-Azhar in Asyut, became the spiritual advisor to al-Gama'ah al-Islamiyyah, now one of the largest student groups in the country. Sheikh Omar's important tasks included issuing religious rulings (fatwas) to justify actions from a jihadist perspective. Eventually he became its leader (Amir) and religious ruling head (Mufti).[99]

In 1980–1981, the two wings of the jihadists in Egypt, al-Jihad group and al-Gama'ah, worked together, led by Muhammad 'Abd al-Salam Faraj, in planning the assassination of President Sadat. Sheikh Omar became the religious ruling head for both wings. Upon the assassination of President Sadat on October 6, 1981, Sheikh

Omar was arrested and was accused of issuing fatwas regarding the excommunication of the ruler and setting up the Islamic state through jihad even though he claimed that he did not know about the assassination of Sadat until after it took place. He was released from prison on October 2, 1984.[100]

A controversy surrounding the leadership of the jihadists erupted in prison among al-Gama'ah and the Jihad group after the execution of their leader Faraj. Ayman al-Zawahiri and Sheikh Omar took opposite stands. Some suggested that Sheikh Omar was the best man to lead the two wings of the jihadists. Al-Zawahiri countered that Islamic law (Shari'ah) states that the leader (Amir) cannot be blind. Sheikh Omar replied that the Shari'ah also stipulates that a prisoner, that is, 'Abboud al-Zumar, cannot be a leader. These endless claims and counterclaims only drove a deep wedge between the two groups, and since then both groups have been "decimated by defections and arrests."[101]

Despite his imprisonment and poor health, Sheikh Omar continues to be the spiritual leader of al-Gama'ah al-Islamiyyah of Egypt, who led a bloody armed struggle against Egyptian President Hosni Mubarak, Mubarak's regime, and the tourism sector in the late 1980s and in the 1990s. It was reported in 2001 that Sheikh Omar's two sons, As'ad and Ahmad, were serving as advisors to Bin Laden in Afghanistan.[102] Sheikh Omar continues to remind Muslims of their obligation to jihad, that is, to struggle for their religion by "stating the truth, enjoining good and forbidding evil." Sheikh Omar describes his early struggle in Egypt against dictatorship, which brought him suffering and imprisonment, as being an embodiment of this central principle of jihad, struggle for the sake of Allah. Likewise, Sheikh Omar explains that his travels to Europe and the United States were for the same purpose "but ended with being framed with this fraudulent case and with a prison sentence." Sheikh Omar stresses that "the word of truth comes with its own liabilities. Enjoining good and, particularly, forbidding evil also has its liabilities . . . although enjoining good and forbidding evil is the dynamo and motor behind Islamic work. It is the aspect that preserves Islamic principles."

Sheikh Omar reminds Muslims in the West that their responsibilities toward their religion "are to unite and develop themselves financially." He stresses that "they must have money. Money is the element of life, the mainstay of life. A strong Muslim is better and more beloved by Allah than a weak Muslim. Muslims must get the strength of money, to have their media outlets, to have strong productivity and to unite in industrial and agricultural organizations." On the other hand, according to Sheikh Omar, Muslims have to preserve their religion, remain distinguished, and not mix in a way that will make them let go of their religion.[103]

Sheikh/Mullah Fateh Krekar and Ansar al-Islam

Another prominent and controversial Islamist who was deeply influenced by Qutb is Sheikh/Mullah Fateh Krekar, a native of Iraqi Kurdistan and a resident of Norway. Fateh Krekar had never met Qutb, having been born in 1956, and was ten years old when Sayyid Qutb was executed in 1966. Qutb's thought had a profound impact on him, however. Krekar named his children after Sayyid Qutb and his books. He named his eldest son Sayyid Qutb; thus people address him in the Arab tradition as "Abu Sayyid Qutb" (the Father of Sayyid Qutb). Krekar gave his eldest daughter the name of Qutb's most controversial work, Ma'alim (Milestones), and he gave his younger daughter the name of Zilal (Shades), in reference to Qutb's outstanding work *Fi Zilal al-Qur'an* (In the Shades of the Qur'an). Krekar gave his younger son the name of the doyen of jihadist Islam, Ibn Taymiyyah,[104] who is quoted very often by jihadist Islamists including Sayyid Qutb. Fateh Krekar joined the Islamic movement in eastern Kurdistan in June 1988, having become the head of the military wing and the office of planning and implementation in the 1990s.[105]

The jihadist trend emerged in Kurdistan in 1978 and 1979 directly as a result of the success of the Iranian Revolution and Soviet invasion of Afghanistan. In 1980, jihadists established their armed presence in Kurdistan. Like many other Kurds, they fled their homes to the Iranian borders and Iranian refugee camps following the attack by Iraqi forces on the city of Halabjah. Following the 1991 Gulf War, many of the Islamists and jihadists returned from Iran. On December 10, 2001, three jihadist groups, Jund al-Islam (The Soldiers of Islam), the Kurdish HAMAS, and al-Tawhid group, merged into one group under the name of Ansar al-Islam (Supporters of Islam). Mullah Fateh Krekar became the leading figure in this jihadist organization, which was influenced ideologically by Sayyid Qutb and the Egyptian Jihad group, among others.[106]

In September 2002, Mullah Krekar, also known as Najmuddin Faraj, made the headlines when Dutch authorities arrested him for suspected ties to al-Qaʿeda and for heading a Qaʿeda affiliate in Iraqi Kurdistan, that is, Ansar al-Islam (Supporters of Islam). Eventually Krekar was released and returned to Norway, where he has been living under a refugee status since 1991. On March 21, 2003, he was ordered arrested by Norwegian law enforcement agencies to ensure "he did not leave the country while accusations that he had threatened terrorist attacks were investigated."[107]

On the eve of the U.S. invasion of Iraq in 2003, Ansar al-Islam controlled dozens of villages and mountain peaks in eastern Kurdistan close to the Iranian borders, an area that traditionally has been under the control of the secular Patriot Union of Kurdistan (PUK) of Jalal al-Talabani. Many times, PUK soldiers and other members were ambushed and killed. It is believed that many Afghan Arabs joined Ansar al-Islam who were accused by Americans and their allies of giving safe haven to al-Qaʿeda's top leader in Iraq, Abu Musʿab al-Zarqawi, the Jordanian native who had been sentenced to death in absentia. On March 23, 2003, as the Iraqi war was underway, PUK fighters and American ground and air forces attacked, and al-Ansar's enclave was destroyed. Many Islamists were killed, and some were captured. Following the U.S. invasion and destruction of al-Ansar's enclave in eastern Kurdistan in March 2003, Ansar al-Islam, al-Zarqawi, and other jihadist groups including Ansar al-Sunna have managed to regroup. They have been accused since then of being behind the many devastating suicide car bombings that have been taking place in Iraq in 2003, 2004, and 2005, such as those targeting the Jordanian Embassy, U.N. Headquarters, Najaf Mosque, the CIA building in Arbil, Shiʿite shrines, churches, police stations, police personnel, American military convoys, and personnel.[108]

Epilogue

Conclusions concerning the various aspects of Qutb's intellectual career are contained in the individual chapters of this study. My concluding remarks, therefore, focus on Qutb's pre-1952 career and his career between 1952 and 1966, his execution in August 1966, and the impact of his thought.

The following question was raised in the prologue regarding Qutb's pre-1952 intellectual career and his emergence as an Islamic da'iyah (propagator): What were the factors that led Qutb to change his outlook from that of a secularist adib (man of letters) in the 1930s and 1940s to that of an Islamic da'iyah in the late 1940s, 1950s, and 1960s?

It was pointed out that a simplistic, unsubstantiated explanation—like that offered by Muhammad Tawfiq Barakat, who suggests that Qutb's change of attitude resulted from listening to a speech given by the General Guide and founder of the Muslim Brothers, Hassan al-Banna, which had a "magic" effect on him—does not warrant any consideration. That explanation fails to take into account the various forces that shaped Qutb's personality and outlook, for example, the state of Egyptian life and society in the first half of this century, Qutb's upbringing and religious training, and his personal disappointments in life.

With the consideration of these and other possible influences, the early chapters of this study set out to examine Qutb's milieu, namely, the state of Egyptian political and intellectual life and society in the fifty years preceding the July 23, 1952, military revolution. The findings indicate clearly that Qutb was a product of a society that had been going through major political and cultural dislocations at a time when Egypt's transition from a traditional society to a modern one was taking place.

Qutb can be seen as an embodiment of this transition. In his childhood biography, one can observe the conflicting forces of tradition and modernity that were shaping his personality and worldview. One can see, for example, the shift from traditional education to secular training, that is, from the kuttab (Qur'anic school) to the madrassah (elementary school). In the process one can also see the schism that was developing in the educational system between those who had received a religious education and those who had received a secular one.

In the 1920s, when Qutb was in his teens and early twenties in Cairo, having left his village, Musha, to live with his uncle, liberal nationalist forces spearheaded by the Wafdists appeared to have gained the upper hand and managed to leave their mark on the intellectual life of the country. In his formative stage, Qutb was very much influenced by these forces, especially the Wafdists, the modernist al-'Aqqad, and the Diwan literary school's rebellion against neoclassicism. It is also at this stage that Qutb acquired secular ideas, such as those concerning the separation of religion and literature, which were expressed forcefully in his writings in the 1930s.

By the mid-1930s, however, there was a widespread reaction in Egypt against rampant Westernization and the failure of the liberal national establishment to achieve the independence of the Nile valley and a solution to society's pressing problems. This reaction ranged from the proliferation of Muslim clubs and societies to the articulation of anti-Western views, the promotion of pan-Eastern ideas and an increased interest in Islamics among liberal literati. Qutb's writings reflected the "East versus West" theme, especially in his rebuttal of Taha Hussayn's work on the future of culture in Egypt. In addition, in 1939, Qutb began to take a serious interest in the Qur'an, albeit for literary purposes.

World War II (1939–1945) and the economic, political, and social dislocations it caused further alienated one-time adherents of liberal nationalist ideals like Qutb. The war's impact on Qutb cannot be overemphasized. Its adverse effects are very much reflected in Qutb's writing, as it was in this period that many drastic changes began to take place in Qutb's outlook. Likewise, during the seven-year period preceding the July 1952 military revolt, the country was dominated by a sense of anger, grief, and despair at the established order, which was only exacerbated by the Egyptian defeat in the 1948 Palestine War. This state of mind is reflected in the intellectual activity of the time, including that of Qutb. During this period, Qutb became totally alienated from the establishment and, as a result, he chose to forsake literature permanently for the Islamic da'wah (propagation).

Another factor of great significance in Qutb's change of outlook was his upbringing. His early life in Musha was crucial, since it was at this stage that Qutb mastered the traditional culture, that is, Arabic and the memorization of the Qur'an. Moreover, traditional Islamic values were firmly implanted in his total conception. This early experience, according to Qutb, came back later to haunt him, eventually leading him back to Islam from his uncertain secular-oriented world. The impact of traditional life on the mind of Qutb the adib is reflected in the large space he devotes in his childhood biography to his Islamic upbringing, the customs and manners of the villagers, and popular religious practices.

When Qutb moved to Cairo in his teens, he came to experience life in a modern and urban social structure very different from the rural setting in which he grew up. As a result, he became a product of two conflicting worlds, traditional and modern, with two outlooks. It is thus very important to realize that when one deals with the question of Qutb's transformation from secularist adib to an Islamic da'iyah, one must not assume that Qutb possessed at one time a vigorous rationalist spirit, which he later abandoned. Qutb's earliest literary works, especially his poetry, clearly indicate subjective and spiritual orientations. He attributes much of this spiritualism to his early upbringing.

When Qutb became interested in the Qur'an and its artistic aspects beginning in 1939, the more traditional component of his outlook began to reassert itself gradually, even though his modern outlook continued to exert itself prominently, as can be seen in his work on social justice in Islam, where he calls for the outright adoption of Western technology regardless of the consequences. It can also be seen (in the same work) in his call for Muslims not to be afraid of using any man-made social legislation and systems, as long as they do not conflict with the principles of Islam.

Qutb's interest in the Qur'an was not merely an "intellectual and psychological luxury," as he termed the literary analysis of the sa-

cred Book, but was apparently a psychological and spiritual necessity. The Qur'an was a comforting refuge from the pain of the environment in which Qutb lived. His unhappiness in Cairo was very
much evident in his poetry and prose works in the 1930s and 1940s.
Furthermore, the death of Qutb's mother, his shattered love affair,
and his poor health in the 1940s, together with his alienation from
the status quo, prompted him to turn increasingly toward his religion for his personal needs and for answers to his nation's ills.

Qutb's emergence as a student of the Qur'an and his articulation
of Qur'anic ideology beginning in 1946 are significant. Henceforth
all Qutb's Islamic writings were to be grounded in and justified by
quotations from the Qur'an. These quotations assumed a crucial role
in the 1950s and 1960s while Qutb was in prison. In the revised
portions of his Qur'anic commentary and in his controversial
Ma'alim, which he wrote during his imprisonment, he validates and
justifies Islamic revolution against the Jahili way of life on Qur'anic
grounds.

Qutb's revolutionary writings revolve around the idea that all societies on earth, including the so-called Muslim societies, are pagan
societies based on ignorance of the Divine guidance. This line of
Qutb's thought led eventually, after his execution in 1966, to radical interpretation of his writings and to the rise of takfir (excommunication) of these pagan societies. There is no doubt that the
prison environment and repression inside President Nasser's prisons
were the nurseries that hatched these takfir jihadist ideas seen in
Qutb's *Milestones on the Road* (1964), which has become since then
a manifesto for jihadist Islamists throughout the world. The first
kafir (infidel) in Qutb's mind during his imprisonment, 1954–1964,
1965–1966, was President Nasser. Had the Nasser regime not executed Qutb in August 1996, the possibility was fair that Qutb
would have clarified many of the controversial terms he had posited
in his prison writings. Instead, with Qutb gone, his writings were
left wide open for radical interpretations which led many circles in
the West since September 11, 2001, to dub him the ideologue of
Osama Bin Laden, Ayman al-Zawahiri, and al-Qa'eda, as well as
the philosopher of Islamic terror. For this reason, Qutb's controversial writings should not be interpreted in an absolutely literal
way. Qutb was not a religious scholar or a jurisprudent, and his
words should be accompanied by a reader's guide. The best person
to guide the reader through Sayyid Qutb's works is his younger
brother Muhammad Qutb, professor of Islamic studies at King 'Abd

al-ʿAziz University in Saudi Arabia, who worked very closely with his older brother and who is more capable "in specifying the intentions of his brother Sayyid, his ideas, his opinions and his independent judgements."[1]

Despite positive views of the late President Gamal ʿAbd al-Nasser and his leadership of the liberation movement in the Arab world and the nonaligned movement in the 1950s, the execution of Sayyid Qutb and others in August 1966 had no justification. The Nasserite regime in 1966 was too strong to be shaken by an individual or a group. However, shortly after the execution of Sayyid Qutb and his two comrades, the greatest Arab defeat occurred, the defeat of 1967. Islamists consider this defeat a Divine revenge from the regime of the late president and his repressive measures against the Muslim Brothers and Sayyid Qutb. What is nearer to the truth is that the defeat was a decisive indication of the bankruptcy of the bureaucratic, autocratic, unitary Arab order, which has ultimately led to defeat after defeat since 1948. Israel was not victorious only because of its military might or its economical and social ingenuity. The confrontation was not on equal terms. Israel was victorious because the Arab order was very weak economically, politically, and militarily. The Arab masses and the educated were alienated by the aggravation of despotism and its institutions in the Arab world, which uprooted Arab ingenuity and creative forces and caused many Arab intellectuals to leave their Arab countries.

Violence, which the Arab citizen in the Arab world has been reaping the bloody consequences of, is the result of the deeply rooted despotism and absence of social justice in Arab societies in recent decades. The safety valve that provides opportunities for all, including the opposition, to participate in the democratic game, which is well-known in a pluralistic system, is not available in most Arab societies. This in turn has led and is still leading to frustration and despair among young people and to waves of violence and anti-violence in society, which eventually destroys the society's internal texture.

In order to get out of this swamp of violence, it is necessary to have pluralism and dialogue. Pluralism and dialogue require adopting democracy as a constant value politically, economically, socially, and intellectually, as well as practicing it and translating it into a perceptible reality at home, at school, at work, and in the street. The Arab educational strategy should include a comprehensive program to spread democratic concepts as a constant value. This strategy should ultimately connect the democratic process to the economic needs of society and guide the Arab individual toward economic production. Political stability will remain a mere illusion if it is not supported by self-sufficiency, production, and social justice. This pluralistic formulation will enable all Arab elements, including Islamists, nationalists, socialists, and others, to participate effectively in building successful Arab societies. Any other strategy that is not tied to the democratic project is only a futile attempt to adhere to the despotic unitary order in its different manifestations, which has brought only successive catastrophes for the Arab people. Adopting a pluralistic system does not mean abandoning our culture and our cultural specificity, or blind mimicry of the materialistic civilization. Rather, it means tolerance and acceptance of others who differ from us, with an open mind.

Notes

PREFACE

1. See, for example, Gilles Kepel, *Jihad: The Trail of Political Islam*, translated by Anthony F. Roberts (Cambridge, MA: 2002); and Lawrence Davidson, *Islamic Fundamentalism*, rev. ed. (Westport, CT and London: 2003).

2. See Sayyid Qutb, *Milestones*, translated to English by International Islamic Federation of Student Organizations (Kuwait, Salimiah: 1977), 7–19.

3. On this issue and other issues related to the controversial thought of Qutb, see for example and not exclusively these Arabic-language works: Salim al-Bahnasawi, *Sayyid Qutb Between Emotion and Objectivity* (Alexandria: 1986); by the same writer, *Governing and the Issue of Making the Muslim Infidel* (Cairo: 1975); Ja'afar Sheikh Idris, "The Issue of Methodology of Sayyid Qutb in Milestones on the Road," in the *Symposium of the Trends of Contemporary Islamic Thought*, Bahrain, February 22–25, 1985, Office of Arab Education for the Gulf States, 1987, 531–65; Sharif Younes, "Sayyid Qutb . . . Milestones on the Road of Killing," *al-Qahira*, November 1994, 99–144; and Ahmed Madi, "God's Law on Earth in the Thought of Sayyid Qutb," *Arabic Philosophical Magazine* vol. 3, no. 3 (December 1994): 23–30.

4. Mohammad Tawfiq Barakat, *Sayyid Qutb* (Beirut, n.d.), no. 1, 16.

5. Salah 'Abd al-Fattah al-Khalidi, *Nazariyyat al-taswir al-fanni 'inda Sayyid Qutb* (Amman, Jordan: 1983), 3–4.

6. 'Abd al-Baqi Muhammad Hussayn, *Sayyid Qutb: Hayatuhu wa adabuhu* (al-Mansoura, Egypt: 1986), 114–15.

CHAPTER 1

1. J.C.B. Richmond, *Egypt, 1798–1952: Her Advance Towards a Modern Identity* (New York: 1977), 172–74, 177; and see, for example, V. Lutsky, *Modern History of the Arab Countries*, translated by Lika Nasser (Moscow: 1969), 377–83.

2. Jean Lacouture and Simone Lacouture, *Egypt in Transition*, translated by Francis Scarfe (New York: 1958), 91.

3. P. J. Vatikiotis, *The History of Egypt*, 2nd ed. (Baltimore: 1980), 258–60.

4. Nadav Safran, *Egypt in Search of Political Community: An Analysis of the Intellectual and Political Evolution of Egypt, 1804–1952* (Cambridge, MA: 1961), 74.

5. Hisham Sharabi, *Arab Intellectuals and the West: The Formative Years, 1875–1914* (Baltimore: 1970), 131–32.

6. Nadav Safran, *Egypt in Search of a Political Community: An Analysis of the Intellectual and Political Evolution of Egypt, 1804–1952* (Cambridge, MA: 1961), 108.

7. See ʻAli ʻAbd al-Raziq, *al-Islam wa-usul al-hukm: Bahth fil Khilafah wal Hukumah fil-Islam*, 2nd printing (Cairo: 1925).

8. For a detailed account of this controversy, see Mukhtar al-Tuhami, *Thalath maʻarik fikriyah* (Cairo: 1977), 53–143; Anwar al-Jundi, *al-Maʻarik al-adabiyah* (Cairo: n.d.), 318–28; and Safran, *Egypt in Search of a Political Community*, 140–43.

9. al-Tuhami, *Thalath maʻarik fikriyah*, 147–85; al-Jundi, *al-Maʻarik al-adabiyah*, 328–59; and Safran, *Egypt in Search of a Political Community*, 153–56.

10. Salma Khadra Jayyusi, *Trends and Movements in Modern Arabic Poetry* vol. 1 (Leiden: 1977), 154.

11. R.C. Ostle, "Iliya Abu Madi and Arabic Poetry in the Inter-war Period," in *Studies in Modern Arabic Literature*, edited by R.C. Ostle (London: 1975), 40–41.

12. Vatikiotis, *History of Egypt*, 306–7.

13. Ibid., 309–11.

14. Taha Hussayn, *Mustaqbal al-Thaqafah fi Misr*, 2 vols. (Cairo: 1938).

15. J. Heyworth-Dunne, *Religious and Political Trends in Modern Egypt* (Washington, DC: 1950), 9, 11–13.

16. See, for example, Richard P. Mitchell, *The Society of the Muslim Brothers* (London: 1969), 1–11; and Abd al-Fattah M. El-Awaisi, "Emergence of a Militant Leader: A Study of the Life of Hassan Al-Banna: 1906–1908," *Journal of South Asian and Middle Eastern Studies* (Fall 1998): 46–63.

17. Ibrahim Iskandar Ibrahim, *The Egyptian Intellectuals between Tradition and Modernity*, unpublished Ph.D. dissertation, St. Antony's College (Oxford: 1967), 161–79; and Muhammad Jabir al-Ansari, *Tahawwulat al-fikr wa-al-siyasah fi al-Sharq al-ʻArabi, 1930–1970* (Kuwait: 1980), 37–54.

18. 'Abd al-'Azim Ramadan, *Tatawwur al-harakah al-wataniyah fi Misr, min sanat 1937 ila sanat 1948* vol. 1 (Cairo: 1973), 283.

19. For an overview of these Islamic works, see Samih Karim, *Islamiyat Taha Hussayn, al-'Aqqad, Hussayn Haykal, Ahmad Amin, Tawfiq al-Hakim*, 2nd printing (Beirut: 1977).

20. Safran, *Egypt in Search of a Political Community*, 139–40.

21. Charles D. Smith, "The Crisis of Orientation: The Shift of Egyptian Intellectuals to Islamic Subjects in the 1930's," *International Journal of Middle East Studies* no. 4 (October 1973): 384.

22. Ibrahim, *Egyptian Intellectuals*, 20, 27, 29.

23. Ibid., 23, 30, 31, 33.

24. For an account of these political developments, see Yunan Labib Rizq, *Tarikh al-wizarat al-Misriyah, 1878–1953* (Cairo: 1975), 261–527.

25. Vatikiotis, *History of Egypt*, 349; and Peter Mansfield, *The British in Egypt* (London: 1971), 277–79.

26. See Richmond, *Egypt, 1798–1952*, 201–202; and Ramadan, *Tatawur al-harakah al-wataniyah* vol. 2, 344–69.

27. Daniel Lerner, *The Passing of Traditional Society: Modernizing the Middle East*, pbk. ed. (New York: 1964), 218–19; Charles Issawi, *Egypt at Mid-Century: An Economic Survey* (London: 1954), 55, 60.

28. Issawi, *Egypt at Mid-Century*, 262; and see 'Asim Ahmad al-Disuqi, *Misr fi al-Harb al-'Alamiyah al-Thaniyah, 1939–1945* (Cairo: 1976), 204–12.

29. See, for example, Mansfield, *The British in Egypt*, 279.

30. Safran, *Egypt in Search of a Political Community*, 185.

31. Mahfouz's work has been reprinted several times and was translated into English. See Naguib Mahfouz, *Midaq Alley*, translated by Trevor Le Gassick (Beirut: 1966 and London: 1974); and see *Critical Perspectives on Naguib Mahfouz*, edited by Trevor Le Gassick (Washington, DC: 1991).

32. Hamdi Sakkut, *The Egyptian Novel and Its Main Trends, from 1913 to 1952* (Cairo: 1971), 124.

33. Mansfield, *The British in Egypt*, 278.

34. Don Peretz, *The Middle East Today*, 2nd ed. (Hinsdale, IL: 1971), 208–10.

35. Quoted from Beinin and Lockman, *Workers in the Nile*, 267, as cited in Joel Beinin, "Egypt: Society and Economy, 1923–1952," *The Cambridge History of Egypt* vol. 2, edited by M. W. Daly (Cambridge, England: 1998), 329.

36. Nathan J. Brown, *Peasant Politics in Modern Egypt*, 108–9, as cited in Joel Beinin, "Egypt: Society and Economy," 330.

37. Vatikiotis, *History of Egypt*, 360, 364, 365.

38. Anouar Abdel-Malek, *Egypt: Military Society*, translated by Charles Lam Markman (New York: 1968), 22–23.

39. Vatikiotis, *History of Egypt*, 358–59; and for a detailed study of

class conflict, see Mahmoud Hussein, *Class Conflict in Egypt, 1945–1970*, translated by Michel Chirman and Susanne Chirman (New York and London: 1973), 15–92.

40. Beinin, "Egypt: Society and Economy," 330.

41. Anouar Abdel-Malek, *Egypt: Military Society*, 24–25.

42. See, for example, Abd al-Fattah M. El-Awaisi, "Emergence of a Militant Leader: A Study of the Life of Hasan Al-Banna" *Journal of South Asian and Middle Eastern Affairs*, Fall 1998, 46–63.

43. Heyworth-Dunne, *Religious and Political Trends*, 19.

44. Mitchell, *Society of Muslim Brothers*, 272–74.

45. Ibid., 274, 281.

46. Vatikiotis, *History of Egypt*, 360.

47. Mitchell, *Society of Muslim Brothers*, 94–103.

48. Pierre Cachia, *Taha Husayn: His Place in the Egyptian Literary Renaissance* (London: 1956), 64–65.

49. Taha Hussayn, *al- Mu'adhdhabun fi al-'ard* (Cairo: 1952), 8–9.

50. Ibid., 5–7.

51. Khalid Muhammad Khalid, *Min huna nabda'*, 4th ed. (Cairo: 1950), 46–47.

52. Ibid., 48–49.

53. Ibid., 96–97.

54. Ibid., 3–63.

55. Vatikiotis, *History of Egypt*, 460–62; and see Israel Gershoni, *The Emergence of Pan-Arabism in Egypt* (Tel-Aviv: 1981); and Ramadan, *Tatawwur al-harakah al-wataniyah* vol. 2, 351–69.

56. See Richmond, *Egypt 1798–1952*, 201–2; and Ramadan, *Tatawwur al-harakah al-wataniyah* vol. 2, 344–69.

57. Derek Hopwood, *Egypt: Politics and Society 1945–1981* (London: 1982), 28–29.

58. Vatikiotis, *History of Egypt*, 437.

59. Tariq al-Bishri, *al-Harakah al-siyasiyah fi Misr, 1945–1952* (Cairo: 1972), 304–7, 479, 488–89, 501–8, 517.

60. Mitchell, *Society of Muslim Brothers*, 92–93.

61. Vatikiotis, *History of Egypt*, 370–71, 374–475.

62. Mitchell, *Society of Muslim Brothers*, 94–103.

63. Selma Botman, "Egyptian Communists and the Free Officers: 1950–1954," *Middle Eastern Studies* vol. 22, no. 3 (July 1986): 350.

64. Vatikiotis, *History of Egypt*, 371.

CHAPTER 2

1. For a review of Qutb's childhood biography, see Wadi' Filastin's review in *al-Risalah* no. 670 (May 6, 1946): 510–11.

2. See Ibrahim Iskandar Ibrahim, *The Egyptian Intellectuals between Tradition and Modernity* (Oxford: 1967), 18–31.

3. Sayyid Qutb, *al-Atyaf al-arba'ah* (Cairo: 1945), 166.

4. Ibrahim, *Egyptian Intellectuals*, 310–11.

5. Taha Hussayn, *al-Ayyam*, 2 vols. (Cairo: 1929–1939).

6. See Sayyid Qutb, "Min Laghwi al-sayf," *al-Risalah* no. 681 (July 22, 1946): 796–98.

7. See the dedication page in Sayyid Qutb, *Tifl min al-qaryah* (Beirut: 1973). I relied on the Dar al-Hikmah edition (Beirut) in my analysis of Qutb's childhood.

8. Ibid., 80.

9. See Muhammad Ramzi, *al-Qamus al-jughrafi lil-bilad al-Misriyah* vol. 4 (Cairo: 1963), 26, 29.

10. Qutb's conversation with Abulhasan 'Ali Nadvi in the latter's *Mudhakkirat sa'ih fi al-Sharq al-'Arabi*, 2nd rev. ed. (Beirut: 1975), 153.

11. Sayyid Qutb, *Tifl min al-qaryah*, 187–93.

12. Ibid., 31, 139.

13. See the dedication page in Sayyid Qutb, *Mashahid al-qiyamah fi al-Qur'an* (Cairo: 1966).

14. Sayyid Qutb, *Tifl min al-qaryah*, 194.

15. Sayyid Qutb, *al-Atyaf al-arba'ah* (Cairo: 1945).

16. Sayyid Qutb, *Tifl min al-qaryah*, 194.

17. See the dedication page in Sayyid Qutb, *al-Taswir al-fanni fi al-Qur'an* (Cairo: 1962).

18. Sayyid Qutb, *Tifl min al-qaryah*, 16, 17.

19. Ibid., 31–35.

20. Ibid., 40.

21. Ibid., 38.

22. Sayyid Qutb, *al-Taswir al-fanni fi al-Qur'an*, 7, 8.

23. Sayyid Qutb, *Tifl min al-qaryah*, 40, 140.

24. Ibid., 113.

25. Ibid., 118, 120, 122–23, 132–35.

26. Ibid., 140–42.

27. Ibid., 144.

28. Ibid., 16, 17.

29. Ibid., 73.

30. Ibid., 17, 23.

31. Ibid., 26.

32. Ibid., 91.

33. Ibid., 172–84.

34. Ibid., 185–86.

35. Popular religious practices in rural Egypt, which were observed in Qutb's work, are discussed in E. W. Lane, *Manners and Customs of Modern Egyptians* (London: 1954), 228–69; and Winfred S. Blackman, *The Fel-*

lahin of Upper Egypt (London: 1968), 227–51. Also see Shihata Siyam, *al-Din al-Sha'bi fi Misr: Naqd al-'aql al-mutahayil* (Alexandria, Egypt: 1995).

36. Sayyid Qutb, *Tifl min al-qaryah*, 5–7.

37. Ibid., 90–117.

38. Ibid., 201–4.

39. Ibid., 202.

40. Salah 'Abd al-Fattah al-Khalidi, *Sayyid Qutb min al-milad ila al-istishhad* (Beirut, Damascus: 1994), 19.

41. Abd al-Baqi Muhammed Hussayn, *Sayyid Qutb* (al-Mansurah, Egypt: 1986), 122.

42. Ibid., 56; and al-Khalidi, *Sayyid Qutb min al-milad ila al-istishhad*, 100.

43. Nadvi, *Mudhakkirat sa'ih fi al-Sharq al-'Arabi*, 93.

44. Sayyid Qutb, "Bayna al-'Aqqad wa-al-Rafi'i," *al-Risalah* no. 257 (June 6, 1938): 937.

45. See, for example, Sayyid Qutb, "Bayt al-Maghrib fi Misr," *al-Risalah* no. 282 (November 28, 1938): 1937.

46. Sayyid Qutb, "Naqd 'Mustaqbal al-thaqafah fi Misr," *Sahifat Dar al-'Ulum* Sana 5, no. 4 (April 1939): 69.

47. Roger Allen, 'Abbas Mahmud al-'Akkad, in the *Encyclopedia of Islam*, Supplement (Fascicules 1–2), (Leiden: E. J. Brill, 1980), 57–58; and for a detailed study of al-'Aqqad, see 'Abd al-Hayy Diyab, *'Abbas al-'Aqqad naqidan* (Cairo: 1965).

48. Salma Khadra Jayysui, *Trends and Movements in Modern Arabic Poetry* vol. 1 (Leiden: 1977), 152–75; and M. M. Badawi, *A Critical Introduction to Modern Arabic Poetry* (Cambridge: 1975), 84–114, 154.

49. Sayyid Qutb, "al-Ittijahat al-hadithah fi al-shi'r al-'Arabi," *Sahifat Dar al-'Ulum* Sana 7, no. 4 (April 1941): 58–65.

50. Cairo, 1932.

51. Sayyid Qutb, *Muhimmat al-sha'ir fi al-hayah wa-shi'r al-jil al-hadir* (Beirut: Dar al-Shuruq), n.d., 10.

52. Ibid., 13–15.

53. Ibid., 17. For an examination of Qutb's *Muhimmat al-sha'ir*, see Ahmad al-Badawi, *Sayyid Qutb* (Cairo: 1992), 11–51.

54. For a review of Sayyid Qutb's diwan by Mahmud al-Khafif, see *al-Risalah* no. 101 (June 10, 1935): 959–60.

55. For a brief examination of Sayyid Qutb's *al-Shati' al-majhul*, see Mahmud al-Shihabi, "Sayyid Qutb min khilali Shi'rihi," *al-Adib* (Beirut), January–April 1979, 47–49.

56. *Sahifat Dar al-'Ulum* Sana 1, no. 3 (January 1935): 82–86. This poem was also published in his first diwan in 1935.

57. See *al-Risalah* no. 66 (October 8, 1934): 1667.

58. See "al-Hayah al-ghaliyah," *al-Risalah* no. 69 (October 29, 1934): 1789.

59. See al-Shihabi, "Sayyid Qutb min khilali Shi'rihi," 48–49.

60. From his 1935 diwan, *al-Shati al majhul*, 204 as cited in 'Abd Allah Khabbas, *Sayyid Qutb al-adib al-naqid* (al-Zarqa, Jordan: 1983), 148.

61. Sayyid Qutb, *Muhimmat al-sha'ir fi al-hayah*, 91–93.

62. Badawi, *Critical Introduction*, 128; and 'Abd al-'Aziz al-Dasuqi, "Qadaya wa-mulahazat," *al-Thaqafah* no. 92 (May 1981): 42–43.

63. Sayyid Qutb, "Khawatir mutasawiqah fi al-naqd wa-al-adab wa-al-fann," *al-Risalah* no. 597 (December 11, 1944): 1087–88.

64. Nadvi, *Mudhakkirat sa'ih fi al-Sharq al-'Arabi*, 96.

65. 'Abd al-Baqi Muhammad Hussayn, *Sayyid Qutb*, 23–24, 144–45

66. Ibid., 144–45.

67. Sayyid Qutb, "Ila al-thalathin," in *al-Muqtataf* vol. 90, no. 3 (March 1, 1937): 323.

68. The planned publication of Qutb's second anthology was announced in footnotes to Qutb's poems in *al-Risalah* no. 224 (October 18, 1937): 1709; no. 226 (November 1, 1937): 1789; no. 229 (November 22, 1937): 1912; and *Sahifat Dar al-'Ulum* Sana 4, no. 2 (October 1937): 144.

69. *Sahifat Dar al-'Ulum* Sana 1, no. 4 (April 1935): 75.

70. *al-Risalah* no. 226 (November 1, 1937): 1789.

71. *al-Shabab* (Cairo), October 5, 1938, as reprinted in Ahmad 'Abd al-Latif al-Jada' and Husni Adham Jirar, *Shi'r al Da'wah al-Islamiyah fi al-'asr al-hadith* vol. 4 (Beirut: 1978), 39–40.

72. Salah 'Abd al-Fattah al-Khalidi, *Nazariyyat al-taswir al-fanni'ind Sayyid Qutb* (Amman: 1983), 46–57.

73. Sayyid Qutb, *Muhimmat al-sha'ir fi al-hayat*, 24–29.

74. Files of Sayyid Qutb in the Ministry of Education and the Egyptian archives as cited in Abd al-Baqi Muhammad Hussayn, *Sayyid Qutb*, 28, 30, 43.

75. Sayyid Qutb's own account of his assignment in *al-Ahram* is presented in 'Abd al-'Aziz al-Dasuqi, "Qadaya wa-mulahazat," *al-Thaqafah* no. 94 (July 1981): 47, 48.

76. Sayyid Qutb's views are summarized in al-Dasuqi, "Qadaya wa-mulahazat," *al-Thaqafah* no. 91 (April 1981): 49–53.

77. Ibid., 53; Qutb's literary battle with the Apolo group is seen in al-Badawi, *Sayyid Qutb*, 52–66.

78. 'Abd al-'Aziz al-Dasuqi, *Jama'at Apullu* (Cairo: 1971), 485–86.

79. Sayyid Qutb, "Apullu wa-al-shu'ara'," *al-Usbu'* no. 43 (September 19, 1934) as reprinted in al-Dasuqi, "Qadaya wa-mulahazat," *al-Thaqafah* no. 94 (July 1981): 51–53.

80. Ibid., 53–54.

81. Sayyid Qutb, "Mawakib al-'ajazah aw lawhat al-i'lan," *al-Usbu'* no. 44 (September 26, 1934) as reprinted in al-Dasuqi, "Qadaya wa-mulahazat," *al-Thaqafah* no. 95 (August 1981): 58–60.

82. Sayyid Qutb, "Dajjah mufta'alah, *al-Wadi*, September 21, 1934, as cited in al-Dasuqi, *Jama'at Apullu*, 495–96.

83. For an overview of these debates, see Anwar al-Jundi, *al-Ma'arik al-adabiyyah* (Cairo: n.d.), 253–75; and al-Badawi, *Sayyid Qutb*, 63–66.

84. *Diwan: Kitab fi al-naqd wa-al-adab* (Cairo: 1921), 79–84; and al-Jundi, *al-Ma'arik al-adabiyyah*, 408, 410–12.

85. al-Jundi, *al-Ma'arik al-adabiyyah*, 408, 409.

86. Ibid., 413–15; 542–55.

87. Sayyid Qutb, "al-Dalalah al-nafsiyyah lil-alfaz wa-al tarakib al-'Arabiyyah," *Sahifat Dar al-'Ulum* Sana 4, no. 3 (January 1938): 23.

88. Ibid., 27–29.

89. See, for example, Marun 'Abbud. *'Ala al-mihak*, 2nd ed. (Beirut: 1963), 193–237; and al-Badawi, *Sayyid Qutb*, 65–66.

90. Sayyid Qutb, "Bayna al-'Aqqad wa-al-Rafi'i," *al-Risalah* no. 251 (April 25, 1938): 694.

91. Sayyid Qutb, "Bayna al-'Aqqad wa-al-Rafi'i," *al-Risalah* no. 257 (June 6, 1938): 936.

92. Sayyid Qutb, "Bayna al-'Aqqad wa-al-Rafi'i wa-bayni wa-bayna al-rafi'iyin," *al-Risalah* no. 280 (November 14, 1938): 1865; and al-Badawi, *Sayyid Qutb*, 203–9.

93. 'Adel Hammuda, *Sayyid Qutb min al-qaryah ila al-mashnaqah* (Cairo: 1996), 45.

94. *Al-Usbu'* vol. 3, no. 35 (July 25, 1934): 8 as cited in al-Khalidi, *Sayyid Qutb min al-milad ila al-istishhad*, 95–96.

95. Nadvi, *Mudhakkirat sa'ih fi al-Sharq al-'Arabi*, 96.

96. Sayyid Qutb, *Khasa'is al-tasawwur al-Islami wa-muqawwimatih* (Cairo: 1962), 21, 146.

97. Qutb, *Muhimmat al-sha'ir fi al-hayah*, 46.

98. Ibid., 17.

99. Sayyid Qutb, *Hadha al-din* (Cairo: 1962), 22–23.

100. Sayyid Qutb, *Khasa'is al-tasawwur al-Islami*, 213.

101. Sayyid Qutb, *Muhimmat al-sha'ir fi al-hayah*, 13–14.

102. Ibid., 23.

103. Ibid.

104. Sayyid Qutb, *Hadha al-din*, 38.

105. Salah 'Abd al-Fattah al-Khalidi, *Sayyid Qutb al-Shahid al-hay* (Amman: 1981), 109.

106. Nadvi, *Mudhakkirat sa'ih fi al-Sharq al-'Arabi*, 96.

107. Hisham Sharabi, *Arab Intellectuals and the West: The Formative Years, 1875–1914* (Baltimore: 1970).

108. Sayyid Qutb, "Bayna al-'Aqqad wa-al-Rafi'i," *al-Risalah* no. 263 (July 18, 1938): 1179–80.

109. Ibid., 1180.

110. Ibid., 1179–80.

111. Ibid., 1180.

112. Sayyid Qutb, "Manhaj al-adab," *al-Ikhwan al-Muslimun* (Cairo), year 1, no. 1 (May 20, 1954): 14; and see al-Badawi, *Sayyid Qutb*, 194–95.

113. Sayyid Qutb, "al-Dalalah al-nafsiyah lil-alfaz wa-al-tarakib al-'Arabiyah," *Sahifat Dar al-'Ulum* (January 1938): 27.

114. Sayyid Qutb, "Naqd mustaqbal al-thaqafah fi misr," *Sahifat Dar al-'Ulum* (April 1939): 32–38.

115. *al-'Alam al-'Arabi* Sana 1, no. 1 (April 1947).

CHAPTER 3

1. See, for example, *al-Risalah* no. 682 (July 29, 1946): 847.

2. Muhammad al-Nuwayhi, *Thaqafat al-naqid al-adabi*, 2nd ed. (Beirut: 1969), 62.

3. Ibid., 59–64.

4. *al-Adab al-'Arabi fi athar al-darisin* (Beirut: 1961), 62.

5. Sayyid Qutb, *al-Naqd al-adabi: usuluhu wa-manahijuhu* (Cairo: 1947), 247–48; and see Ahmad Badawi, *Sayyid Qutb* (Cairo: 1992), 169–76.

6. *al-Adab al-'Arabi fi athar al-darisin*, 362–63.

7. See, for example, Qutb, *al-Naqd al-adabi*, 56 and for the same author, "Ra'y fi al-shi'r," *al-Kitab* (Cairo) Sana 3, no. 2 (February 1948): 255.

8. Badawi, *Sayyid Qutb*, 84–85.

9. Ibid., 209–11.

10. 'Abd al-Baqi Muhammad Hussayn, *Sayyid Qutb*, 85–87.

11. al-Khabbas, *Sayyid Qutb al-adib al-naqid*, 269–70.

12. Sulayman Fayyad, "Sayyid Qutb bayna al-naqd al-adabi wa-jahiliyyat al-qarn al 'ishrin," *al-Hilal* (September 1986): 58–59.

13. See Fu'ad Duwarah, *'Asharat udaba' yatahaddathun* (Cairo: 1965), 280.

14. Sayyid Qutb, " 'Ala hamish al-naqd: Khan al-Khalili," *al-Risalah* no. 650 (December 17, 1945): 1364; and see Badawi, *Sayyid Qutb*, 143–49.

15. Cited in 'Abd al-Baqi Muhammad Hussayn, *Sayyid Qutb*, 386–94.

16. Sayyid Qutb, *al-Madinah al-mashurah* (Cairo: 1946), 9.

17. For a listing of these and other works of Qutb, see *Dalil al-matbu'at al-Misriyah, 1940–1956* (Cairo: 1975).

18. Sayyid Qutb, *al-Taswir al-fanni fi al-Qur'an* (Cairo: 1962), 7–8. I utilized the following works in my quotation of Qur'anic verses: Muhammad M. Pickthall, *The Meaning of the Glorious Qur'an: Text and Explanatory Translation* (Mecca: 1977); and Muhammad Isma'il Ibrahim, *Mu 'jam al-alfaz wa-al-a 'lam al-Qur'aniyah*, 2nd ed. (Cairo: 1968).

19. Sayyid Qutb, *al-Taswir al-fanni fi al-Qur'an*, 8.

20. Ibid.

21. Abulhasan 'Ali Nadavi, *Mudhakkirat sa'ih fi al-Sharq al-'Arabi* (Beirut: 1975), 189.

22. Sayyid Qutb, *Fi Zilal al-Qur'an* vol. 1, 2nd ed. (Cairo: 1953), 5.

23. Sayyid Qutb, *al-Taswir al-fanni fi al-Qur'an*, 8, 9.

24. Sayyid Qutb, "al-Taswir al-fanni fi al-Qur'an al-karim," *al-Muqtataf* vol. 94, no. 2 (February 1, 1939): 206–7.

25. Ibid., 206.

26. Ibid., 207.

27. Ibid., 209–11.

28. Sayyid Qutb, "al-Taswir al-fanni fi al-Qur'an al-karim," *al-Muqtataf* vol. 94, no. 3 (March 1, 1939): 313–15.

29. Ibid., 315–17.

30. Ibid., 317–18.

31. Sayyid Qutb, *al-Taswir al-fanni fi al-Qur'an*, 9.

32. Ibid., 9–10.

33. Sayyid Qutb, "al-Ma'ani wa-al-zilal," *al-Risalah* no. 581 (August 21, 1944): 690–93, and no. 583 (September 4, 1944): 728–31.

34. Sayyid Qutb, *Mashahid al-qiyamah fi al-Qur'an* (Cairo: 1966), 9.

35. Ibid., 9–10.

36. Ibid., 12.

37. Yusuf al-'Azm, *Ra'id al-fikr al-Islami al-mu 'asir al-shahid Sayyid Qutb* (Damascus, Beirut: 1980), 247.

38. One encounters numerous references to this work, for example, Qutb's commentary on the Qur'anic Surah "al-Baqarah" in his *Fi Zilal al-Qur'an* vol. 1 (Beirut: 1973), 28, 46, 55, 65, 71, 80, 268, 290, 293.

39. Sayyid Qutb, *al-Taswir al-fanni fi al-Qur'an*, 10.

40. Ibid., 12–14.

41. Ibid., 19, 21–22.

42. Ibid., 24–26.

43. Ibid., 26–30, 32–33.

44. Ibid., 34–36.

45. Ibid., 62–71.

46. Ibid., 73.

47. Ibid., 120–28.

48. Ibid., 128–40.

49. Muhammad Rajab al-Bayyumi, "Sayyid Qutb bayna al-'Aqqad wa-al-Khuli," *al-Thaqafah* Sana 5, no. 53 (February 1988): 50–51; and see Muhammad Muhammad Ahmad Khallaf Allah, *al-fann al-qassasi fi-al-Qur'an al-karim*, 4th printing (Cairo: 1972), 1–12.

50. See 'Abd al-Baqi Muhammad Hussayn, *Sayyid Qutb*, 87–90; and Badawi, *Sayyid Qutb*, 225–28.

51. *Al-Risalah*, April 23, 1945, as cited by Mas 'ud Ghanayim, "Bayna Sayyid Qutb wa-Najib Mahfouz," in *al-Manbar* (Tamrah) no. 8 (1995): 58; and Badawi, *Sayyid Qutb*, 222–24.

52. Sayyid Qutb, *Mashahid al-qiyamah fi al-Qur'an*, 38.

53. Ibid., 13–37.

54. Ibid., 37–42.

55. Ibid., 57–58.

56. Samih Karim, *Islamiyat Taha Hussayn al-'Aqqad, Hussayn Haykal, Ahmad Amin, Tawfiq al-Hakim* (Beirut: 1977).

57. Sayyid Qutb, *al-Atyaf al-Arba 'ah* (Cairo: 1945), 6.

58. Ibid., 167–68.

59. Ibid., 165.

60. Ibid., 3.

61. Ibid., 33.

62. Sayyid Qutb, *Ashwak* (Cairo: n.d.).

63. Ibid., 3.

64. *al-Thaqafah* Sana 5, no. 236 (July 6, 1943): 24. This is a slightly revised version of a poem with the same title which appeared in *al-Muqtataf* vol. 102, no. 5 (May 1, 1943): 460.

65. Sayyid Qutb, "Nida' al-kharif," *al-Risalah* no. 538 (October 25, 1943): 449.

66. Sayyid Qutb, "al-fakihah al-muharramah," *al-Risalah* no. 541 (November 15, 1943): 912–13.

67. Sayyid Qutb, "ma' nafsi . . . !" *al-Risalah* no. 569 (May 29, 1944): 449.

68. *al-Risalah* no. 376 (September 16, 1940): 1450.

69. *al-Risalah* no. 645 (November 12, 1945): 1225.

70. *al-Risalah* no. 681 (July 22, 1946): 796.

71. *al-Da 'wah* (Cairo) Sana 1, no. 47 (January 8, 1952): 3, and no. 48 (January 15, 1952): 3; and see Sulayman Fayyad, "Sayyid Qutb bayna al-naqd al-adabi, wa-jahiliyyat al-qarn al-'ishrin," 64–65.

72. Nadvi, *Mudhakkirat sa'ih fi al-Mashriq al-'Arabi*, 189.

73. Sayyid Qutb, "Fi al-tayh," *al-Risalah* no. 544 (December 6, 1943): 973.

74. Ibid.

75. *al-Risalah* no. 691 (September 30, 1946): 1081–82.

76. Ibid., 1081.

77. Ibid.

78. Sayyid Qutb, "Qiyadatuna al-ruhiyyah," *al-Risalah* no. 705 (January 16, 1947): 29.

79. Ibid.

80. Ibid., 28.

81. Ibid.

82. Ibid., 29.

83. Richard P. Mitchell, *The Society of the Muslim Brothers* (London: 1969), 209–11.

CHAPTER 4

1. Sayyid Qutb, *Ashwak*, 69.

2. Mahmud 'Abd al-Halim, *al-Ikhwan al-Muslimun: ahdath sana'at al-tarikh, ru'yah min al-dakhil* vol. 1 (Alexandria: 1979), 191–92.

3. Sayyid Qutb, *Ma'rakat al-Islam wa-al-ra'smaliyah*, 2nd printing (Cairo: 1952), 38–39.

4. Sayyid Qutb, "al-Ghina' al-marid," *al-Risalah* no. 374 (September 2, 1940): 1382.

5. Ibid.

6. Ibid., 1383.

7. Sayyid Qutb, "al-Mutribun wa-al-mutribat," *Sahifat Dar al-'Ulum* Sana 7, no. 1 (July 1940).

8. Sayyid Qutb, "al-Ghina' al-marid," 1383.

9. Sayyid Qutb, "Firaq li-mukafahat al-ghina' al-marid!," *al-Risalah* no. 395 (January 27, 1941): 94.

10. Sayyid Qutb, "al-Ghina' al-marid," 1383.

11. Sayyid Qutb, "Min laghwi al-sayf: suq al-raqiq," *al-Risalah* no. 683 (August 6, 1946): 858.

12. Ibid.

13. Sayyid Qutb, "Min laghwi al-sayf: suq al-raqiq," *al-Risalah* no. 685 (August 19, 1946): 912.

14. See *al-Risalah* no. 622 (June 4, 1945): 579–81.

15. Sayyid Qutb, "Min laghwi al-sayf: suq al-raqiq," 912.

16. Ibid.

17. Ibid. Muhammad ibn 'Abd al-Wahhab is an eighteenth-century cleric after whom the Wahhabi movement in Arabia is named. He allied himself with the Saudi family who provided him with manpower and political clout. Together, in the name of purification of Islam and the return to pristine Islam and its primary sources—the Qur'an, the Sunnah of the Prophet, and the example set by the Prophet's companions and their immediate successors—they succeeded in a short period in the eighteenth and nineteenth centuries in controlling all of the Arabian Peninsula as well as invading Iraq and Syria. They established an Islamic state based on the strict and fundamentalist Hanbalite school of Orthodox Islam, headed by the Saudi kings. The founder of modern Saudi Arabia is King 'Abd al-'Aziz ibn Sa'ud, the father of ruling kings and princes past and present: Sa'ud, Faisal, Khaled, Fahd, 'Abdallah, and others. For further details, see Lawrence Davidson,

Islamic Fundamentalism: An Introduction, rev. ed. (Westport, CT and London: 2003), 49–56.

18. Sayyid Qutb, "al-'Alam yajri!!," *al-Risalah* no. 17 (September 15, 1933): 12–13.

19. Ibid., 12.

20. Ibid., 13.

21. Ibid., and for further information on Ibn Khaldun, see Albert Hourani, *A History of the Arab Peoples* (New York: 1992), 1–4, 209–10.

22. Ibid.

23. Sayyid Qutb, "Muluk al-Tawa'if wa-nazarat fi tarikh al-Islam," *al-Ahram*, June 27, 1934, as reprinted in Anwar al-Jundi, *Kamil al-Kilani fi mir'at al-tarikh* (n.p., 1962): 97–98.

24. Sayyid Qutb, "Naqd Mustaqbal al-thaqafah fi Misr'," *Sahifat Dar al-'Ulum* Sana 5, no. 4 (April 1939): 28–29, 78–79.

25. Ibid., 49–54.

26. Ibid., 55–56.

27. Ibid., 61–62.

28. Ibid., 62.

29. Ibid., 31–47.

30. Ibid., 31–32.

31. Ibid., 32–33.

32. Ibid., 33–35.

33. Ibid., 35.

34. Ibid., and for further details concerning the Umayyad and Abbasid states, see W. Montgomery Watt, *The Majesty That Was Islam (The Islamic World 661–1100)* (New York: 1974).

35. Sayyid Qutb, "Naqd Mustagbal al-thaqufah fi Misr," 36–37.

36. Ibid., 37–38.

37. Ibid., 38.

38. Ibid., 38–39.

39. Ibid., 39–41.

40. Ibid., 41.

41. Ibid., 41–43.

42. Ibid., 43–44.

43. Ibid., 45.

44. Ibid.

45. Ibid.

46. Ibid., 45–46.

47. Ibid., 46.

48. Ibid.

49. Sayyid Qutb, *Social Justice in Islam*, translated by John B. Hardie (New York: 1980), 247–52.

50. Sayyid Qutb, "Naqd Mustaqbal al-thaqafah fi Misr'," 46–47.

51. Ahmad Amin's paraphrased ideas as quoted in ibid., 47.

52. Ibid., 48–49.

53. Ibid., 49.

54. Yusuf al-'Azm, *Ra'id al-fikr al Islami al-mu'asir al-shahid Sayyid Qutb* (Beirut: 1980), 125–26.

55. *al-Thaqafah* no. 272 (March 14, 1944): 21–22.

56. Sayyid Qutb, "al-Lughah al-wahidah al-lati yafhamuha al-Injilis," *al-Risalah* no. 659 (February 18, 1946): 184.

57. Sayyid Qutb, "Min laghwi al-sayf: suq al-raqiq," 912.

58. Sayyid Qutb, "Hadhihi hiya Faransa," *al-Risalah* no. 624 (June 18, 1945): 632.

59. Ibid.

60. Sayyid Qutb, "Ayna anta ya Mustafa Kamil," *al-Risalah* no. 1309 (December 3, 1945): 1309–10.

61. Ibid., 1310.

62. Ibid.

63. Sayyid Qutb, "Mantiq al-dima' al-bari'ah fi Yawm al-Jala," *al-Risalah* no. 661 (March 4, 1946): 238.

64. Ibid.

65. Ibid., 239.

66. Sayyid Qutb, "al-Damir—al-Amrikanit . . . ! wa-qadiyat Filastin," *al-Risalah* no. 694 (October 21, 1946): 1155.

67. Ibid.

68. Sayyid Qutb, "Ila al-ahzab al-Misriyah 'addilu baramijakum aw in-sahibu qabla fawat al-awan," *al-Risalah* no. 627 (June 9, 1945): 723–24.

69. Sayyid Qutb, "Min laghwi al-sayf: ha'ula' al-aristuqrat," *al-Risalah* no. 687 (September 2, 1946): 961–62.

70. Sayyid Qutb, "Madaris lil-sakht . . . ?!," *al-Risalah* no. 691 (September 30, 1946): 1081.

71. Ibid., 1082.

72. Ibid.

73. Sayyid Qutb, "Khawatir mutasawiqah fi al-naqd wa-al-adab wa-al-fann," *al-Risalah* no. 597 (December 11, 1944): 1087–88.

74. Sayyid Qutb, "Ila ustadhina al-Duktur Ahmad Amin," *al-Thaqafah* no. 633 (September 10, 1951) as cited in Muhammad Rajab al-Bayyumi, "Sayyid Qutb bayna al-'Aqqad wa-al-Khuli," *al-Thaqafah* Sana 5, no. 53 (February 1978): 54, 89.

75. Sayyid Qutb, "Ra'y fi al-shi'r bi-munasabat Luzumiyat Mukhay-mar," *al-Kitab* (Cairo) Sana 3, no. 2 (February 1948): 248–49.

76. Ibid., 248.

77. Ibid., 248, 249.

78. Ibid., 254–57; Sayyid Qutb, *al-Naqd al-adabi: usuluhu wa-manahijuhu* (Cairo: 1947), 16–18; and al-Badawi, *Sayyid Qutb*, 78–80, a critical view of Qutb's approach.

79. See Rabindranath Tagore, *One Hundred and One Poems* (Bombay and Calcutta: 1966), xxxii.

80. Ibid., xxii.

81. Sayyid Qutb, "Bad' al-ma'rakah: al-damir al-adabi fi Misr, shubban wa-shuyukh," *al-'Alam al-'Arabi* (Cairo) Sana 1, no. 4 (July 1947): 52.

82. Ibid., 53.

83. Ibid., 53–54.

84. Ibid., 54.

85. Fu'ad Duwarah, *'Asharat udaba' yatahaddathun* (Cairo: 1965), 289–90.

CHAPTER 5

1. Sayyid Qutb, "al-Damir al-Amirkani . . . wa qadiyat Filastin," *al-Risalah* no. 694 (October 21, 1946): 1156.

2. Ibid., 1157.

3. Sayyid Qutb, "Lughat al-'abidt . . . ," *al-Risalah* no. 709 (February 3, 1947): 136.

4. M. Benaboud and J. Cagne, "Le Congress du Maghreb Arabe de 1947 et les debuts d'Bureau du Maghreb Arab au Caire L'Operation Ibn Abd al-Karim," *Revue D'Histoire Maghribine* (Tunis) no. 25–26 (June 1982): 17, no. 2. The authors incorrectly identify Qutb as one of the leaders of the Muslim Brothers; Qutb did not join the Brothers until 1953.

5. See *al-'Alam al-'Arabi*, Sana 1, no. 5 (August 1947): 4.

6. Sayyid Qutb, "Ahdafuna wa-baramijuna," *al-'Alam al-'Arabi* Sana 1, no. 1 (April 1947): 1.

7. Ibid.

8. Ibid.

9. Sayyid Qutb, "Qiyadatuna al-ruhiyah," *al-Risalah* no. 705 (January 6, 1947): 29.

10. J. Heyworth-Dunne, *Religious and Political Trends in Modern Egypt* (Washington, DC: 1950), 97.

11. Interview with al-Damardash al-'Iqali in Sulayman al-Hakim, *Asrar al-'ilaqah al-khasah bayna 'Abd al-Nasser wa al-Ikhwan* (al-Gizah, Egypt: 1996), 3, 48.

12. Heyworth-Dunne, *Religious and Political Trends*, 97, no. 63; and *Majallat al-Fikr al-Jadid*, a three-page handwritten memo, believed by this researcher, as a result of handwriting analysis, to have been written by Sayyid Qutb. This memo was found with clippings dealing with events leading to the dissolution of the Muslim Brothers which are part of the University of Michigan's J. Heyworth-Dunne acquisition (henceforth referred to as Qutb's memo).

13. Qutb's memo, 2, 3.

14. Heyworth-Dunne, *Religious and Political Trends*, 57.
15. Ibid.
16. Qutb's memo, 3.
17. Heyworth-Dunne, *Religious and Political Trends*, 57.
18. Qutb's memo, 1.
19. Ibid.
20. Heyworth-Dunne, *Religious and Political Trends*, 97, no. 63.
21. *al-Fikr al-Jadid* no. 1 (January 1948): 1.
22. Heyworth-Dunne, *Religious and Political Trends*, 97, no. 63.
23. Qutb's memo, 3.
24. See Chapter 6 in this book.
25. Sayyid Qutb, *al-'Adalah al-ijtima 'iyyah fi al-Islam* (Cairo: 1949); and al-'Azm, *Ra'id al-fikr al-Islami al-mu'asir al-shahid Sayyid Qutb*, 154–55.
26. Yusuf al-'Azm, *Ra'id al-fikr al-Islami al-mu'asir al-shahid Sayyid Qutb* (Beirut: 1980), 154–55.
27. Sayyid Qutb, *Limadha a'damuni?* (Saudi Arabia: n.d.), 11.
28. al-'Azm, *Ra'id al-fikr al-Islami*, 154–55.
29. For a critical examination of Qutb's *al-'Adalah* in its various editions, see William Shepard, *Sayyid Qutb and Islamic Activism: A Translation and Critical Analysis of "Social Justice in Islam"* (Leiden: 1996).
30. See Yvonne Yazbeck Haddad, "The Qur'anic Justification of an Islamic Revolution: The view of Sayyid Qutb," *The Middle East Journal* vol. 37, no. 1 (Winter 1983): 14–29.
31. J.C.B. Richmond, *Egypt, 1798–1952: Her Advance Towards a Modern Identity* (New York: 1977), 214.
32. Derek Hopwood, *Egypt: Politics and Society 1945–1981*, 28–29.
33. Sayyid Qutb, *Social Justice in Islam*, translated by John B. Hardie (New York: 1980), 15–16.
34. See Ahmad 'Abbas Salih, "al-Ta'assub wa al-khiyanah' nash'at al al-khawarij," *al-Kitab* (Cairo) Year 6, no. 62 (May 1966): 29–37. Indeed, it is not an uncommon practice in the Arab world to accuse dissident groups of being *khawarij*. Thus in 1948 and 1954 during a crackdown on the Muslim Brothers, the Egyptian government accused them of being *khawarij*. See Richard P. Mitchell, *The Society of the Muslim Brothers* (London: 1969), 320, no. 63; and for clarification of the term *Kharijite* or *Khawarij*, see W. Montgomery Watt, *The Majesty That Was Islam (The Islamic World 661–1100)* (New York, Washington: 1974), 62–65.
35. For a study of the Qutb's concept of Jahiliyya, see William E. Shepard, "Sayyid Qutb's Doctrine of Jahiliyya," *International Journal of Middle East Studies* vol. 35 (November 2003): 521–45.
36. Sayyid Qutb, *Ma'alim fi al-tariq* (Beirut: n.d.), 105–06.
37. Sayyid Qutb, *Social Justice in Islam*, 227–28.
38. Ibid., 15–16.

39. Ibid., 17–18; and for an overview of philosophical movements in Islam, see F. E. Peters, *Aristotle and the Arabs* (New York: 1968).

40. Ibid., 19, 20, 29, 30.

41. Ibid., 35.

42. Ibid., 44.

43. Ibid., 47.

44. Ibid., 48.

45. Ibid., 56.

46. Ibid., 65–66.

47. Ibid., 73, 74.

48. Ibid., 77.

49. Ibid., 93.

50. Ibid., 95.

51. Ibid.

52. Ibid., 100.

53. Ibid., 110.

54. Ibid., 111–15.

55. Ibid., 116–17.

56. Ibid., 118.

57. Ibid., 118, 124–33.

58. Ibid., 135, 138.

59. Ibid., 205, 228–29; for an overview of early Islamic political developments, see Watt, *The Majesty That Was Islam*, 7–21.

60. Ibid., 229.

61. Ibid.

62. Ibid., 228–29.

63. Ibid., 234–35.

64. Ibid., 235.

65. Ibid., 247–48.

66. Ibid., 251.

67. Ibid., 252.

68. Ibid., 259–60.

69. Ibid., 260.

70. Ibid., 260, 266, 270.

71. Ibid., 270–71.

72. Ibid., 267–76.

73. Ibid., 277.

74. Ibid.

CHAPTER 6

1. See Yusuf al-'Azm, *Ra'id al-fikr al-Islami al-mu'asir al-shahid Sayyid Qutb* (Beirut: 1980), 206–7; and Salah 'Abd al-Fattah al-Khalidi, *Amrika*

min al-dakhil bi-minzar Sayyid Qutb (Jeddah, Saudi Arabia: 1985), 16–17. Al-Khalidi's work is basically an anthology of Qutb's writings on America resulting from his stay during 1948–1950. For an excellent account of Qutb's visit to America, see John Calvert, "The World Is an Undutiful Boy!: Sayyid Qutb's American Experience," *Islam and Christian-Muslim Relations* vol. 11, no. 1 (2000): 87–103.

2. 'Adel Hammuda, *Sayyid Qutb min al-qaryah ila al-mashnaqah: Sirat al-ab al-ruhi li-jama'at al-'unf* (Cairo: 1996), 85–86.

3. Al-Khalidi, *Amrika min al-dakhil*, 19–20.

4. Paul Berman, *Terror and Liberalism* (New York and London: 2004), 61.

5. Zafar Bangash, "Remembering Sayyid Qutb: An Islamic Intellectual and Leader of Rare Insight and Integrity," 1–15, www.muslimedia.com/archives/features99/qutb.htm, September 1999, 1, 2.

6. Calvert, "The World Is an Undutiful Boy," 95.

7. Sayyid Qutb, "Ru'ya 'ala al-ufuq: Musiqa al-wujud," *al-Kitab* (Cairo) Sana 5, no. 4 (April 1950): 326, 328.

8. Calvert, "The World Is an Undutiful Boy," 92.

9. Al-Khalidi, *Amrika min al-dakhil*, 20–27.

10. al-Taher Ahmad Makki, "Sayyid Qutb wa thalath rasa'il lam tun-shar ba'd," *al-Hilal* (Cairo), October 1986, 127–28.

11. Ibid., 128.

12. Sayyid Qutb, "Hama'im fi New York!!!," *al-Kitab* Sana 4, no. 10 (December 1949): 666–67.

13. Sayyid Qutb, *al-Islam wa-mushkilat al-hadarah*, 4th legal printing (Beirut: 1978), 75–76.

14. Ibid., 77.

15. Ibid., 82–84.

16. Ibid., 84–85.

17. Sayyid Qutb, "Hama'im fi New York!!!" 666–67.

18. National Public Radio (NPR), "Sayyid Qutb's America," May 6, 2003, in http://discover.npr.org/features/feature.jhtml?wfld=1253796, 1.

19. Calvert, "The World Is an Undutiful Boy," 95.

20. Sayyid Qutb, "Amrika allati ra'ayt: fi mizan al-qiyam al-insaniyah," *al-Risalah* no. 959 (November 19, 1951): 1201.

21. Ibid., no. 962 (December 3, 1951): 1357.

22. Cited in al-'Azm, *Ra'id al-fikr al-Islami al-mu'asir*, 152–53.

23. Ibid., 210.

24. NPR, "Sayyid Qutb's America," 1.

25. Berman, *Terror and Liberalism*, 61.

26. *al-Risalah* no. 961 (December 3, 1951): 1360.

27. Cited in full in al-'Azm, *Ra'id al-fikr al-Islami al-mu'asir*, 153–54.

28. Sayyid Qutb, "Adwa' min ba 'id," *al-Kitab* Sana 5, no. 2 (February 1950): 145.

29. *al-Risalah* no. 887 (July 3, 1950): 756.

30. Sayyid Qutb, "Du 'a al-gharib," *al-Kitab* (June 1950): 497.

31. Jonathan Raban, "The Roots of Fundamentalism as a Theology of Rebellion," *The Guardian* of London, March 2, 2002, www.guardian.co.uk, 6.

32. Sayyid Qutb, *Limadha a'damuni?*, 10–11.

33. Richmond, *Egypt, 1798–1952*, 215.

34. al-'Azm, *Ra'id al-fikr al-Islami al-mu'asir*, 158–59.

35. For a favorable review of Qutb's work, see *al-Risalah* no. 921 (February 26, 1951): 260–62, and no. 923 (March 12, 1951): 314–15.

36. Sayyid Qutb, *Ma 'rakat al-Islam wa-al-ra'smaliyah*, 2nd printing (Cairo: 1952), 5.

37. Ibid., 7–8.

38. Ibid., 9, 10, 12–14.

39. Ibid., 15, 17–19.

40. Ibid., 20–21, 24, 27, 29–30.

41. Ibid., 30–35, 43–44, 47.

42. Ibid., 70–72, 75–76, 79.

43. Ibid., 80–118.

44. See *Britannica Book of the Year 1951* (Chicago, Toronto, London: 1951), xxii.

45. Sayyid Qutb, *Islam and Universal Peace* (Indianapolis: 1977), 4.

46. Ibid., 9, 15.

47. Ibid., 16–29.

48. Ibid., 30–67.

49. Ibid., 69.

50. Ibid., 71.

51. Ibid., 72–73.

52. Ibid., 73–74.

53. Ibid., 74–75, 81.

54. al-'Azm, *Ra'id al-fikr al-Islami al-mu'asir*, 210.

55. Sayyid Qutb, *al-Salam al-'alami wal-al-Islam* (n.p.: 1967), 157–58.

56. Ibid., 159–60, 162.

57. Ibid., 160, 162, 163.

58. Ibid., 163–64.

59. Ibid., 166–70.

60. Ibid., 176–77.

61. Derek Hopwood, *Egypt: Politics and Society, 1945–1981* (London: 1982), 30, 44; and *Texts of Selected Speeches and Final Communiqué of the Asian-African Conference*, Bandung, Indonesia, April 18–24, 1955 (New York: 1955).

62. Sayyid Qutb, "Lil-Azhar risalah. . . . Wa-lakinnahu la yu'addiha. . . ," *al-Risalah* no. 937 (June 18, 1951): 685–86.

63. Sayyid Qutb, "Idha ja'a nasr Allah wa-al-fath," *al-Risalah* no. 951 (September 25, 1951): 1246.

64. For details, see Richard P. Mitchell, *The Society of Muslim Brothers* (London: 1969), 65–67.

65. Ibid., 71–72, 80, 84.

66. Ibid., 78, 84.

67. Ibid., 85, 87.

68. Ibid., 89, 116–224.

69. An anthology of articles, including this article, bearing the same title appeared following Qutb's death. See, for example, Sayyid Qutb, *Fi-al-tarik . . . fikrah wa-minhaj* (Beirut: 1974), 37–61.

70. Sayyid Qutb, *Fi Zilal al-Qur'an* vol. 1, 2nd ed. (Cairo: 1953), 5.

71. Sayyid Qutb, " 'Abbi'u al-sha'b lil-kifah," *al-Da'wah* Sana 1, no. 37 (October 30, 1951): 3.

72. Sayyid Qutb, " 'Aqidah wa-kifah," *al-Da 'wah* Sana 1, no. 38 (November 6, 1951): 3.

73. Mitchell, *Society of Muslim Brothers*, 89, 92.

74. Sayyid Qutb, "Ayna al-tariq," *al-Da'wah* Sana 1, no. 41 (November 27, 1951): 3.

75. Sayyid Qutb, "al-Haqiqah tankashif," *al-Da'wah* Sana 1, no. 43 (December 11, 1951): 3.

76. *al-Da'wah* Sana 1, no. 48 (January 15, 1952): 3.

77. *al-Da'wah* Sana 1, no. 50 (January 29, 1952): 3.

78. *al-Misri* (Cairo), January 1, 1952, as cited and in Tariq al-Bishri, *al-Harakah al-siyasiyah fi Misr, 1945–1952* (Cairo: 1972), 376–77.

79. Mitchell, *Society of Muslim Brothers*, 89–90.

80. Sayyid Qutb, "Faqaqi'," *al-Risalah* no. 974 (March 3, 1952): 237–38.

81. See, for example, Sayyid Qutb, *Ma'rakat al-Islam wa-al-ra'smaliyah*, 2nd printing (Cairo: 1952). The date of this printing is April 1952. The last page in this work lists the author's published works. The Brothers' publishing house is credited with the third printing of Qutb's renowned work on social justice in Islam as well.

82. Sayyid Qutb, "Nuqtat al-bad'," *al-Risalah* no. 955 (July 28, 1952): 827.

83. Isma'il al-Shatti, "Ma' al-Shahid Sayyid Qutb," *al-Mujtama'* (Kuwait) no. 215 (August 17, 1974): 17.

CHAPTER 7

1. Richard P. Mitchell, *Society of Muslim Brothers* (London: 1969), 104.

2. Ibid., 106.

3. Ibid., 107.

4. Ibid.

5. Ibid.

6. Ibid., 109.

7. Christina Harris, *Nationalism and Revolution in Egypt: The Role of the Muslim Brotherhood* (Stanford, CA: 1964), 214; and see Hamadan Husni Ahmed Muhammad, *al-Tanzimat al-siyasiyyah li-Thawrat Yulyu 1952 (1953–1961)*, (Cairo: 2002), 70–72, 76–77.

8. Sayyid Qutb, "Nahnu al-sha'b nurid," *al-Risalah* no. 1005 (October 6, 1952): 1105.

9. Interview with Attorney al-Damardash al-'Iqali in Sulayman al-Hakim, *Asrar al-'ilaqah al-khasah bayna 'Abd al-Nasser wa-al-Ikhwan* (Cairo: 1996), 50.

10. Sayyid Qutb, *Limadha a'damuni?* (n.d.), 13–14.

11. Sulayman Fayyad, "Sayyid Qutb bayna al-naqd al-adabi wa-jahiliyyat al-qarn al-'ishrin," 62–63.

12. *Kalimat al-Haqq* Sana 1, no. 2 (May 1967): 38 as cited in Salah 'Abd al-Fattah al-Khalidi, *Sayyid Qutb min al-milad ila al-istishhad*, 300–301.

13. 'Adel Hammuda, *Sayyid Qutb min al-qaryah ila al-mashnaqa: Sirat al-ab al-ruhi li-jama'at al-'unf* (Cairo: 1996), 117.

14. Salah 'Abd al-Fattah al-Khalidi, *Sayyid Qutb min al-milad ila al-istishhad* (Beirut and Damascus: 1994), 300–301.

15. *al-Ahram* (Cairo), August 13, 1952, 8. Also the *Communique Ratified by the Founding Body of the Muslim Brothers in Its Extraordinary Meeting Held at the Headquarters* (Cairo), August 1, 1952.

16. Sana' al-Misri, *al-Ikhwan al-Muslimun wa-al-tabaqa al 'amilah* (Cairo: 1992), 76, 77, 83.

17. *Akhbar al-yawm* (Cairo), August 8, 1952, as cited in Abdallah Imam, *'Abd al-Nasser wal-al-Ikhwan*; and in 'Adel Hammuda, *Sayyid Qutb min al-qaryah ila al-mashnaqa: Sirat al-ab al-ruhi li-jama'at al-'unf* (Cairo: 1996), 119.

18. Hammuda, *Sayyid Qutb min al-qaryah ila al-mashnaqa*, 119–20.

19. Muhammad Naguib, *Mudhakirrat (Kuntu ra'isan li-Misr)*, 2nd printing (Cairo: 1988), 181.

20. Al-Damardash al-'Iqali's statement as cited in al-Hakim, *Asrar al-'ilaqah al-khasah bayna 'Abd al-Nasser wa-al-Ikhwan*, 50.

21. Sayyid Qutb, *Limadha a'damuni?*, 12.

22. al-Damardash al-'Iqali in al-Hakim, *Asrar al-'ilaqah al-khasah bayna 'Abd al-Nasser wa-al-Ikhwan*, 50–51.

23. al-Tahir Ahmad Makki, "Sayyid Qutb wa-thalath rasa'il lam tun-shar min qabl," 125–26.

24. Sayyid Qutb, *Limadha a'damuni?*, 12, 31.

25. Mitchell, *Society of Muslim Brothers*, 124.

26. Ibid., 126.

27. Ibid.

28. Ibid., 126 n. 59.

29. Ibid., 126–28.

30. Ibid., 128–30. For an Egyptian account of the Nasser-Naguib struggle, see 'Abd al-'Azim Ramadan, *al-Sira' al-ijtima'i wa-al-siyasi fi Misr min Thawrat 23 Yuliyu ila azmat Mars 1954* (Cairo: 1975), 85–117.

31. Mitchell, *Society of Muslim Brothers*, 136–39.

32. Ibid., 141.

33. Ibid., 151.

34. Ibid., 151–62.

35. Ibid., 87.

36. Ibid., 171.

37. Ibid., 171, 172.

38. Ibid., 187.

39. Ibid., 189.

40. Ibid., 189–90.

41. Sayyid Qutb, "Sahhihu akadhib al-tarikh," *al-Risalah* no. 1001 (September 8, 1952): 993–94.

42. Sayyid Qutb, "Akhrisu hadhihi al-aswat al-danisah," *al-Risalah* no. 1003 (September 22, 1952): 1049–50.

43. Sayyid Qutb, " 'Aduwwuna al-awwal al-rajul al-abyad," *al-Risalah* no. 1009 (November 3, 1952): 1217–19.

44. Sayyid Qutb, "Ya li-jirahat al-watan al-Islami," *al-Risalah* no. 1011 (November 17, 1952): 1273–75.

45. Sayyid Qutb, "Faransa amm al-hurriyah," *al-Risalah* no. 1015 (December 15, 1952): 1285–1387.

46. Sayyid Qutb, " 'Adalat al-ard wa-damm al-Shahid Hassan al-Banna," *al-Risalah* no. 1022 (February 2, 1953): 161–63.

47. Sayyid Qutb, "Nahnu nad'u ila 'alamin afdal," *al-Da'wah* no. 106 (February 24, 1952): 3.

48. See Sayyid Qutb, Dirasat Islamiyyah (Cairo, Egypt: 1953).

49. See Sayyid Qutb, Nahwa mujtama' Islami (Amman, Jordan: 1969).

50. See "Qissat al-'adad al-awwal," *al-Ikhwan al-Muslimun* (Cairo), Sana 1, no. 1 (May 20, 1954): 8.

51. See, for example, Mitchell, *Society of Muslim Brothers*, 187.

52. *al-Ikhwan al-Muslimun* Sana 1, no. 2 (May 27, 1954): 9.

53. Ibid., no. 7 (July 1, 1954): 3.

54. Ibid., no. 1 (May 20, 1954): 14.

55. Ibid., no. 5 (June 17, 1954): 14.

56. Ibid., no. 6 (June 24, 1954): 3.

57. 'Abd al-'Azim Ramadan, "al-Ikhwan al-Muslimun," *al-Hadaf* (Kuwait), January 22, 1981, 19; and Mitchell, *Society of Muslim Brothers*, 187.

58. Sayyid Qutb, *Dirasat Islamiyah* (Beirut: n.d.), 48–61.

59. (Damascus: 1953); and see ibid., 62–72.

60. Yusuf al-'Azm, *Ra'id al-fikr al-Islami al-mu'asir al-shahid Sayyid Qutb* (Beirut: 1980), 47. See al-Ikhwan al-Muslimun. *Qism Nashr al-Da 'wah. Hatta ya'lam al-Ikhwan; al qawl al-fasl* (Cairo: 1954).

61. Mitchell, *Society of Muslim Brothers*, 141.

62. Ibid., and *Akhbar al-Yawm* (Cairo), November 27, 1954, 1, 2.

63. *Akhbar al-Yawm*, November 20, 1954, 1; and *al-Ahram*, November 19, 1954, 1.

64. See Mahkamat al-Sha'b. al-Kitab al-Thani. *Muhakamat Hassan al-Hudaybi wa-A'da' Maktab al-Irshad*, prepared by Kamal Kirah (Cairo: 1954), 71–74.

65. al-'Azm, *Ra'id al-fikr al-Islami al-mu'asir*, 39.

66. Sayyid Qutb, *Limadha a'damuni?*, 12, 14–15.

67. Hassan Hanafi, *al-Din wa-al-thawrah* vol. 5 (Cairo: n.d.), 219–20.

68. See Gilles Kepel, *The Prophet and the Pharaoh: Muslim Extremism in Egypt*, translated from the French by Jon Rothschild (Berkeley and Los Angeles: 2003), 28. And see Jabir Rizq, *Madhbahat al-Ikhwan fi Liman Turah* (Cairo: 1979).

69. al-'Azm, *Ra'id al-fikr al-Islami al-mu'asir*, 39, 251.

70. Muhammad 'Amarah, "Min amrad al-sahwah al-Islamiyyah al-mu'asirah," *al-Hilal* (Cairo), September 1986, 70. On Mawdudi's influence in the Arab world, see Fathi Osman, "Mawdudi's Contribution to the Development of Modern Islamic Thinking in the Arabic-Speaking World," *The Muslim World* vol. 93, (July–October 2003): 465–85. Also see Hanafi, *al-Din wal-al-Thawrah* vol. 5, 123–65; and Sayyid Vali Reza Nasr, "A Reexamination of the Origins of Islamic Fundamentalism," *Contention* vol. 4, no. 2 (Winter 1995): 57–73.

71. Hammuda, *Sayyid Qutb min al-qaryah ila al-mashnaqa*, 153.

72. Abu al-Hassan 'al-Nadvi, *Madha khasira al-'alam bi-inhitat al-Muslimin*, 2nd printing (Cairo: 1951), 8–11.

73. Sayyid Qutb, *Milestones*, 7–19.

74. Paul Berman, *Terror and Liberalism* (New York and London: 2004), 65.

75. Sayyid Qutb, *Fi Zilal al-Qur'an* vol. 1, 2nd ed. (Cairo: 1953), 5.

76. Ibid.

77. Sayyid Qutb, *In the Shade of the Qur'an* vol. 30, with an introduction by Professor Muhammad Qutb, translated by M. A. Salahi and A. A. Shamis (London: 1979), xvi.

78. Sayyid Qutb, *Milestones*, 14–18.

79. See, for example, Sami Jawhar, *al-Mawta yatakallamun*, 133–35, 178–79.

80. Radwan al-Sayyid, "Harkat al-Islam al-siyasi al-mu'asirah," *al-'Arabi* (Kuwait) no. 466 (September 1997): 42.

81. *al-Qahirah* (Cairo), November 1994, 106. The issue of this journal is devoted to the study of Sayyid Qutb's thought.

82. For example, see Nash'at al-Taghlibi, "Ma'alim fi al-Tariq: dustur al-ikhwanjiyyah," *Majallat al-Quwwat al-Musallahah* no. 446 (October 1, 1965): 6, 13.

83. Ja'far Sheikh Idris, "Qadiyyat al-manhaj 'inda Sayyid Qutb fi (Ma'alim fi al-tariq)," *Symposium on Trends in Contemporary Islamic Thought*, al-Bahrayn, February 22–25, 1985 (al-Riyad, Saudi Arabia: 1997), 535.

84. Sayyid Qutb, *Khasa'is al-tasawwur al-Islami wa-muqawwimatih*, 4th legal printing (Beirut: 1978), 5, no. 1.

85. Ibid., 5–6.

86. Ibid., 16–17.

87. Ibid., 51–84.

88. Ibid., 85–108.

89. Ibid., 109–35.

90. Ibid., 136–71.

91. Ibid., 172–91.

92. Ibid., 192–213.

93. Ibid., 214–36.

94. Sayyid Qutb, *al-Islam wa-mushkilat al-hadarah*, 4th legal printing (Beirut: 1978), 5–12.

95. Ibid., 31–32.

96. Ibid., 34–37.

97. Ibid., 39–40.

98. Ibid., 46–49.

99. Ibid., 57–61.

100. Ibid., 75–77, 82–86.

101. Ibid., 95–105.

102. Ibid., 109, 115.

103. Ibid., 156–62.

104. Ibid., 169–76.

105. See, for example, al-'Azm, *Ra'id al-fikr al-Islami al-mu'asir*, 164–65.

106. Sayyid Qutb, *The Religion of Islam*, translated by the International Islamic Federation of Students' Organizations (Kuwait: 1977), 2.

107. Ibid., 7–9.

108. Ibid., 30.

109. Ibid., 43.

110. Ibid., 65–66.

111. Ibid., 86.

112. Ibid., 98.

113. Sayyid Qutb, *Islam, the Religion of the Future*, translated by the International Islamic Federation of Students' Organizations (Kuwait: 1977), 9.

114. Ibid., 11–12.

115. Ibid., 34–35.

116. Ibid., 50–51.

117. Ibid., 61, 63, 69, 77.

118. Ibid., 102, 104.

119. Ibid., 117.

120. Ahmad 'Abd al-Latif al-Jada' and Husni Adham Jirar, *Shi'r al-Da'wah al-Islamiyyah fi al-'asr al-hadith* vol. 4 (Beirut: 1978), 41–47.

121. Interview with the wife of Muhammad Yusuf Hawwash, *al-Da'wah* no. 109, Muharram 1422 (March–April 2002), as cited in full in www.zawaj.com/articles/interview-hawwash.html, 1; and Jabir Rizk, "Shuhada' 'ala al-tariq, Sayyid Qutb wa-sahibah," *al-Da'wah* Sana 30 (426), no. 52 (September 1980): 22–23.

122. Sayyid Qutb, *Limadha a'adamuni?* 27–38.

123. Ibid., 72.

124. 'Umar al-Talmasani, *Dhikrayat la mudhakirrat* (Memories No Memoirs) (Shobra, Egypt: 1985), 280–81.

CHAPTER 8

1. See Zaynab al-Ghazali, *Ayyam min hayati* (Days from My Life), as cited fully in www.ikhwan.net/books, 1–4.

2. Sayyid Qutb, *Limadha a'adamuni?*, 42–60; and Sami Jawhar, *al-Mawta ya-takallamun*, 111–46 and 160–82.

3. Sayyid Qutb, *Limadha a'adamuni?*, 91.

4. Jawhar, *al-Mawta ya-takallamun*, 50–59, 185.

5. Ibid., 73–77.

6. Ibid., 32–38.

7. Hassan Hanafi, *al-Din wa-al-Thawrah* vol. 5, 250.

8. Sayyid Qutb, *Milestones*, 16–18, 32, 34, 148, 152, 234; and for an examination of the doctrine of "Jahiliyya," see William E. Shepard, "Sayyid Qutb's Doctrine of Jahiliyya," *International Journal of Middle East Studies* vol. 35, no. 4 (November 2003): 521–45.

9. See Zafar Bangash at www.muslimedia.com/archives/features99/qutb.htm.

10. See Robert Irwin, "Is This the Man Who Inspired Bin Laden?" *The Guardian*, November 1, 2001, at www.guardian.co.uk.

11. John C. Zimmerman, "Sayyid Qutb's Influence on the 11 September Attacks," *Terrorism and Political Violence* vol. 16, no. 2 (Summer 2004): 238–40 and endnotes no. 92–116, 250–52.

12. Ibid.

13. Ziad Abu 'Amr, *al-Harakah al-Islamiyyah fi al-Diffah al-Gharbiyyah wa-Qita' Ghazza* (Acres 1989), 119.

14. 'Abd al-Ghani 'Imad, *Hakimiyyat Allah wa-sultan al-faqih: Qi-*

ra'ah fi khitab al-harakat al-Islamiyyah al-mu'asirah (Beirut: 1997), 50–
53; and see Sa'id Hawwa, *Jundu Allah thaqafatan wa-akhlaqan*, rev. ed.
(Beirut, Amman: 1988).

15. Muqbil ibn Haadee al-Wadi'ee, "The Inflexible Ruling Concerning
Reading the Writings of Sayyid Qutb," translated by Maaz Qureshi, at
www.troid.org/articles/manhaj/innovation/qutbees/print/inflexibleruling.
htm.

16. Salih al-Fawzan, "On the Generalised Statements of Takfir of Salman
al-'Awdah," *al-Ajwibah al-Mufeedah*, 151, at www.jihadonline.brave
pages.com/takfirawadah.htm.

17. Ahmad an-Najmee, "Refuting the Mistakes of Sayyid Qutb, Hassan
al-Banna et al," *al-Fataawa al-Jaliyyah 'anil-Manaahij al-Da'wiyyah* 31,
question no. 41 at www.fatwa-online.com.

18. Sayyid Qutb, *Muqawwimat al-tasawwur al-Islami* (Beirut: 1995), 7.

19. Ibid., 30.

20. Ibid., 35.

21. Ibid., 41.

22. Ibid., 44.

23. Ibid., 48.

24. Ibid., 62.

25. Ibid., 110, 112–14.

26. 'Imad, *Hakimmiyat Allah wa-sultan al-faqih*, 128–30.

27. Yvonne Yazbeck Haddad, "The Qur'anic Justification for an Islamic
Revolution: The View of Sayyid Qutb," *The Middle East Journal* vol. 34,
no. 1 (Winter 1980): 3–12.

28. Sayyid Qutb, *Muqawwimat al-tasawwur al-Islami*, 38–39.

29. Ibid., 39–40.

30. Michael J. Thompson, "Sayyid Qutb and the Philosophical Roots of
Islamic Fundamentalism," part one. See www.lapismagazine.org/thomp
son2.htm, 1; and for a look at the Reformation in Europe, see, for example,
Lewis W. Spitz, *The Renaissance and Reformation Movements* (Chicago:
1971).

31. 'Imad, *Hakimmiyat Allah wa-sultan al-faqih*, 38–39.

32. Hassan Isma'il al-Hudaybi, *Du'at la-qudat: abhath fi al-'aqidah al-
Islamiyyah wa-manhaj al-da'wah ila Allah*, 2nd printing (Beirut: 1978),
220–21.

33. Yusuf al-Qaradawi, "Waqfah ma' al-Shaheed Sayyid Qutb," 6–7.
See www.Attajdid.ma/qaradawi/p.5.asp. Al-Qaradawi's book on Sayyid
Qutb appeared in May 2004. See www.almotamar.net/10244.htm. On the
translation of the Qur'an, I utilized *The Meaning of the Glorious Qur'an:
Text and Explanatory Translation* by Muhammad Marmaduke Pickthall
(Mecca: Muslim World League, 1977).

34. al-Qaradawi, "Waqfah ma' al-Shaheed Sayyid Qutb," 6–7.

35. Sayyid Qutb, *Milestones*, 126.

36. Ibid., 150.

37. Pickthall, *The Meaning of the Glorious Qur'an*, 182.

38. Hans Wehr: *A Dictionary of Modern Written Arabic*, edited by Milton Cowan, 2nd printing (Ithaca, NY: 1966), 142–43; and Majid Khadduri, *War and Peace in the Law of Islam* (Baltimore, MD: 1955), 55.

39. Khadduri, *War and Peace in the Law of Islam*, 55–56.

40. Ibid., 60; also see Kenneth Church, "Jihad," in *Collateral Language*, edited by John Collins and Ross Glover (New York: 2002), 109–24.

41. Sayyid Qutb, *Milestones*, 93.

42. For an overview of Ibn Taymiyya's political thought, see Qamar al-Din Khan, *Ibn Taymiyyah wa-fikrihi al-siyassi*, translated by Ahmad Mubarak al-Baghdadi (Kuwait: 1985). For a detailed list of Ibn Taymiyya's works, see 225–42.

43. Sayyid Qutb, *Milestones*, 14.

44. Ibid., 137, 139.

45. Ibid., 131.

46. Ibid., 100.

47. Ibid., 110–11.

48. Ibid., 94.

49. Ibid., 94–95.

50. Ibid., 94, 95, 114.

51. Ibid., 115–16.

52. See, for example, *al-Musawwar* (Cairo), no. 3009 (June 11, 1982): 30–31.

53. Salim 'Ali al-Bahnasawi, *al-Hukm wa-qadiyat takfir al-Muslim* (Cairo: 1977), 4–42.

54. Salim 'Ali al-Bahnasawi, *Sayyid Qutb bayna al-'atifah wa al-mawdu'iyyah* (Alexandria: 1986), 91.

55. For a detailed presentation of the Islamic system as seen by Hizb al-Tahrir, see Taqiy al-Din al-Nabhani, *Nizam al-Islam*, 5th printing (Jerusalem/al-Quds: 1953); and for an overview of the Islamic Constitution as seen by the Islamic group, see Hizb al-Tahrir, *Muqaddimat al-Dustur aw al-asbab al-mujibah lahu* (n.p.: 1963).

56. 'Abd al-'Ati Muhammad Ahmad, *al-Harakat al-Islamiyyah fi Misr wa-qadaya al-tahawwul al-dimuqrati* (Cairo: 1995), 120–21; and 'Adel Hammuda, *al-Hijrah ila al-'unf: al-tatarruf al-dini min Hazimat Yunyu ila Ightiyal October* (Cairo: 1987), 29–51.

57. Hammuda, *al-Hijra ila al-'unf*, 46–47.

58. Ibid., 171–73; and Shukri Mustafa at www.pwhce.org/shukri.html.

59. For a detailed study, see Gilles Kepel, *The Prophet and the Pharaoh: Muslim Extremism in Egypt*, 70–102; and Hammuda, *al-Hijra ila al-'unf*, 229–47 for the ideas of Shukri Mustafa.

60. 'Abd al-'Ati Muhammad Ahmad, *al-Harakat al-Islamiyyah fi Misr wa-qadaya al-tahawwul al-dimuqrati*, 120; and Hammuda, *al-Hijra ila al-'unf*, 181–82.

61. See Kepel, *Prophet and Pharaoh*, 102; and for a comparative study

of the two groups, see David Zeidan, "Radicalism in Egypt: A Comparison of Two Groups," *MERIA Journal* vol. 3, no. 3 (September 1999).

62. Zeidan, "Radicalism in Egypt," 4.

63. See Majid Khadduri, *War and Peace in the Law of Islam* (Baltimore: 1955), 60.

64. See Muhammad 'Abd al-Salam Faraj, *al-Farida al-gha'ibah*, 5–11, as cited fully in www.e-prism.org/images/ALFAREDA.doc.

65. See www.pwhce.org/faraj.html.

66. Rif'at Sayyid Ahmad, *al-Harakat al-Islamiyyah al-radikaliyyah fi Misr* (Beirut: 1998), 7–10 and 64, no. 4; and see 'Adel Hammuda, *Ightiyal al-ra'is bi-al-watha'iq: Asrar ightiyal al-Sadat* (Cairo: 1985).

67. Ahmad, *al-Harakah al-Islamiyyah al-radikaliyya*, 9–10.

68. See, for example, Lawrence Davidson, *Islamic Fundamentalism: An Introduction*, rev. ed. (Westport, CT: 2003), 83–84, xxi–xxii, and for an excellent overview of the life of Ayman al-Zawahiri, see Lawrence Wright, "The Man Behind Bin Laden," *New Yorker*, September 16, 2002.

69. Wright, "The Man Behind Bin Laden," 7–9; and Muntasir al-Zayyat, "Ayman al-Zawahiri . . . kama 'ariftahu," *al-Quds* (Arab Jerusalem), January 14, 2002, 17. Much of this information is based on the Egyptian state investigation with Ayman al-Zawahiri following his arrest in the aftermath of Sadat's assassination on October 6, 1981, as reported by al-Zayyat.

70. Quoted by Scott Baldauf of the *Christian Science Monitor*: see www.csmonitor.com/2001/1031/p's1-wosc.html, 2.

71. See Muhammad Jamal Barut's article about al-Zawahiri in *al-Bayan*, November 14, 2001, as cited fully in *Akhbar al-Sharq*, November 14, 2001. See www.thisissyria.net/11-2001/14/articles.html, 2–3.

72. Ahmad, *al-Harakah al-Islamiyyah al-radikaliyyah*, 8; and Wright, "The Man Behind Bin Laden," 12, 14, 15.

73. al-Zayyat, "Ayman al-Zawahiri . . . kama 'ariftahu," *al-Quds* (Arab Jerusalem), January 14, 2002, 17.

74. Ayman al-Zawahiri, "Knights Under the Prophet's Banner," translated published extracts appearing in serialized form in London's Arabic language daily *al-Sharq al-Awsat*, December 2001, as printed in *Foreign Broadcast Information Services*, NES-2002-0100 (December 2, 2001), 1. For excerpts of text, see www.fas.org/irp/world/para/ayman_bk.html.

75. Ibid., 14–16.

76. See, for example, excerpts from 'Abdallah 'Azzam's book *'Imlaq al-fikr al-Islami al-shaheed Sayyid Qutb* (The Giant of Islamic Thought, Martyr Sayyid Qutb), 25–26 as cited on www.khayma.com/alattar/selection/sqotb2.htm. 'Azzam's experiences and views of Afghanistan are seen in his work *Ayat al-Rahman fi jihad al-Afghan* (The Verses of the Merciful in the Jihad of the Afghan), Lahore, Pakistan: 1983; also see *al-Manara al-mafqudah* (The Missing Minaret), Peshawar, Pakistan: 1987, concerning the destruction of the Islamic caliphate.

77. See www.intelligence.org.il/eng/sib/11_4/legacy.gtm, 2, 7, 13.

78. Ibid., 3, 4.

79. Wright, "The Man Behind Bin Laden," 23, 25, 26, and interview with Bin Laden in 1996. See www.islam.org.au/articles/15/laden.htm, 1.

80. Wright, "The Man Behind Bin Laden," 27.

81. Quoted from ibid., 28.

82. Ibid., 29.

83. See Barut, "al-Zawahiri," 6.

84. Wright, "The Man Behind Bin Laden," 33, 34.

85. Ibid., 35.

86. Ibid., 38, 40.

87. See Scott Baldauf of the Christian Science Monitor, 1.

88. Profile: Ayman al-Zawahiri at www.english.aljazeera.net, March 20, 2004, 2.

89. Ibid., 1.

90. See text and excerpts of the audiotape at www.english.aljazeera.net, Saturday, October 2, 2004, 1–2; www.story.news.yahoo.com, Friday, October 1, 2004, 1–2; and *al-Quds* daily (Arab Jerusalem), October 2, 2004, 6.

91. John C. Zimmerman, "Sayyid Qutb's Influence on the 11 September Attacks," 222–23.

92. Ibid., 222.

93. "Sheikh Omar Abd al Rahman Page," at www.islam.co.za/saiin/abdulrahman.htm, 1–2.

94. See *al-Quds* (Arab Jerusalem), August 22, 2004, 19.

95. Omar 'Abd al-Rahman, *Kalimat Haq: Murafa'at al-Duktur 'Omar 'Abd al-Rahman fi qadiyyat al-Jihad* (n.p., Dar al-I'tisam: n.d.), 16.

96. Ibid., 13.

97. Wright, "The Man Behind Bin Laden," 11.

98. Ibid.

99. Ahmad, *al-Harakat al-Islamiyyah al-radikaliyyah fi Misr*, 49.

100. al-Rahman, *Kalimat Haq*, 81–165.

101. al-Zayyat, "Ayman al-Zawahiri . . . kama 'ariftahu," *al-Quds* (Arab Jerusalem), January 14, 2002, 17; and Wright, "The Man Behind Bin Laden," 21, 31; and for a further look at the strife between the two groups, that is, al-Jihad and al-Gama'ah, see Barut, "al-Zawahiri," 4–6.

102. See Scott Baldauf of the *Christian Science Monitor*, 2.

103. Interview with Dr. Omar 'Abd al-Rahman in *Nida'ul Islam*, no. 16, December–January 1996–1997 as cited fully at www.islam.org.au/articles/16/dromar.htm, 1, 2, 3.

104. Interview with Sheikh Fateh Krekar in the 20th issue of *Nida'ul Islam*, September–October 1997. See www.islam.org.au/articles/20/kurds.htm, 1.

105. Ibid.

106. Hani al-Siba'i, "Ansar al-Islam, Ansar al-Sunnah Army, Abu Mus'ab al-Zarqawi and Abu Hafs Brigades" was posted March 14, 2004, on al-Basra.net cited by *Foreign Broadcast Information Service.* See www.galeropia.org/temp/jihadist_movement_iraq.html, 1–14.

107. See www.frontpage.com/articles/printable.asp?ID=5571, 1; and www.en.wikipedia.org/wiki/Ansar_al-Islam, September 10, 2004, 1.

108. www.en.wikipedia.org/wiki/Ansar-al-Islam, 1; and see Catherine Taylor, "Taliban-Style Group Grows in Iraq," *Christian Science Monitor*, March 15, 2002, www.csmonitor.com/2002/0315/p01s04-wome.html, 1–4; and see Jonathan Schanzer, "Ansar al-Islam: Back in Iraq," *Middle East Quarterly*, Winter 2004, at www.meforum.org/article/579, 1–8.

EPILOGUE

1. For clarifications by Muhammad Qutb concerning alleged excommunicating ideas of Sayyid Qutb, see the periodical *al-Mujtama'* (Kuwait), October 21, 1975, as cited in Salim al-Bahnasawi, *Sayyid Qutb bayna al-'atifa wa-al-mawdu'iyyah* (Alexandria, Egypt: 1986), 88–91.

Bibliography

ORIGINAL WORKS BY SAYYID QUTB

Qutb, Sayyid. *al-'Adalah al-Ijtima 'iyyah Fi al-Islam* [Social Justice in Islam]. Cairo: Lajnat al-Nashr lil-Jami'iyyin, 1949.

———. *Ashwak* [Thorns]. Cairo: Dar Sa'd Misr, n.d. First published in Cairo, 1947.

———. *al-Atyaf al-arba'ah* [The Four Phantoms]. Cairo: Lajnat al-Nashr lil-Jami'iyyin, 1945.

———. *A Child from the Village*. Edited and translated with an introduction by John Calvert and William Shepard. Syracuse, NY: Syracuse University Press, 2004.

———. *Fi Zilal al-Qur'an* [In the Shade of the Qur'an]. 1st and 2nd eds. 20 vols. Cairo: Dar Ihya' al-Kutub al-'Arabiyyah, 1952–1959.

———. *Fi Zilal al-Qur'an* [In the Shade of the Qur'an]. Rev. ed. 20 vols. Beirut: Dar al-Ma'rifah and Dar Ihya' al-Turath al-'Arabi, 1971.

———. *Fi Zilal al-Qur'an* [In the Shade of the Qur'an]. Rev. ed. 6 vols. Beirut: Dar al-Shuruq, 1973–1974.

———. *Hadha al-din* [The Religion of Islam]. Cairo: Dar al-Qalam, 1962.

———. *In the Shade of the Qur'an* [Fi Zilal al-Qur'an]. Vol. 30. With an introduction by Muhammad Qutb, translated by M. A. Salahi and A. A. Shamis. London: MWH Publishers, 1979.

———. *Islam and Universal Peace* [al-Salam al-'alami wa-al-Islam]. Indianapolis: American Trust Publication, 1977.

————. *Islam, the Religion of the Future* [al-Mustaqbal li-hadha al-din]. Delhi: Marakaz Maktaba Islami, 1974, and Kuwait: International Islamic Federation of Student Organizations, 1977.

————. *al-Islam wa-mushkilat al-hadarah* [Islam and the Problem of Civilization]. Cairo: Dar Ihya' al-Kutub al-'Arabiyah, 1962.

————. *Khasa'is al-tasawwur al-Islami wa-muqawwimatih* [The Characteristics and Components of Islamic Conception]. Cairo: Dar Ihya' al-Kutub al-'Arabiyyah, 1962.

————. *Limadha a'damuni?* [Why Did they Execute Me?] The Saudi Company for Research and Marketing, n.d. Sayyid Qutb's written statement as requested by investigators in the aftermath of his arrest in 1965.

————. *Ma'alim fi al-tariq* [Milestones on the Road]. Beirut: Dar al-Shuruq, n.d. First published in Cairo, 1964.

————. *al-Madinah al-mashurah* [The Bewitched City]. Beirut: Dar al-Shuruq, 1974. First published in Cairo, 1946.

————. *Ma'rakat al-Islam wa-al-ra'smaliyah* [The Battle of Islam and Capitalism]. 2nd printing. Cairo: Dar al-Ikhwan lil-Sihafah wa-al-Tiba'ah, 1952. First published in Cairo, 1951.

————. *Mashahid al-qiyamah fi al-Qur'an* [Scenes of Resurrection in the Qur'an]. Cairo: Dar al-Ma'arif, 1966. First published in Cairo, 1947.

————. *Milestones* [Ma'alim]. Translated by International Islamic Federation of Student Organizations, n.p., Kuwait, Salimiah, 1977.

————. *Muhimmat al-sha'ir fi al-hayah wa-shi'r al-jil al-hadir* [The Mission of the Poet in Life and the Poetry of the Present Generation]. Beirut: Dar al-Shuruq, n.d. First published in Cairo, 1932.

————. *Muqawwimat al-tasawwur al-Islami* [Components of Islamic Conception]. Beirut: Dar al-Shuruq, 1995. First published twenty years after Qutb's execution in 1966, circa 1986.

————. *al-Mustaqbal li-hadha al-din* [Islam the Religion of the Future]. Cairo: Maktabat Wahbah, 1965.

————. *al-Naqd al-Adabi: Usuluhu wa-Manahijuhu* [Literary Criticism: Its Sources and Methods]. Cairo: Dar al-Fikr al-'Arabi, 1947.

————. *The Religion of Islam* [Hadha al-din]. Delhi: Markazi Maktaba Islami, 1974, and Kuwait: International Islamic Federation of Student Organizations, 1977.

————. *al-Salam al-'alami wa-al-Islam* [Islam and Universal Peace]. N.p., 1967. First published in Cairo, 1951.

————. *al-Shati' al-Majhul* [The Unknown Shore]. Cairo, 1935.

————. *Social Justice in Islam* [al-'Adalah al-Ijtima'Iyah Fi al-Islam]. Translated by John B. Hardie. New York: Octagon Books, 1980.

————. *al-Taswir al-fanni fi al-Qur'an* [Artistic Portrayal in the Qur'an]. Cairo: Dar al-Ma'arif, 1962. First published in Cairo, 1945.

————. *Tifl min al-qaryah* [Child from the Village]. Beirut: Dar al-Hikmah, n.d. First published in Cairo, 1946.

PERIODICALS

al-'Alam al-'Arabi [The Arab World]. (Cairo), 1947.
al-Da'wah [The Call]. (Cairo), 1951–1953.
al-Fikr al-Jadid [Modern Thought]. (Cairo), 1948.
al-Hilal [The Crescent]. (Cairo), 1986.
al-Ikhwan al-Muslimun [The Muslim Brothers]. (Cairo), 1954.
al-Katib al-Misri [The Egyptian Author]. (Cairo), 1946.
al-Kitab [The Book]. (Cairo), 1946–1951.
al-Mabahith al-Qada'iyah [Judicial Themes]. (Cairo), 1950.
al-Muqtataf [Selection]. (Cairo), 1934–1943.
al-Musawwar [The Illustrated]. (Cairo), 1982.
al-Muslimun [The Muslims]. (Cairo), 1951–1954.
al-Quds. (East Jerusalem), 2004.
al-Risalah [The Message]. (Cairo), 1933–1953.
al-Thaqafah [Culture]. (Cairo), 1943, 1978, 1981.
Ruz al-Yusuf. (Cairo), 1976.
Sahifat Dar al-'Ulum [Dar al-'Ulum Review]. (Cairo), 1934–1941.

ANTHOLOGIES OF SAYYID QUTB'S ARTICLES

Qutb, Sayyid. *Dirasat Islamiyyah* [Islamic Studies]. Cairo: Maktabat Laj-
    nat al-Shabab al-Muslim, 1953.
———. *Fi-al-tarikh, fikrah wa-minhaj* [In History, Idea and Method].
    Beirut: Dar al-Shuruq, 1974. First published in Saudi Arabia, 1967.
———. *Kutub wa-Shakhsiyat* [Books and Personalities]. Beirut: Dar al-
    Shuruq, n.d. First published in Cairo, 1946.
———. *Nahwa mujtama' Islami* [Toward an Islamic Society]. Amman:
    Maktabat al-Aqsa, 1969.
———. *Naqd 'Kitab mustaqbal al-thaqafah'* [Criticism of the Future of
    Culture in Egypt]. Cairo, n.p., 1939.

SPECIAL COLLECTIONS

Richard P. Mitchell Collection on the Muslim Brothers. Ann Arbor: Uni-
    versity of Michigan Library, 1977.

UNPUBLISHED MATERIAL

Majallat *al-Fikr al-Jadid* (Modern Thought), a copy of a three-page hand-
    written memo, believed by this researcher, as a result of handwriting

analysis, to have been written by Sayyid Qutb. This memo was found with newspaper clippings dealing with events leading to the dissolution of the Muslim Brothers. These materials are housed at the University of Michigan Graduate Library.

WEB SITES

www.abc.net.au
www.akhbarelyom.org
www.alasr.ws
www.alinaam.org.za
www.almaqdese.com
www.almotamar.net
www.as-sahwah.com
www.atimes.com
www.attajdid.ma
www.biu.ac.il
www.cpjustice.org
www.crisisweb.com
www.csmonitor.com
www.cybcity.com
www.disinfo.com
www.e-prism.org
www.en.wikipedia.org
www.english.aljazeera.net
www.enterstageright.com
www.fas.org
www.fatwa-online.com
www.frontpage.com
www.galeropia.org
www.google.com
www.guardian.co.uk

www.icna.org
www.ikhwan.net
www.islaam.com
www.islam.co.za
www.islam.org.au
www.islamic-world.net
www.jannah.org
www.jihadonline.bravepages.com
www.khayma.com
www.lapismagazine.org
www.meforum.org
www.muslimedia.com
www.nationmaster.com
www.outsidethebeltway.com
www.pwhce.org
www.secularislam.net
www.the-idler.com
www.thisissyria.net
www.troid.org
www.weekly.ahram.org.eg
www.weeklystandard.com
www.yahoo.com
www.youngmuslims.ca
www.zawaj.com

WORKS ON SAYYID QUTB

Akhavi, Shahrough. "The Dialectic in Contemporary Egyptian Social Thought: The Scripturalist and Modern Discourses of Sayyid Qutb and

Hasan Hanafi." *International Journal of Middle East Studies* 29 (1997).

al-'Azm, Yusuf. *Ra'id al-fikr al-Islami al-mu'asir al-shahid Sayyid Qutb*. Damascus, Beirut: Dar al-Qalam, 1980.

al-Badawi, Ahmad. *Sayyid Qutb*. Cairo: al-Hay'ah al-Misriyyah al-'Amah lil-Kuttab, 1992.

Badrul Hasan, S. *Syed Qutb Shaheed*. Karachi: International Islamic Publishers, 1980.

al-Bahnasawi, Salim 'Ali. *Sayyid Qutb bayna al-'atifah wa-al-mawdu'iyyah*. Alexandria, Egypt: Dar al-Da'wah, 1986.

al-Balihi Ibrahim ibn 'Abd al-Rahman. *Sayyid Qutb*. al-Riyad: Kulliyat al-Shari'ah, 1972.

Barakat, Muhammad Tawfiq. *Sayyid Qutb*. Beirut: Dar al-Da'wah, n.d.

Barut, Muhammad Jamal. *al-Dawla wa-al-nahda wa al-hadatha: Muraja'at naqdiyyah*. al-Ladhiqiyya, Syria: Dar al-Hiwar lil-Nashr, 2000.

al-Bayyumi, Muhammad Rajab. "Sayyid Qutb bayna al-'Aqqad wa-al-Khuli." *al-Thaqafah* Sana 5, no. 53 (February 1978).

Berman, Paul. "The Philosopher of Islamic Terror." *New York Times Sunday Magazine*, March 23, 2003.

Bouzid, Ahmed. *Man, Society and Knowledge in the Islamist Discourse of Sayyid Qutb*. Unpublished doctoral dissertation, Virginia Polytechnic Institute and State University, Blacksburg, Virginia, April 1998.

Calvert, John. "The Individual and the Nation: Sayyid Qutb's *Tifl min al-Qarya*" (Child from the Village). *The Muslim World* vol. 90 (Spring 2000).

———. "The World Is an Undutiful Boy! Sayyid Qutb's American Experience." *Islam and Christian-Muslim Relations* vol. 11, no. 1 (2000).

Fadl Allah, Mahdi. *Ma' Sayyid Qutb fi fikrihi al-siyasi wa-al dini*. Beirut: Mu'assasat al-Risalah, 1979.

Fayyad, Sulayman. "Sayyid Qutb bayna al-naqd al-adabi wa-jahiliyyat al-qarn al-'ishrin." *al-Hilal* (Cairo), September 1986.

Haddad, Yvonne Yazbeck. "The Qur'anic Justification of an Islamic Revolution: The View of Sayyid Qutb." *The Middle East Journal* vol. 37, no. 1 (Winter 1983).

Hammuda, 'Adel. *Sayyid Qutb min al-qaryah ila al-mashnaqa: Sirat al-ab al-ruhi li-jama'at al-'unf*. 3rd printing. Cairo: Dar al-Khayyal, 1996.

Hanafi, Hassan. "Athar al-Imam al-Shahid Sayyid Qutb 'ala al-harakat al-diniyya al-mu'asirah." In *al-Din wa-al-Thawrah fi Misr, 1952–1981*, vol. 5. Cairo: Maktabat Madbuli, n.d.

Husayn, 'Abd al-Baqi Muhammad. *Sayyid Qutb: Hayatuhu wa adabuhu*. al-Mansoura, Egypt: Dar al-Wafa', 1986.

Jawhar, Sami. *al-Mawta yatakallamun*. Cairo: al-Maktab al-Misri al-Hadith, 1977.

Johns, A. H. "Let My People Go! Sayyid Qutb and the Vocation of Moses." *Islam and Christian-Muslim Relations* vol. 1, no. 2 (December 1990).

Kashmiri, Bashir Ahmad. *'Abqari al-Islam Sayyid Qutb*. Cairo: Dar al-Fadilah, n.d.

Khabbas, 'Abd Allah. *Sayyid Qutb al-adib al-naqid al-Zarqa'*, Jordan: Maktabat al-Manar, 1983.

al-Khalidi, Salah 'Abd al-Fattah. *Amrika min al-dakhil bi-minzar Sayyid Qutb*. Jeddah, Saudi Arabia: Dar al-Manara, 1985.

———. *Nazariyyat al-taswir al-fanni 'inda Sayyid Qutb*. Amman, Jordan: Dar al-Furqan, 1983.

———. *Sayyid Qutb min al-milad ila al-istishhad*. 2nd printing. Beirut and Damascus: Dar al-Qalam and al-Dar al-Shamiyyah, 1994.

———. *Sayyid Qutb al-Shahid al-hayy*. Amman: Maktabat al-Aqsa, 1981.

Khatab, Sayed. "Arabism and Islamism in Sayyid Qutb's Thought on Nationalism." *The Muslim World* (Hartford, CT) vol. 94 (April 2004).

———. "Citizenship Rights of Non-Muslims in the Islamic State of Hakimiya Espoused by Sayyid Qutb." *Islam and Christian-Muslim Relations* vol. 13, no. 2 (2002).

———. "Hakimiyyah and Jahiliyyah in the Thought of Sayyid Qutb." *Middle Eastern Studies* vol. 38, no. 3 (July 2002).

Madi, Ahmad. "al-Hakimiyya li-Allah fi fikr Sayyid Qutb." *al-Majallah al-Falsafiyyah al-'Arabiyyah* vol. 3, no. 3 (December 1994).

Makki, al-Tahir Ahmad. "Sayyid Qutb wa-thalath rasa'il lam tunshar min qabl." *al-Hilal* (Cairo), October 1986.

Moussalli, Ahmad S. *Radical Islamic Fundamentalism: The Ideological and Political Discourse of Sayyid Qutb*. Beirut: American University of Beirut, 1992.

Musallam, Adnan. *In Search of Self in a Disturbed World: The Life and Thought of Islamic Ideologue Sayyid Qutb, 1906–1966* (in Arabic). Jerusalem: Emerezian, 2000.

———. "Prelude to Islamic Commitment: Sayyid Qutb's Literary and Spiritual Orientation, 1932–1938." *The Muslim World* (Hartford, CT), July–October 1990.

———. *Sayyid Qutb: The Emergence of the Islamist 1939–1950*. 2nd ed. Jerusalem: The Palestinian Academic Society for the Study of International Affairs (PASSIA), December 1997.

———. "Sayyid Qutb and Social Justice, 1945–1948." *Journal of Islamic Studies* (Oxford) 4:1 (1993).

———. "Sayyid Qutb's View of Islam, Society and Militancy." *Journal of South Asian and Middle Eastern Studies* (Villanova University) vol. 22, no. 1 (Fall 1998).

Qutb, Muhammad 'Ali. *Sayyid Qutb al-Shahid al-a'zal*. Cairo: Dar al-Mukhtar al-Islami, 1975.

Rizq, Jabir. "Shuhada' 'ala al-tariq; Sayyid Qutb wa-sahibah." *al-Da'wah* Sana 30 (426), no. 52 (September 1980): 22–23.

al-Shatti, Isma'il. "Ma' al-Shahid Sayyid Qutb." *al-Mujtama'* (Kuwait), no. 215 (August 27, 1974).

Shehadeh, Lamia Rustum. "Women in the Discourse of Sayyid Qutb." *Arab Studies Quarterly* vol. 22, no. 3 (Summer 2000).

Shepard, William E. "Islam as a System in the Later Writings of Sayyid Qutb." *Middle Eastern Studies* (January 1989).

———. *Sayyid Qutb and Islamic Activism: A Translation and Critical Analysis of "Social Justice in Islam."* Leiden: E. J. Brill, 1996.

———. "Sayyid Qutb's Doctrine of Jahiliyya." *International Journal of Middle East Studies* vol. 35, no. 4 (November 2003).

al-Shihabi, Mahmud. "Sayyid Qutb min khilali Shi'rihi." *al-Adib* (Beirut), January–April 1979, 47–49.

Thompson, Michael J. "Sayyid Qutb and the Philosophical Roots of Islamic Fundamentalism." Parts one and two. *Lapis Magazine Online*, www.lapismagazine.org/thompson2.htm.

al-Zarqani, Muhammad. "Awwal risalah jami'iyah 'an al-Shahid Sayyid Qutb." *al-Mukhtar al Islami* (Cairo), Sana 2, no. 14 (August 1980): 44–51.

Zimmerman, John C. "Sayyid Qutb's Influence on the 11 September Attacks." *Terrorism and Political Violence* vol. 16, no. 2 (Summer 2004): 222–52.

GENERAL WORKS IN ARABIC

Abbud, Marun. *'Ala al-mihak.* 2nd ed. Beirut: Dar al-thaqafah, 1963.

'Abd al-Halim, Mahmud. *al-Ikhwan al-Muslimun: ahdath sana 'at al-tarikh ru'yah min al-dakhil.* 2 vols. Alexandria, Egypt: Dar al-Da'wah, 197?–1981.

'Abd al-Nasser, Gamal. *Falsafat al-Thawrah* [Philosophy of the Revolution]. Cairo: Dar al-Ma'arif, 1953 or 1954.

'Abd al-Rahman, Omar. *Kalimat haq: Murafa'at al-Duktur 'Omar 'Abd al-Rahman fi qadiyyat al-Jahad* [A Word of Truth]. Cairo (?): Dar al-I'tisam, n.d.

'Abd al-Raziq, 'Ali. *al-Islam wa-usul al-hukm: Bahth fil Khilafah wal Hukumah fil-Islam* [Islam and the Principles of Government]. 2nd printing. Cairo: Matba'at Misr, 1925.

Abu 'Amr, Ziad. *al-Harakah al-Islamiyyah fi al-Diffa al-Gharbiyyah wa-Qita' Ghazza.* Acres: Dar al-Aswar, 1989.

al-Adab al-'Arabi fi athar al-darisin. Beirut: Dar al-'Ilm lil-Malayin, 1961.

Ahmad, 'Abd al-'Ati Muhammad. *al-Harakat al-Islamiyyah fi Misr wa-qadaya al-lahawwul al-dimuqrali.* Cairo, 1995.

Ahmad, Rif'at Sayyid. *al-Harakat al-Islamiyyah al-radikaliyyah fi Misr.* Beirut: Markaz al-Dirasat al-Istratijiyyah wa-al-Buhuth wa-al-Tawthiq, 1998.

————. *al-Nabi al-musallah.* 2 vol. London: Riad El-Rayyes Books, 1991.

'Amarah, Muhammed. "Min amrad al-sahwa al-Islamiyyah al-mu'asirah." *al-Hilal* (Cairo), September 1986, 68–75.

al-Ansari, Muhammad Jabir. *Tahawwulat al-fikr wa-al-siyasah fi al-Sharq al-'Arabi, 1930–1970.* Kuwait: al-Majlis al-Watani lil-Thaqafah wa-al-Funun wa-al-Adab, 1980.

al-'Aqqad, 'Abbas Mahmud. *Ana.* Cairo: Dar al-Hilal, 1964.

————. *Hayat qalam.* Cairo: Dar al-Hilal, 196?.

————. *al-Majmu'ah al-kamilah li-mu'allafat al-Ustadh 'Abbas Mahmud al-'Aqqad.* 23 vols. Beirut: Dar al-Kitab al-Lubnani, 1974–1982.

al-'Aqqad, 'Abbas Mahmud, and al-Mazini, Ibrahim 'Abd al-Qadir. *al-Diwan: Kitab fi al-naqd wa-al-adab* [The Diwan: A Book on Criticism and Literature]. Cairo, n.p., 1921.

al-'Ashmawi, Hasan. *al-Ikhwan wa-al-thawrah.* Vol. 1. Cairo: al-Maktab al-Misri al-Hadith, 1977.

'Azzam, 'Abdallah. *Ayat al-Rahman fi jihad al-Afghan.* Lahore, Pakistan: Ittihad al-Talabah al Muslimin-Pakistan, 1983.

————. *Al-Difa' 'an aradi al-Muslimin aham furud al-a'yan.* 2nd ed. Amman: Maktabat al-Rissalah al-Hadithah, 1987.

————. *'Imlaq al-fikr al-Islami al-shahid Sayyid Qutb.* Selections cited in www.khayma.com/alattar/selection.sqotb2.htm.

————. *al-Manarah al mafqudah.* Peshawar, Pakistan: Matbu'at Majallat al-Jihad, 1987.

al-Bahi, Muhammad. *al-Fikr al-Islami al-hadith wa-silatahu bi-al-isti'mar al-gharbi.* 8th ed. Cairo: Maktabat Wahbah, 1975.

al-Bahnasawi, Salim 'Ali. *al-Hukm wa-qadiyat takfir al-Muslim.* Cairo: Dar al-Ansar, 1977.

al-Banna, Hassan. *Majmu'at rasa'il al-Imam al-Shahid Hassan al-Banna.* Beirut: Mu'assasat al-Risalah, n.d.

————. *Mudhakkirat al-Da'wah wa-al-da'iyah.* Beirut: al-Maktal al-Islami, 1974.

al-Bishri, Tariq. *al-Harakah al-siyasiyah fi Misr, 1945–1952.* Cairo: al-Hay'ah al-Misriyah al-'Amah lil-Kuttab, 1972.

Dalil al-matbu'at al-Misriyah, 1940–1956. Cairo: Qism al-Nashr bi-al-jami'ah al-Amrikiyah, 1975.

al-Dasuqi, 'Abd al-'Aziz. *Jama'at Apullu.* Cairo: al-hay'ah al-misriyah al-'Amah lil-ta'lif wa-al-Nashr, 1971.

————. "Qadaya wa-mulahazat." *al-Thaqafah* (Cairo) no. 91 (April 1981): 49–53; no. 92 (May 1981): 42–47; no. 94 (July 1981): 44–54; no. 96 (September 1981): 61–64.

al-Disuqi, 'Asim. *Misr fi al-Harb al-'Alamiyah al-Thaniyah, 1939–1945.* Cairo: Jami'at al-Duwal al-'Arabiyah, al-Munazzamah al-'Arabiyah lil-Tarbiyah wa-al-Thaqafah wa-al-'Ulum, 1976.

Diyab, 'Abd al-Hayy. *'Abbas al-'Aqqad naqidan*. Cairo: al-Dar al-Qawmiyah, 1965.

Duwarah, Fu'ad. *'Asharat udaba' yatahaddathun*. Cairo: Dar al-Hilal, 1965.

Faraj, Muhammad 'Abd al-Salam. *Al-Jihad / al-Faridah al-Gha'ibah*. Text in www.e-prism.org/images/ALFARIDA.doc. N.p., 1981.

al-Ghazali, Muhammad. *Min huna na'lam*. 5th printing. Cairo: Dar al-Kutub al-Hadithah, 1965. First published in Cairo, 1950.

al-Hakim, Sulayman. *Asrar al-'ilaqah al-khasah bayna 'Abd al-Nasser wa al-Ikhwan*. Cairo, al-Gizah: Markaz al-Hadarah al-'Arabiyya lil-I'lam wa-al-Nashr, 1996.

Hammuda, 'Adel. *al-Hijra ila al-'unf: al-tatarruf al-dini min Hazimat Yunyu ila ightiyal October*. Cairo: Sina Publishing, 1987.

———. *Ightiyal al-ra'is bi-al-watha'iq: Asrar ightiyal al-Sadat*. Beirut: Dar al-Sharq, 1985.

Hamrush, Ahmad. *Qissat Thawrat 23 Yuliyu*. 4 vols. Beirut: al-Mu'assasah al-'Arabiyah lil-Dirasat wa-al-Nashr, 1974–1977.

Hawa, Sa'id. *Jundu Allah thaqafatan wa-akhlaqan*. Beirut, Amman: Dar 'Ammar, 1988.

Hizb al-Tahrir. *Muqaddimat al-Dustur aw al-asbab al-mujibah lahu*. N.p., 1963.

al-Hudaybi, Hassan Isma'il. *Du'at la-qudat: Abhath fi-al-'aqidah al-Islamiyyah wa-manhaj al-da'wah ila Allah*. 2nd printing. Beirut: Dar al-Salam, 1978.

Hussayn, Muhammad Muhammad. *al-Ittijahat al-wataniyah fi al-adab al-mu'asir*. 2 vols. Beirut: Dar-Irshad, 1970.

Hussayn, Taha. *al-Ayyam* [The Stream of Days]. 2 vols. Cairo, 1929–1939.

———. *Fi al-adab al-jahili* [On Pre-Islamic Literature]. Cairo, 1927.

———. *Fi al-shi'r al-jahili* [On Pre-Islamic Poetry]. Cairo, 1926.

———. *Al-Mu'adhabun fi al-'ard* [The Tormented on Earth]. Cairo: Dar al-Ma'aref, 1952.

———. *Mustaqbal al-Thaqafah fi Misr* [The Future of Culture in Egypt]. 2 vols. Cairo: Matba'at al-Ma'arif wa-Maktabatuha, 1938.

Hussein, Mahmoud. *Class Conflict in Egypt, 1945–1970*. Translated by Michel Chirman and Sussanne Chirman. New York and London, 1973.

Ibrahim, Hasanayn Tawfiq. *al-Nizam al-siyassi wa-al-Ikhwan al-Muslimun fi Misr min al-tasamuh ila al-muwajaha, 1981–1996*. Beirut: Dar al-Tali'ah, 1998.

Ibrahim, Muhammad Isma'il. *Mu'jam al-alfaz wa-al-a'lam al-Qur'aniyah*. 2nd ed. Cairo: Dar al-Fikr al-'Arabi, 1968.

'Imad, 'Abd al-Ghani. *Hakimiyyat Allah wa-sultan al-faqih: Qira'a fi khitab al-harakat al-Islamiyyah al-mu'asirah*. Beirut: Dar al-Tali'ah, 1997.

Imam, 'Abdallah. *'Abd al-Nasser wa al-Ikhwan al-Muslimun*. Cairo: Dar al-Khayyal, 1997.

al-Jada', Ahmad 'Abd al-Latif, and Jirar, Husni Adham. *Shi'r al-Da'wah al-Islamiyah fi al-'asr al-hadith*. Vol. 4. Beirut: Mu'assasat al-Risalah, 1978.

al-Jundi, Anwar. *al-Ma'arik al-adabiyyah*. Cairo, n.d.

———. *Kamil al-Kilani, fi mir'at al-tarikh*. N.p., 1962.

Karim, Samih. *Islamiyat Taha Hussayn, al-'Aqqad, Hussayn Haykal, Ahmad Amin, Tawfiq al-Hakim*. 2nd printing. Beirut: Dar al-Qalam, 1977.

Khalaf Allah, Muhammad Ahmad. *al-Fann al-qassasi fi al-Qur'an al-Karim*. 4th printing. Cairo: The Anglo Egyptian Bookshop, 1972.

Khalid, Khalid Muhammad. *Min huna nabda'* [From Here We Begin]. 4th ed. Cairo: Maktabat al-Khanji wa-Maktabat Wahbah, 1950.

Khan, Qamar al-Din. *Ibn Taymiyya wa-fikrihi al-siyassi*. Translated by Ahmad Mubarak al-Baghdadi. Kuwait: Maktabat al-Falah, 1985.

Mahkamat al-Sha'b, al-Kitab al-Thani. *Muhakamat Hassan al-Hudaybi wa-A'da' Maktab al-Irshad*. Prepared by Kamal Kirah. Cairo, 1954.

al-Misri, Sana'. *al-Ikhwan al-Muslimun wa-al-tabaqa al-'amilah al-Misriyyah*. Cairo, n.p., 1992.

Muhammad, Hamadah Husni Ahmad. *al-Tanzimat al-siyasiyyah li-Thawrat yulyu 1952 (1953–1961)*. Cairo: al-Hay'ah al-Misriyyah al-'Amah lil Kuttab, 2002.

Nabhani, Taqiy al-Din. *Nizam al-Islam*. 5th printing. Jerusalem, Al-Quds: Hizb al-Tahrir Publications, 1953.

Nadvi, Abulhasan 'Ali. *Madha khasira al-'alam bi-inhitat al-Muslimin* [What Did the World Lose by the Degeneration of the Muslims?]. 4th rev. ed. Cairo: Maktabat Dar al-'Urubah, 1961.

———. *Mudhakkirat sa'ih fi al-Sharq al-'Arabi*. 2nd rev. ed. Beirut: Mu'assasat al-Risalah, 1975.

Naguib, Muhammad. *Mudhakirrat (Kuntu ra'isan li-Misr)*. 5th printing. Cairo: al-Maktab al-Misri al-Hadith, 1988.

al-Nuwayhi, Muhammad. *Thaqafat al-naqid al-adabi*. 2nd ed. Beirut: Maktabat al-Khanji, 1969.

Ramadan, 'Abd al-'Azim. *al-Sira' bayna al-Wafd wa-al-'Arsh, 1936–1939*. Beirut: al-Mu' assasah al-'Arabiyah lil-Dirasat wa-al-Nashr, 1979.

———. *al-Sira' al-ijtima'i wa-al-siyasi fi Misr min Thawrat 23 Yuliyu ila azmat Mars 1954*. Cairo: Maktabat Madbuli, 1975.

———. "al-Tanzim al-jadid lil-Ikhwan al-Muslimin." *Ruz al-Yusuf* (Cairo) no. 2518 (September 13, 1976): 5–6, 53.

———. *Tatawwur al-harakah al-wataniyah fi Misr, min sanat 1918 ila sanat 1936*. Cairo: Dar al-Katib al-'Arabi, 1986.

———. *Tatawwur al-harakah al-wataniyah fi Misr, min sanat 1937 ila sanat 1948*. 2 vols. Cairo, 1973.

Ramzi, Muhammad. *al-Qamus al-jughrafi lil-bilad al-Misriyah*. Vol. 4. Cairo: Matba'at Dar al-Kutub al-Misriyah, 1963.

Rizq, Jabir. *Madhbahat al-Ikhwan fi Liman Turah*. Cairo, 1979.

Rizq, Yunan Labib. *Tarikh al-wizarat al-Misriyah, 1878–1953*. Cairo: Markaz al-Dirasat al-Siyasiyah wa-al-Istratijiyah bi-al-Ahram, 1975.

al-Sakkut, Hamdi, and Jones, Marsden. *Taha Husayn*. 2nd rev. ed. Beirut and Cairo: Markaz al-Dirasat al-'Arabiyah bi-al-Jami'ah al-Amrikiyah, 1982.

al-Sayyid, Radwan. "Harakat al-Islam al-siyasi al-mu'asirah: ta'amullat fi bi'atiha al-aydiyulujiyyah wa-al-siyasiyyah." *al-'Arabi* (Kuwait) no. 466, September 1997.

al-Sharif, Ahmad Ibrahim. *al-Madkhal ila shi'r al-'Aqqad*. Beirut: Dar al-Jil, 1974.

Siyam, Shihata. *al-Din al-Sha'bi fi Misri: Naqd al-'aql al-mutahayil*. al-Iskandariyya: Ramtan lil-Nashr, 1995.

al-Talmasani, 'Umar. *Dhikrayat la mudhakirrat*. Shobra, Egypt: Dar al-Tiba'ah wa-al-Nashr al-Islamiyyah, 1985.

al-Tuhami, Mukhtar. *Thalath ma'arik fikriyah*. Cairo, 1977.

GENERAL WORKS IN ENGLISH

Abdel-Malek, Anouar. *Egypt: Military Society*. Translated by Charles Lam Markmann. New York: Random House, 1968.

Abdelnasser, Walid M. "Islamic Organizations in Egypt and the Iranian Revolution of 1979: The Experience of the First Few Years." *Arab Studies Quarterly* vol. 19, no. 2 (Spring 1997).

Abu Khalil, Asa'd. "The Incoherence of Islamic Fundamentalism: Arab Islamic Thought at the End of the 20th Century." *Middle East Journal* vol. 48, no. 4 (Autumn 1994).

Abu Lughod, Ibrahim. *Arab Rediscovery of Europe: A Study in Cultural Encounters*. Princeton: Princeton University Press, 1963.

Adams, Charles C. *Islam and Modernism in Egypt*. London: Oxford University Press, 1933.

Ahmed, Jamal Mohammed. *The Intellectual Origins of Egyptian Nationalism*. London: Oxford University Press, 1960.

Allen, Roger. " 'Abbas Mahmud al-'Akkad." In the *Encyclopedia of Islam*, Supplement (Fascicules 1–2). Leiden: E. J. Brill, 1980.

Aly, 'Abd al-Moneim Sa'id, and Wenner, Manfred W. "Modern Islamic Reform Movements: The Muslim Brotherhood in Contemporary Egypt." *Middle East Journal* vol. 36, no. 3 (Summer 1982): 336–61.

Asad, Muhammad. *The Road to Mecca*. New York: Simon and Schuster, 1954.

Ayubi Nazih, N.M. "The Political Revival of Islam: The Case of Egypt."

International Journal of Middle East Studies vol. 12 (December 1980): 481–99.

Badawi, M.M. *A Critical Introduction to Modern Arabic Poetry*. Cambridge, England: Cambridge University Press, 1975.

Beinin, Joel. *Was the Red Flag Flying There: Marxist Politics and the Arab-Israeli Conflict in Egypt and Israel*. Berkeley: University of California Press, 1990.

Berman, Paul. *Terror and Liberalism*. New York and London: W.W. Norton and Company, 2004.

Blackman, Winfred S. *The Fellahin of Upper Egypt*. London: Frank Cass, 1968.

Botman, Selma. "Egyptian Communists and the Free Officers: 1950–1954." *Middle Eastern Studies* vol. 22, no. 3 (July 1986).

Britannica Book of the Year 1951. Chicago, Toronto, London: 1951.

Cachia, Pierre. *Taha Husayn: His Place in the Egyptian Literary Renaissance*. London: Luzac, 1956.

The Cambridge History of Egypt. Vol. 2, edited by M.W. Daly. Cambridge, England: Cambridge University Press, 1998.

Casandra. "The Impending Crisis in Egypt." *Middle East Journal* vol. 49, no. 1 (Winter 1995).

Chapra, M. Umer. "Mawlana Mawdudi's Contribution to Islamic Economics." *The Muslim World* vol. 94 (April 2004): 163–80.

Choueiri, Youssef M. *Islamic Fundamentalism*. Rev. ed. London: Pinter, 1997.

Collateral Language. Edited by John Collins and Ross Glover. New York and London: New York University Press, 2002.

Colombe, Marcel. *L'Evolution de l'Egypt, 1924–1950*. Paris: Maisonneuve, 1951.

Cragg, Kenneth. *Counsels in Contemporary Islam*. Edinburgh: Edinburgh University Press, 1965.

Critical Perspectives on Naguib Mahfouz. Edited by Trevor Le Gassick. Washington, DC: Three Continents Press, 1991.

Davidson, Lawrence. *Islamic Fundamentalism: An Introduction*. Rev. ed. Westport, CT and London: Greenwood Press, 2003.

Deeb, Marius. *Party Politics in Egypt: The Wafd and Its Rivals 1919–1939*. London: Middle East Center, St. Antony's College, Oxford, 1979.

Dekmejian, R. Harir. "The Anatomy of Islamic Revival: Legitimacy Crisis, Ethnic Conflict and the Search for Islamic Alternatives." *Middle East Journal* vol. 34, no. 1 (Winter 1980): 1–12.

Dessouki, Ali E. Hillal, ed. *Islamic Resurgence in the Arab World*. New York: Praeger Publishers, 1982.

El-Awaisi, abd al-Fattah M. "Emergence of a Militant Leader: A Study of the Life of Hasan Al-Banna." *Journal of South Asian and Middle Eastern Affairs*. Fall 1998.

Eliraz, Giora. "Tradition and Change: Egyptian Intellectuals and Linguistic Reform, 1919–1939." *Asian and African Studies* (Haifa) no. 20 (1986).

Enayat, Hamid. *Modern Islamic Political Thought*. Austin: University of Texas Press, 1982.

Fandy, Mamoun. "Egypt's Islamic Group: Regional Revenge." *Middle East Journal* vol. 48, no. 4 (Autumn 1994).

Gershoni, Israel. *The Emergence of Pan-Arabism in Egypt*. Tel-Aviv: Shiloah Center for Middle Eastern Studies, [c.1981].

Gibb, Hamilton A. R. *Modern Trends in Islam*. Chicago: University of Chicago, 1947.

Gilsenan, Michael. *Saint and Sufi in Modern Egypt: An Essay in the Sociology of Religion*. Oxford: Clarendon Press, 1973.

Gulalp, Haldum. "Islamism and Postmodernism." *Contention: Debates in Society, Culture and Science* vol. 4, no. 2 (Winter 1995): 57–73.

Haddad, Yvonne Yazbeck. *Contemporary Islam and the Challenge of History*. Albany: State University of New York Press, 1982.

———. "Islamists and the (Problem of Israel): The 1967 Awakening." *Middle East Journal* vol. 46, no. 2 (Spring 1992).

Harris, Christina. *Nationalism and Revolution in Egypt: The Role of the Muslim Brotherhood*. Stanford, CA: Hoover Institution, 1964.

Heyworth-Dunne, J. *An Introduction to the History of Education in Modern Egypt*. London: Luzac, 1938.

———. *Religious and Political Trends in Modern Egypt*. Washington, DC, 1950.

Hopwood, Derek. *Egypt: Politics and Society 1945–1981*. London: George Allen and Unwin, 1982.

Hourani, Albert. *Arabic Thought in the Liberal Age*. London and New York: Oxford University Press, 1962.

———. *A History of the Arab Peoples*. New York: Warner Books, 1992.

Humphreys, R. Stephen. "Islam and Political Values in Saudi Arabia, Egypt and Syria." *Middle East Journal* vol. 33, no.1 (Winter 1979): 1–19.

Husaini, Ishak Musa. *The Moslem Brethrens the Greatest Modern Islamic Movements*. Beirut: Khayat's, 1956.

Ibrahim, Ibrahim Iskandar. *The Egyptian Intellectuals between Tradition and Modernity*. Unpublished Ph.D. dissertation, St. Antony's College, Oxford, 1967.

Ismail, Salwa. "Confronting the Other: Identity, Culture, Politics and Conservative Islamism in Egypt." *International Journal of Middle East Studies* 30 (1998): 199–225.

Issawi, Charles. *Egypt at Mid-Century: An Economic Survey*. London: Oxford University Press, 1954.

Jayyusi, Salma Khadra. *Trends and Movements in Modern Arabic Poetry*. 2 vols. Leiden: E. J. Brill, 1977.

Karpat, Kemal, ed. *Political and Social Thought in the Contemporary Middle East*. New York: Frederick A. Praeger, 1968.

Kepel, Gilles. *Jihad: The Trail of Political Islam*. Translated by Anthony F. Roberts. 2nd printing. Cambridge, MA: Belknap Press of Harvard University Press, 2002.

———. *The Prophet and the Pharaoh: Muslim Extremism in Egypt*. Translated by Jon Rothschild. Berkeley and Los Angeles: University of California Press, 2003.

Khadduri, Majid. *War and Peace in the Law of Islam*. Baltimore: Johns Hopkins University Press, 1955.

Kuran, Timur. "The Economic System in Contemporary Islamic Thought: Interpretation and Assessment." *International Journal Middle East Studies* vol. 18, no. 2 (May 1986).

Lacouture, Jean, and Lacouture, Simone. *Egypt in Transition*. Translated by Francis Scarfe. New York: Methuen, 1958.

Lane, E. W. *Manners and Customs of Modern Egyptians*. London: J. M. Dent, 1954.

Lerner, Daniel. *The Passing of Traditional Society: Modernizing the Middle East*. New York: Free Press, 1964.

Lutsky, V. *Modern History of the Arab Countries*. Translated by Lika Nasser. Moscow: Progress Publishers, 1969.

Mahfouz, Naguib. *Midaq Alley* [Zuqaq al-Midaqq]. Translated by Trevor LeGassick. Beirut: Khayats, 1966 and London: Heinemann, 1974.

Mansfield, Peter. *The British in Egypt*. London: Weidenfeld and Nicolson, 1971.

Martin, Maurice, and Massad, Rose Marie. "al-Takfir wa-al-Hijrah: A Study in Sectarian Protest." *Cenam Reports*. Beirut: Dar al-Mashriq, 1977, 135–56.

Maududi, Abul A'la. *A Short History of the Revivalist Movement in Islam*. Lahore, Pakistan: Islamic Publications, 1963.

———. *Towards Understanding Islam*. Translated from Urdu and edited by Khurshid Ahmad. Indianapolis: American Trust Publications, 1977.

Mazrui, Ali A. "Islamic and Western Values." *Foreign Affairs* (Washington, DC), vol. 76, no. 5, September/October 1997.

Mitchell, Richard P. *The Society of the Muslim Brothers*. London: Oxford University Press, 1969.

Mohaddessin, Mohammad. *Islamic Fundamentalism: The New Global Threat*. Washington, DC: Seven Locks Press, 1993.

Mortimer, Edward. *Faith and Power: The Politics of Islam*. New York: Random House, 1982.

Moussalli, Ahmad S. *Moderate and Radical Islamic Fundamentalism: The Quest for Modernity, Legitimacy, and the Islamic State*. Gainesville: University Press of Florida, 1999.

Najjar, Fawzi M. "The Debate on Islam and Secularism in Egypt." *Arab Studies Quarterly* no. 2 (Spring 1996).

Osman, Fathi. "Mawdudi's Contribution to the Development of Modern Islamic Thinking in the Arabic-Speaking World." *Muslim World* vol. 93 (July/October 2003): 465–85.

Ostle, R. C. "Iliya Abu Madi and Arabic Poetry in the Inter-war Period." In *Studies in Modern Arabic Literature*. Edited by R. C. Ostle. London, 1975.

Peretz, Don. *The Middle East Today*. 2nd ed. Hinsdale, Illinois: Dryden Press, 1971.

Peters, F. E. *Aristotle and the Arabs*. New York: New York University Press, 1968.

Pickthall, Muhammad M. *The Meaning of the Glorious Qur'an: Text and Explanatory Translation*. Mecca: Muslim League Rabita, 1977.

Quraishi, Zaheer Masood. *Liberal Nationalism in Egypt: Rise and Fall of the Wafd Party*. Allahabad: Kitab Mahal, 1967.

Richmond, J.C.B. *Egypt, 1798–1952: Her Advance Towards a Modern Identity*. New York: Columbia University Press, 1977.

Safran, Nadav. *Egypt in Search of Political Community: An Analysis of the Intellectual and Political Evolution of Egypt, 1804–1952*. Cambridge, MA: Harvard University Press, 1961.

Sakkut, Hamdi. *The Egyptian Novel and Its Main Trends, from 1913 to 1952*. Cairo: American University in Cairo Press, 1971.

al-Sayyid-Marsot, Afaf Lutfi. *Egypt's Liberal Experiment, 1922–1936*. Berkeley: University of California Press, 1977.

Sharabi, Hisham. *Arab Intellectuals and the West: The Formative Years, 1875–1914*. Baltimore: Johns Hopkins University Press, 1970.

———. *Government and Politics of the Middle East in the Twentieth Century*. Princeton, NJ: D. Van Nostrand Company, 1962.

Sivan, Emmanuel. *Radical Islam: Medieval Theology and Modern Politics*. New Haven: Yale University Press, 1985.

Smith, Charles D. "The Crisis of Orientation: The Shift of Egyptian Intellectuals to Islamic Subjects in the 1930's." *International Journal of Middle East Studies* no. 4 (October 1973).

———. "Imagined Identities, Imagined Nationalisms: Print Culture and Egyptian Nationalism in Light of Recent Scholarship: A Review Essay of Israel Gershoni and James P. Jankowski (Redefining the Egyptian Nation, 1930–1945)." *Inter-national Journal of Middle East Studies* 29 (1997).

Smith, Wilfred Cantwell. *Islam in Modern History*. Princeton, NJ: Princeton University Press, 1957.

Spitz, Lewis. *The Renaissance and Reformation Movements*. Chicago: Rand McNally, 1971.

Studies in Modern Arabic Literature. Edited by R. C. Ostle. London: School of Oriental and African Study, 1975.

Studies on the Civilization of Islam. Edited by Stanford J. Shaw and William R. Polk. Boston: Beacon Press, 1962.

Tagore, Rabindranath. *One Hundred and One Poems.* Bombay and Calcutta: Asia Publishing House, 1966.

Texts of Selected Speeches and Final Communiqué of the Asian African Conference. Bandung, Indonesia, April 18–24, 1955. New York: Far East Report, 1955?

Vatikiotis, P. J., ed. *Egypt since the Revolution.* New York: Frederick A. Praeger, 1968.

———. *Egyptian Army in Politics: Pattern for New Nations.* Bloomington: Indiana University Press, 1961.

———. *The History of Egypt.* 2nd ed. Baltimore: Johns Hopkins University Press, 1980.

Warburg, Gabriel R. "Islam and Politics in Egypt: 1952–80." *Middle Eastern Studies* vol. 18, no. 2 (April 1982): 131–57.

Watt, W. Montgomery. *The Majesty That Was Islam (The Islamic World 661–1100).* New York: Praeger Publishers, 1974.

Wehr, Hans. *A Dictionary of Modern Written Arabic.* Edited by Milton Cowan. 2nd printing. Ithaca, NY: Cornell University Press, 1966.

Welch, Alford T., and Cachia, Pierre. *Islam: Past Influence and Present Challenge.* Edinburgh: Edinburgh University Press, 1979.

Wright, Lawrence. "The Man Behind Bin Laden." *New Yorker*, September 16, 2002.

Yapp, M. E. "Contemporary Islamic Revivalism." *Asian Affairs* (London) vol. XI, part II (June 1980).

Zeidan, David. "Radical Islam in Egypt: A Comparison of Two Groups." *MERIA Journal* (Middle East Review of International Affairs) vol. 3, no. 3 (September 1999).

Index

ADNAN A. MUSALLAM is an Associate Professor in History, Politics, and Cultural Studies at Bethlehem University. Active in interfaith dialogue, he has published books and articles in both Arabic and English.